ORTHODOX ANGLICAN IDENTITY

Orthodox Anglican Identity

The Quest for Unity in a Diverse Religious Tradition

CHARLES ERLANDSON

PICKWICK *Publications* · Eugene, Oregon

ORTHODOX ANGLICAN IDENTITY
The Quest for Unity in a Diverse Religious Tradition

Pickwick Publications
An Imprint of Wipf and Stock Publishers
199 W. 8th Ave., Suite 3
Eugene, OR 97401

www.wipfandstock.com

PAPERBACK ISBN: 978-1-5326-7825-7
HARDCOVER ISBN: 978-1-5326-7826-4
EBOOK ISBN: 978-1-5326-7827-1

Cataloguing-in-Publication data:

Names: Erlandson, Charles, author.

Title: Orthodox Anglican identity : the quest for unity in a diverse religious tradition / by Charles Erlandson.

Description: Eugene, OR: Pickwick Publications, 2020 | Includes bibliographical references and index.

Identifiers: ISBN 978-1-5326-7825-7 (paperback) | ISBN 978-1-5326-7826-4 (hardcover) | ISBN 978-1-5326-7827-1 (ebook)

Subjects: LCSH: Anglican Communion. | Church controversies—Anglican Communion. | Christian union—Anglican Communion.

Classification: BX5005 E75 2020 (print) | BX5005 (ebook)

Manufactured in the U.S.A.   APRIL 21, 2020

"For as the body is one and has many members, but all the members of that one body, being many, are one body, so also is Christ."

—1 COR 12:12

Contents

Acknowledgments

DESPITE THE LONELINESS AND individual responsibility involved in writing a book, I have been constantly reminded in my labors that "No man is an island." I would therefore like to acknowledge some of those who are a part of the larger continent to which I and my work have been connected.

Two men were most instrumental in my decision to proceed with the PhD which is the parent of this book, without whose initial encouragement and inspiration I would never have begun: Dr. Peter Newman Brooks and the Rt. Rev. Dr. Ray Sutton.

I was blessed by others with the necessary support to continue my work. My thesis was undoubtedly made stronger and more relevant by the diligent oversight of my supervisor, Dr. Gavin Hyman, of Lancaster University. St. Chrysostom's Reformed Episcopal Church (now Christ Anglican) in Hot Springs, Arkansas, provided me with a loving and supportive community while I finished my work. I can't imagine a more peaceful place of employment from which to write.

Many thanks to my family members who have put up with my incessant discussions of Anglicanism. My dad, Dr. David Erlandson, has been especially encouraging in my many discussions with him. The daily prayers of my children that I might finish have meant more to me than they will ever know.

Finally, my greatest thanks go to my wife, Jackie, who has held up the world for me that I might complete my labors.

Abbreviations

ACC   Anglican Church in Canada

ACC   Anglican Consultative Council

ACI   Anglican Communion Institute

ACN   Anglican Communion Network

ACNA   Anglican Church in North America

AMiA   Anglican Mission in America

CCP   Common Cause Partners

CMS   Church Mission Society

COU   Church of Uganda

ECUSA   Episcopal Church in the United States of America

GAFCON Global Anglican Future Conference

HTB   Holy Trinity, Brompton

PECUSA Protestant Church in the United States of America

REC   Reformed Episcopal Church

SOMA   Sharing of Ministries Abroad

TEC   The Episcopal Church

TSM   Trinity School for Ministry

Introduction

It was the best of times, it was the worst of times, it was the age of wisdom, it was the age of foolishness, it was the epoch of belief, it was the epoch of incredulity, it was the season of Light, it was the season of Darkness, it was the spring of hope, it was the winter of despair, we had everything before us, we had nothing before us, we were all going direct to heaven, we were all going direct the other way—in short, the period was so far like the present period, that some of its noisiest authorities insisted on its being received, for good or for evil, in the superlative degree of comparison only.

THIS FAMOUS OPENING OF Charles Dickens's *A Tale of Two Cities* serves well as an introduction to the complexities and ambiguities of religious identities. Christians (and adherents of other religions) desire to see and experience God clearly in their lives. They usually look back to a Golden Age of the church when things were better: when Christians had true faith and were willing to die for it; when Christians had all things in common and lived in peace and harmony; and when the church was integral to all parts of life. But when they look at the church in their own lives, they are dismayed by the weakness and coldness of faith they observe, the irrelevance and impotence of the church, and, perhaps, the seeming absence of God in their lives. Some are tempted to tell the story of the church in terms of a long period of decline since the purported Golden Age. It's easy to look at Western Christianity and compare it to either the early church or the medieval church and wonder what went wrong.

But what if there's another way to tell the story? What if the church has always simultaneously experienced both the best of times and the worst of times? And what if religious identities, including Christianity, are inherently complex entities, which encompass contrary trends at one and the same time? My own belief is that you could take your finger, randomly run it up and down the timeline, stop anywhere along the line, and you would find that the church's experience was both positive and negative. And if you spun a globe and stopped it with your finger at any given nation, you'd find much the same thing.

Maybe the church in the New Testament was the Golden Age of the church for which we should all long. Who cannot be moved by Luke's account of the early church in Acts 2? But when we read about the church at Corinth, under the oversight of the great apostle Paul, we discover a church filled with sexual immorality, pride, and divisions. Is this the Golden Age for which we are to yearn?

Or maybe it's the High Middle Ages, where the church, state, and culture were unified under the authority and legal influence of the pope. But you don't have to be Martin Luther to know the manifold abuses and corruptions that often prevailed in this mythical Golden Age.

When we grasp the truth that religious identities are inherently complex and that the expressed ideals of Christendom are never fully realized, an opportunity for hope emerges. When we come to the realization that the church as a whole, as well as specific Christian churches, can both say with confidence who they are and at the same time have trouble defining themselves, we may discover a strange sense of peace. How can hope and peace emerge from a complex and ambiguous identity? Because we realize we're not alone in this circumstance and that the church has always had to work out its salvation with fear and trembling.

This book is a personal one. I am a self-professed orthodox Anglican and one who has spent years searching for my Anglican identity beyond the tidy ones I read about in other books. I originally wanted to study Anglican revival but soon realized that to revive or reform people or things you had to have some idea of who they are supposed to be. And so I felt compelled to descend into the maelstrom of Anglican identity. It was not an easy journey, and I was surprised and dismayed at the complexity and confusion I frequently encountered.

Certain fundamental truths emerged from my journey, ones I want to share especially with the Christian and Anglican world. People and institutions experience identity crises in times of great change and transition, such as our own day. Change itself is not an enemy, and identities in organisms require constant renewal. On the one hand, the organism has to establish and defend its identity against the environment outside it. On the other hand, the organism must interact with and partake of the world outside if it is going to continue to survive and thrive. The church is a divine organism. It needs to know who it is, and yet it cannot be who it is without participating in both the life of God and also the world God created. If the church restricts its identity too much, it risks being incapable of ministering to the larger world. But if the church is too tolerant of diversity, it risks losing its identity, becoming like the culture, and also being incapable of ministering to the larger culture.

Organisms other than unicellular organisms have another inherent identity issue: the relation of the parts to the whole. In the church this relationship is played out not only between the one, holy, catholic, and apostolic church and its constituent members but also between the expressed identity of individual churches and the diversity of members, theologies, and practices in that church. This unity in diversity is at the core of ecclesiastical identity crises. Too much coerced unity within a church results in cults and heresies. Too much diversity results in a church nearly indistinguishable from the culture, as well as heresies. Churches must, therefore, on the one hand have a clear idea of who they are, while on the other hand allow for a certain degree of healthy diversity within established norms. A diversity deemed unhealthy to the church is at the heart of the Anglican identity crisis, as well as the renewed orthodox Anglican identity that has emerged.

Undesirable diversity, if unchecked, may eventually lead to the loss of a meaningful identity in continuity with past identities. But undesirable diversity has the unintended benefit of provoking from the church a deeper examination of conscience, as well as a revitalized reassertion of self. The heresies of the first few centuries of church history provoked the great ecumenical councils of the church and confident clarifications of christological and trinitarian theologies. What renewed orthodox Anglican identity might emerge from the challenge of a progressively liberal Anglicanism in the West?

Think of this book as a kind of story: the story of a worldwide church who, when her identity was threatened, took counsel together to renew and revitalize her sense of self. In the process, she not only faced many dangers and difficulties but also learned much about who she was and who she wanted to be. It is the story of losing oneself and finding oneself: a story of identity. The story is told by one who may be considered one of the official storytellers of the church in question, which explains the objective tone of what is, beneath the argumentation and evidence, a very personal story.

The story begins on 2 November 2003, when The Episcopal Church (TEC)[1] consecrated Vicki Gene Robinson, an openly homosexual man, as Bishop of New Hampshire. While many who consider themselves "orthodox" or "conservative" Anglicans had been concerned about the growth of liberalism within Anglicanism for several decades before this action, it was especially TEC's consecration of Robinson that provoked a strong and negative response from many orthodox Anglicans. This response was supported in part on the basis of the 1998 Lambeth Conference, at which a clear majority of Anglican bishops voted for a resolution that rejected homosexuality as incompatible with the Bible. The response of orthodox Anglicans has been both theological and practical, but underlying these responses is the idea of an orthodox Anglican realignment predicated upon a specifically *orthodox* and *Anglican* identity and articulated in contrast to a *liberal* Anglican identity. So sharp are the disagreements over TEC's action that individual provinces have declared themselves out of communion or in impaired communion with TEC over Robinson's consecration.

Since 2003, orthodox Anglicans have responded with a process of ecclesial and theological realignment. The virtues and vices of this realignment have been examined both by those who favor it and those who dislike it, but neither group has given adequate attention to the underlying identity that orthodox Anglicans assume in such a realignment.

Anglicans on all sides of the current crisis generally assume that an entity called "Anglicanism" exists, and discussions of the Anglican identity crisis continue to be written. What is especially lacking, however, is an extended discussion of the nature of the emerging orthodox Anglican identity that orthodox Anglicans are asserting and on which they predicate their realignment. This orthodox Anglican identity has rarely been articulated by orthodox Anglicans themselves in any detail and has largely remained an unexamined assumption.

Given the importance of this orthodox Anglican realignment and the diversity among these orthodox Anglicans, the question, therefore, remains: "How clear and coherent is this orthodox Anglican identity?" *The thesis of this book is that while orthodox Anglicans desire and seek an identity that is*

---

1. At the time of Robinson's consecration in 2003, The Episcopal Church (TEC) was known as the Episcopal Church in the United States of America (ECUSA). Throughout this book, however, I will be using the current name of TEC.

clear and coherent, in actuality, they will live out an identity that is much more ambiguous and messier. This thesis is an illustration of a grander claim that religious identities are inherently complex organisms who create and maintain their identities through a dynamic process of finding unity in diversity.

In chapter 1, I will present both an overview of the crisis precipitated by TEC's consecration of Robinson and of the orthodox Anglican response to this action. I will then introduce you to some of the characters in this story, offering criteria by which we may judge who counts as orthodox Anglicans, and providing examples of key orthodox Anglicans. A discussion of how these orthodox Anglicans typically define liberal Anglicans will follow, as well as the background to the liberal actions of TEC. Chapter 1 will conclude with a discussion of the nature of the orthodox Anglican response, which may be best described as one of realignment.

Before this orthodox Anglican identity, on which the response of realignment is predicated, can be adequately assessed, I must offer some definition of Anglicanism as a whole, since orthodox Anglicans desire to retain a distinctly Anglican identity and since the clarity and coherence of this Anglican identity is the theme of this book. Therefore, in chapter 2, I will examine in turn four kinds of definitions of Anglicanism: *ecclesial, normative, practical,* and *historical.* These ecclesial, normative, and practical definitions will serve as the framework for an examination of the clarity and coherence of orthodox Anglican identity in chapters 3, 4, and 5, respectively.

Since the historical dimension is an important one in understanding how the other three relate, I will present a simplified model of religious identity, one which suggests that one way of understanding Anglican identity may be to look at the relationship between ecclesial authority, norms, and practical aspects of Anglicanism as they have developed over time. This model reveals that the history of Anglican identity has historically developed (since the time of the English Reformation) in three stages: it is also possible that the Anglican identity so described is now entering a fourth, "post-Anglican," stage of identity.

In the remainder of the book, I will examine orthodox Anglican identity in terms of these ecclesial, normative, and practical definitions. My task is a *descriptive* one: rather than *prescribing* what orthodox Anglicanism should be, I am attempting to *describe* the definitions of orthodox Anglicanism that orthodox Anglicans themselves are articulating and actually living out, as well as the challenges to these articulated definitions that are often unacknowledged by the orthodox Anglicans who are asserting them.

Chapter 3 explores the idea that ecclesiastically, orthodox Anglicans desire to live together in a clear and authoritative communion life but are likely to actually live in an ecclesial identity that may not be any clearer than the present ecclesial identity. Ecclesial definitions of Anglicanism involve an equation between Anglicanism and the Anglican Communion, which, however, presents twin dangers. Staying within the structures of the Anglican Communion will only perpetuate the current problems, while the development of new structures, such as GAFCON (Global Anglican Future Conference) and the ACNA (Anglican Church in North America) might not only perpetuate similar ecclesial difficulties but also lead to greater fragmentation. While orthodox Anglicans will seek a clear ecclesial identity for themselves, their ecclesial identity will become increasingly complex and messy, even resembling a networked federation of churches to some degree. This complex identity will, in the end, be likely to continue to allow for increasing diversity.

Chapter 4 demonstrates that, normatively, orthodox Anglicans desire to assert a relatively clear and strong identity by turning to the Bible, the Prayer Book, and the Thirty-nine Articles but that none of these will act as strongly or effectively as many orthodox Anglicans hope they will. A distinctly orthodox Anglican identity is founded most importantly on orthodox interpretations of the Bible; however, while orthodox Anglicans will continue to have a large degree of agreement that the Bible prohibits homosexuality as sinful behavior, they will have increasingly divergent interpretations of Scripture in other areas that relate to Anglican identity. While orthodox Anglicans will make a turn toward using the Thirty-nine Articles and the 1662 Book of Common Prayer as continuing Anglican norms, many orthodox Anglicans will continue to read them in divergent ways or ignore them altogether. Thus, while orthodox Anglicans are defining themselves normatively in terms of clear norms, they will hold to these norms so imperfectly that a clear and coherent identity is undermined.

In chapter 5, I conclude that orthodox Anglicans will, if only implicitly, attempt to base an orthodox Anglican identity on the historical ideal of a comprehension of the various orthodox Anglican spiritualities, which is a species of practical religion or matters of a distinctively Anglican ethos. The traditional Anglican cluster of spiritualities that included Catholic, Evangelical, and Liberal spiritualities is being replaced by an orthodox Anglican identity that includes Anglo-Catholic, Evangelical, Charismatic, and Global spiritualities. Each of these spiritualities, however, is acting to increase the diversity within orthodox Anglicanism and, therefore, to expand the degree of comprehension necessary to contain them all within a single orthodox Anglican identity. The composite effect of such a vast degree of comprehension is that even while orthodox Anglicans desire and assert a clear and coherent identity, they will experience some difficulty saying what this identity is. In this way, a "post-Anglican" Anglican identity is emerging.

Orthodox Anglicans are, therefore, asserting and seeking a clear and coherent identity based on a common ecclesial structure with a clear authority and norms to limit diversity, as well as a common identity based on comprehending the diversity found in their different spiritualities. However, their actual diversity is so great and will continue to increase so that they will achieve the clear norms and markers of identity they desire only very imperfectly. Rather than simply denying that an orthodox Anglican identity exists or is desirable, however, they will live in a complex and ambiguous identity (or identities) that incorporates aspects of both a clear and coherent identity, as well as a more ambiguous and messy identity.

The desire of orthodox Anglicans to assert their own identity against that of a larger, more liberal Anglican identity is only one example of the identity crisis that all Christian churches are experiencing: the identity crisis of Christianity is itself only one example of the systematic identity crisis of the modern world. An examination of this orthodox Anglican quest for identity is, therefore, a lens by which we may see more clearly the complex nature of religious identity in particular. My hope is for a favorable prognosis after what may be a disturbing and discouraging exam. For when the inherent complexity of religious identities, including that of orthodox Anglicanism (the disturbing part of my diagnosis), is seen in the context of a definite and meaningful identity, we may yet find peace.

The story of how orthodox Anglicans are seeking a renewed sense of self in a complex, contested, and fragmented world is a microcosm of our own postmodern searches for meaning and identity. Let us see how they are faring in their search for identity, for this quest holds enticing clues to our own urgent searches for meaning and identity.

Chapter 1 ———————————

Anglican Identity Crisis and Realignment

INTRODUCTION

THE PROFOUND CRISIS WITHIN Anglicanism, as an exemplar of the Christian religion, has been acknowledged by Anglicans for some time. This crisis is at its heart an identity crisis and is evidenced, for example, by the titles of some of the books written in the past few decades, titles such as *The Episcopal Church in Crisis, The Integrity of Anglicanism, Reclaiming Faith, The Renewal of Anglicanism,* and *Reinventing Anglicanism*.[1] This identity crisis is also reflected in the reluctance with which Anglicans are willing to define themselves and by the fact that Anglicans seem to manifest an uncertainty or lack of confidence about the nature of Anglicanism and even about the value of perpetuating it. Paul Avis, for example, warns of the strange habit Anglicans have of talking down the future of Anglicanism and stressing its provisional nature, and he finds that the most radical challenge to the future of Anglicanism is the question: "Do Anglicans really want a future for Anglicanism?"[2] The fact that Anglican identity has become such an issue is itself a marker of the dramatic challenges and changes that are taking place within Anglicanism and the contemporary Western world.

---

1. Booty, *The Episcopal Church in Crisis*; Sykes, *The Integrity of Anglicanism*; Radner and Sumner, *Reclaiming Faith*; McGrath, *The Renewal of Anglicanism*; and Kaye, *Reinventing Anglicanism*.

2. Avis, "Keeping Faith with Anglicanism," 1–2.

While discussions of the Anglican identity crisis before 2003 were more general in nature, after 2003 they have been focused more specifically on the related issues of biblical authority and interpretation, and of homosexuality. Since the consecration of Vicki Gene Robinson, an openly homosexual man, by TEC[3] as a bishop in 2003, the Anglican world in general has begun more visibly to align itself into two broad camps: those who favor homosexuality and allow for homosexual clergy and those who do not, both of which are beliefs associated with particular readings of the Bible. Often, those who favor homosexuality have been called "liberal" or "revisionist," while those who reject homosexuality have been called "orthodox" or "conservative." Particularly in response to TEC's consecration of Robinson, orthodox Anglicans have initiated a more visible and urgent process of realignment in which they clearly distinguish an orthodox Anglican identity from a liberal Anglican identity that has allowed for actions such as Robinson's consecration and the theological beliefs that accompany such actions.

Even while Anglicans have been engaged in the larger process of re-examining their identity, this more immediate and more focused identity crisis over orthodox and liberal Anglican identities has emerged. As orthodox Anglicans begin the process of defining themselves more clearly against their liberal counterparts, it might initially appear that they would be successful in establishing a clearly orthodox Anglican identity. It is relatively easy, for example, to determine who is in favor of the ordination of homosexuals and who is not. As orthodox Anglicans continue the process of convergence, and as new technologies contribute to a smaller world in which orthodox Anglican leaders can more easily communicate and network with one another, on one level, orthodox Anglicans seem to know who they are.

However, the nature of this orthodox Anglicanism has not often been closely examined. Is it possible, for example, that what primarily unites orthodox Anglicans, in addition to their allegiance to the Bible, is a shared rejection of homosexuality and liberalism? The *orthodox* nature of this orthodox Anglican identity, fairly limited as it is, may be relatively clear;

---

3. In 2002 the diocese of New Westminster in the Anglican Church in Canada (ACC) voted to approve a rite for the blessing of same-sex unions. This action provoked a similar but less high-profile response from other Anglicans as have the actions of TEC. Although New Westminster's actions are part of the liberal actions that have precipitated the ongoing Anglican realignment, I'll be discussing the problem of liberalism and the responses of orthodox Anglicans primarily in terms of TEC.

however, the specifically Anglican nature of this identity is less clear. Is there an orthodox Anglican consensus about what the proper limits for a specifically *Anglican* identity are?

A crucial question regarding orthodox Anglicanism, then, is: "Do orthodox Anglicans have a clear and coherent Anglican identity on which they may soundly base their realignment?"

In order to answer such a question in detail, I must first define the terms "orthodox" and "liberal," as commonly understood by orthodox Anglicans. Since an orthodox Anglican identity is being asserted at least partially in response to a growing liberalism, I must also present the background to TEC's consecration of Robinson, as well as the liberal Anglicanism it represents. The growth of this liberal Anglicanism, culminating in the consecration of Robinson, has provoked a vigorous orthodox Anglican response that is best categorized as a realignment composed of three related parts, and so a description of the nature of the ongoing orthodox Anglican realignment will be offered. Chapter 1 will deal with all of these, and yet a discussion of orthodox Anglican identity will also require that an attempt be made to understand Anglican identity as a whole: this discussion will be the focus of chapter 2.

My task is a *descriptive* and not a *prescriptive* one. While more extended analyses of the specifically *orthodox* nature of this orthodox Anglican identity are important, my particular focus is on the clarity and coherence of the *Anglican* nature of this orthodox Anglican identity.

DEFINITIONS OF "ORTHODOX" AND "LIBERAL"

Orthodox[4] Anglicans share four primary characteristics (whether individuals, groups, or churches).

1. *They accept the literal truth of the statements of the historic Christian creeds, such as the virgin birth, the incarnation, and the physical resurrection of Jesus Christ.*

2. *They consider the Bible to be the inspired word of God, the supreme authority in the church, and a trustworthy guide in matters of doctrine and behavior.*

---

4. Sometimes the term "conservative" is used as a synonym for "orthodox," but "orthodox" is both more precise and is also used commonly by those who define themselves as orthodox Anglicans.

3. *Proceeding from their view of the Bible, they adhere to the traditional biblical interpretation that homosexuality is a sin.*

4. *They identify themselves as orthodox.*

Perhaps the best way to understand who orthodox Anglicans are is to list some of the important leaders, churches, and groups most commonly considered orthodox Anglicans. One of the most important groups of leaders to emerge in the continuing orthodox Anglican realignment at the international level is a group of primates and provinces that is generally categorized as the Global South and that includes most of the African, Asian, and Latin American provinces. This constitutes twenty-five out of the thirty-nine provinces that are members of the Anglican Communion. Most significantly, the ACNA, the orthodox Anglican body in North America, was recently added as a member of the Global South. Members of GAFCON, an international orthodox Anglican body which has a large degree of overlap with the Global South, are also solidly and identifiably orthodox. Provincial members of GAFCON include: the ACNA, South Sudan, Nigeria, Uganda, Tanzania, Kenya, Congo, Rwanda, Brazil, Myanmar, Chile, and South America (formerly The Southern Cone). Within North America, the churches that are part of the ACNA are clearly orthodox and consist of thirty dioceses and more than a thousand parishes. The Continuing churches that came out of TEC in the 1970s should also be considered orthodox Anglicans.

In contrast, some of the provinces that are sometimes considered liberal or to have liberal leadership include not only TEC and the Anglican Church in Canada but also the Anglican provinces in Scotland, Ireland, Wales, New Zealand, Australia (with the notable exception of the Diocese of Sydney), Brazil, and South Africa. The Church of England itself, with its recent moves to embrace homosexuality in the church, can no longer be counted as completely orthodox but is instead increasingly liberal.

The number of those within TEC who might be considered orthodox, as far as bishops and dioceses, is now negligible. Within TEC, sixty-three bishops voted for Robinson's consecration in 2003, forty-two voted against, and two abstained. Of these forty-two bishops, twenty might have been considered by orthodox Anglicans to be more clearly orthodox because they signed a statement, after the consecration of Robinson in 2003, stating that TEC had denied the plain teaching of Scripture and the moral consensus of the Church throughout the ages. The ten bishops whose dioceses became part of the Anglican Communion Network were sometimes understood to be more "reliably" orthodox.

More recently, when TEC voted in its 2018 General Council to mandate that all dioceses make provision for allowing same-sex marriage rites, only eight bishops were not in favor, and only one of these has refused the compromise that was offered. This leaves only one diocese/bishop in TEC that is reliably and clearly orthodox in terms of upholding orthodox Anglicans' views of marriage. The lopsided vote of the clergy (ninety-nine "yes," three "no," and four divided) and laity (101 "yes," five "no," and one divided) in favor of same-sex rites confirms the systemic liberalism within TEC.

In addition to these international and North American orthodox Anglicans, most Evangelical and Anglo-Catholic parishes in the UK should be considered orthodox, even while the Churches of England, Scotland, Wales and Ireland, as national churches, should not. Additionally, the bishops, clergy, and laity in the churches of the Global South (as the most convenient and comprehensive measure of orthodox Anglicanism) should also, in very large measure, be counted as orthodox.

As with the term "orthodox," the term "liberal" is used by orthodox Anglicans in a number of related ways. Just as some definitions of "orthodoxy" stand in contrast to the heresies that focus the need for an orthodox articulation of the faith, "liberal" (and its associated term, "revisionist") is often used as a contrast to "orthodox."

In the eyes of orthodox Anglicans, liberalism adapts the faith to the current naturalistic and man-centered worldview and abandons traditional dogmas when convenient or necessary. It views the Bible as a fallible human record of religious thought and experience, and not a divine revelation of truth, and, therefore, doubts the historical facts on which the Bible writers base Christianity. It insists that churches should be undogmatic and tolerant of divergent theologies and holds to an optimistic, evolutionary worldview that sees God's plan as perfecting an immature race rather than redeeming a fallen one. It is a theology of radical inclusion, since God has already accepted all people.

For orthodox Anglicans, this liberal Anglicanism has been growing in influence for some time, but the events of 2003 represented an important enough violation of biblical authority and morality to them that it provoked a vigorous, united response. The liberal Anglicanism to which orthodox Anglicans are reacting is best seen in TEC, the most frequently discussed locus of liberal Anglicanism. TEC is the best example of liberal Anglicanism because in many ways it has acted most clearly and officially in a liberal direction, and it is also the province in which Robinson was consecrated. This provocative action has received more attention than any other liberal action within Anglicanism and is widely regarded as being the action that precipitated the beginnings of a schism within the Anglican Communion. Robinson's consecration is also a primary focus of official Anglican Communion responses. The orthodox Anglicanism that is being asserted and is undergoing a process of realignment is best seen in the documents and writings of orthodox Anglicans as they articulate the reasons for and terms of the realignment they have initiated, as well as in the orthodox Anglican bodies that are uniting. In some ways, the orthodox Anglican realignment is also most clearly taking place in North America, because TEC and the Anglican Church in Canada are at the center of liberal actions that are provoking an orthodox response of realignment. These exemplars of liberal and orthodox Anglicanism will now be discussed in turn.

TEC'S LIBERALISM

Since at least the 1960s, TEC has shown both a willingness to make unilateral innovations to Anglican norms and an unwillingness to discipline theological heterodoxy or heresy. Bishop James Pike is the most famous representative of the trend toward liberalism in TEC in the 1960s, stating, for example, in his 1964 *Time for Christian Candor* that the Trinity was "excess baggage." Demonstrating that theological liberalism and unilateral innovations have often appeared together, Pike ordained a woman as a deacon in 1965, five years before the church gave its formal approval. When the House of Bishops prepared a presentment of Pike, they listed charges of five incorrect teachings concerning the Trinity; the Holy Spirit; the centrality of Christ for salvation; the Incarnation and the Atonement; and the elements of the Chicago-Lambeth Quadrilateral. Wanting to avoid an "oppressive image" and the necessity of dealing with theological definitions, TEC voted to censure Pike but did nothing to inhibit him in the exercise of his office.

The tendency of TEC to promote theological and ecclesiastical innovations became more evident in the 1970s. In 1974, after TEC had already voted twice against women's ordination to the priesthood, eleven women were ordained irregularly, without the approval of their bishops and standing committees. By a vote of one hundred twenty-nine to nine, the House of Bishops declared the ordinations invalid; however, in 1976 a vote to deal with this irregularity was quietly put aside. TEC's approach to Prayer Book revision was also indicative of a willingness to change Anglican norms autonomously. Thus, TEC became the first province to replace the traditional Prayer Book entirely as its liturgical standard and as one of its formularies.[5] In another move designed to make clear a break with Anglican tradition, TEC removed the Thirty-nine Articles from the main body of the Prayer Book in the 1979 Prayer Book to a "Historical Documents of the Church" section where they have been effectively marginalized.

TEC's actions regarding homosexuality have manifested a similar willingness to innovate autonomously and in a liberal direction. When Bishop Moore ordained a professing and practicing lesbian to the priesthood in 1977, the response of the House of Bishops was to do no more than express "disapproval" of Bishop Moore's action. Crucial for subsequent actions of TEC, the 1979 General Council adopted a resolution that declared it was not appropriate to ordain practicing homosexuals. In 1989, however, the Bishop of Newark ordained a practicing homosexual, and although the House of Bishops eventually expressed regret that good order had not been served by such unilateral actions, TEC enacted no censure or discipline. In the 1996 Righter trial, which dealt with Bishop Walter Righter's ordination of an active homosexual, a court of Episcopal bishops found that TEC had "no core doctrine" barring such ordinations, marking an official toleration of liberalism.

TEC's willingness to promote innovations in opposition to established Christian and Anglican norms was most dramatically manifested at its 2003 General Convention. At this General Convention, by a vote of eighty-four to sixty-six, TEC bishops defeated a resolution that directly affirmed Scripture as a standard in TEC that could not be violated. This significant rejection of the authority of Scripture gained little attention, however, because at the same General Convention the lay and clerical deputations, as well as the House of Bishops, voted to consecrate Robinson to the office of bishop. When TEC proceeded with its consecration, in spite of repeated pleas from a wide variety of Anglican leaders not to consecrate Robinson, the orthodox Anglican realignment that is now in progress began to take shape.

---

5. The Australian Prayer Book of 1978 was authorized a year before TEC's new Prayer Book; however, it was intended as a supplement to the 1662 Prayer Book, which, with the Thirty-nine Articles, remained the standard of doctrine and worship.

Most recently, TEC mandated in its 2018 General Convention that every bishop in his diocese provide for same-sex rites, even if the bishop is personally opposed.

ORTHODOX ANGLICAN REALIGNMENT: THE RESPONSE TO LIBERALISM

With some confidence that the larger Anglican Communion supports their interpretation of Scripture concerning homosexuality, orthodox Anglican leaders around the world have responded to the liberal actions of TEC in a variety of ways. These responses may be categorized as an orthodox Anglican realignment composed of three related movements: a *theological realignment*, an institutional or *ecclesial realignment*, and a *practical convergence*.

The response of orthodox Anglicans to TEC's actions is, most importantly, a *theological realignment* in which orthodox Anglicans more clearly distinguish themselves from liberal Anglicans, particularly over the issues of Scripture and homosexuality. What orthodox Anglicans see as substantial violations of Anglican norms, particularly violations of Scripture as the highest authority in Anglicanism and violations of normative Anglican interpretations of Scripture, have precipitated a desire for orthodox Anglicans to identify themselves primarily in terms of their theological commitments to Christian and Anglican orthodoxy. The orthodox theological response to Robinson's consecration, explaining why TEC's action has violated Anglican norms and broken the communion within the Anglican Communion, has been made in numerous publications, coming from a wide variety of individual theologians, church leaders, journals, think tanks, dioceses, provinces, and other groups.

The desire to maintain the historic faith and order of the church has in the minds of orthodox Anglicans also necessitated an institutional or *ecclesial realignment* that reflects the ongoing theological realignment. This ecclesial realignment is reflected in the way that orthodox provinces have viewed and acted towards those who have taken more liberal actions. More specifically, as a result of the actions of TEC's 2003 General Convention, twenty-two of the thirty-eight (at that time) Anglican provinces declared themselves to be either in broken or impaired communion with TEC. Although the exact nature of this "broken" or "impaired" communion is not always clear, the Anglican Church of Tanzania is representative of many provinces when it declared that it was not in communion with "bishops who consecrate homosexuals to the episcopate, ordain them to the priesthood and diaconate, license them to minister, or permit the blessing of same sex unions in their dioceses, as well as all homosexual priests and deacons and clergy who bless same sex unions."[6] Bishops of the Anglican Church of Nigeria stated that they were "breaking relationship not only with the Diocese of New Hampshire but with all the bishops and dioceses in TEC that have joined in this divisive and unscriptural act."[7] Another sign of the broken communion between provinces and primates occurred at the 2005 Primates' Meeting where many orthodox primates refused to participate in a joint communion service with TEC's Presiding Bishop Griswold. As a result of TEC's actions, therefore, a state of broken or impaired communion already exists within the Anglican Communion, which in itself signals some degree of ecclesial realignment.

The most significant ecclesial response to TEC's consecration of Gene Robinson, and consequent actions, has been the formation of GAFCON (Global Anglican Future Conference) and the ACNA (the Anglican Church in North America). GAFCON is the federation of conservative, global Anglican provinces and dioceses that are working both to provide a uniquely orthodox global Anglican body, as well as to find a way to reform the Anglican Communion. The ACNA is the federation of orthodox Anglican dioceses and parishes in North America that the Global South bishops called for, to be able to have one united orthodox Anglican body in North America with whom they could communicate and worship. These new ecclesial bodies are the embodiment of the theological orthodoxy and realignment that is the focus of this work.

Anglican Communion provinces whose leaders consider themselves to be orthodox see themselves as more closely related to orthodox Anglicans outside the official Anglican Communion than they are to TEC, still officially an Anglican Communion province. Their reaction was almost immediate to TEC's consecration of Robinson. Although neither the Reformed Episcopal Church (REC) nor the Anglican Province in America (APA) were official members of the Anglican Communion (since historically only one church in a geographical region can be in communion with

6. "Statement from the House of Bishops, Tanzania," https://www.anglicannews.org/news/2006/12/statement-from-the-house-of-bishops,-tanzania.aspx.

7. "Statement from the Bishops of the Anglican Church of Nigeria," https://www.anglicannews.org/news/2003/11/statement-from-the-bishops-of-the-anglican-church-of-nigeria.aspx.

the See of Canterbury and in the US that church is TEC), in 2005 they signed a covenant with the Church of Nigeria. Under the terms of this covenant, the three churches were united under a common Anglican heritage for the common cause of the gospel of Jesus Christ. Perhaps most importantly, the ministers of the three churches were able to exercise pastoral ministries in each of the other two churches. This willingness to affiliate based on theological orthodoxy over traditional Anglican ecclesial structures is most striking in the case of the ACNA, which is now by far the most significant ecclesial structure for orthodox Anglicans in North America.

While orthodox Anglicans are in large measure agreed upon the necessity of a theological realignment, they do not always share the same strategies regarding how to deal with liberalism. The ecclesial realignment, where it involves separating from TEC at this time, is controversial for some orthodox Anglicans. Some are concerned about not crossing geographical boundaries, and there are differences of opinion about the value of remaining in the Anglican Communion.

This ecclesial realignment, while generally affirmed by orthodox Anglicans, is therefore somewhat less clear than is the theological realignment, when this theological realignment is considered in its orthodox (and not its specifically Anglican) character.

The third kind of realignment that is currently in progress may be termed *convergence* and is represented by the way that different orthodox Anglican groups are working together for the common cause of orthodox Anglicanism. While the ecclesial realignment represents movements away from TEC and its liberalism and has resulted in fragmentation and some degree of chaos, convergence is an attempt to have orthodox Anglican churches and groups work together toward a common, united orthodox Anglicanism. These two aspects of realignment might be seen as complementary in nature, for even as orthodox Anglicans are trying to find ways to realign ecclesiastically, they are also trying to find ways to work together.

Convergence is also taking place on the international level, primarily through GAFCON. The convergence of orthodox Anglicans is expressed by the growing number of orthodox statements, orthodox theological "think-tanks," orthodox coalitions, and other new orthodox groups. While convergence is indeed taking place in terms of an increased orthodox Anglican synergy, the degree of convergence and the specifically Anglican identity that is shared by these orthodox Anglicans is more problematic, a point that will become clearer later.

CONCLUSION

The question of the necessity of realignment is settled for many orthodox Anglicans, and the orthodox nature of their identity, as limited to traditional creedal Christianity and traditional views of human sexuality and biblical authority, is relatively clear. While orthodox Anglicans agree theologically on the authority of the Bible and its teachings on sexual morality, is there theological and ecclesial agreement on specific elements that may be clearly identified as Anglican? The question of Anglican identity remains, therefore, for orthodox Anglicans, even if the question of liberal Anglicanism is answered in a clear and satisfactory way. It may be that not only an Anglican identity crisis exists but also a specifically orthodox Anglican identity crisis. This rapidly realigning orthodox Anglicanism is fairly clearly orthodox in the place it gives the Bible and in its views on homosexuality, but what will specifically identify it as Anglican?

I must attempt a definition of Anglicanism in order to evaluate the clarity and coherence of the identity that orthodox Anglicans are articulating in contrast to a liberal Anglicanism. Any stable orthodox Anglican identity must be able not only to distinguish itself from liberal Anglicanism but must also provide a relatively clear and coherent basis for realignment and convergence and for moving forward in the future.

Chapter 2 ————————————

Definitions of Anglicanism

DECLINING TO DEFINE ANGLICANISM has become an Anglican pastime in recent decades. When I was researching Anglicanism for this book, I sought out many well-known Anglican authorities. One, who, in all honesty, I was hoping would decisively settle the issue for me so that I wouldn't have to, fumbled around for a coherent definition. When I attended a well-known orthodox Anglican conference and a leader asked the question "What is Anglicanism?" the participants gave a Blind Man and the Elephant series of answers, some drawing attention to the liturgy or beauty, some because of its doctrine, etc. When I attended a three-day intensive seminary class on Anglicanism, at the end of the class the professor opened the class up for questions. Immediately, I raised my hand and asked the dreaded question: "What is Anglicanism?" After a few seconds of ponderous silence, the professor did what any good teacher would have done: he turned the question back on the class, saying, "What do *you* think?"

Issues of identity arise when cultures and individuals are fragmented, conflicted, and contested. It's not just Anglicans that are facing an identity crisis but also most churches and religions. A vigorous, nuanced definition of Anglican identity, therefore, has the potential to help all of us better understand and cope with our own identity crises.

Orthodox Anglicans have had some success in asserting a specifically *orthodox* Anglican identity, particularly with the creation of GAFCON and the ACNA. In addition, the actions of TEC, and now also the Church of England, have created an even greater chasm between orthodox and liberal versions of Anglicanism. However, the response of realignment assumes a common orthodox Anglican identity on which this realignment is based.

While the *orthodox* identity of this realigning orthodox Anglican identity may be relatively clear and explicitly articulated by orthodox Anglicans, the specifically *Anglican* nature of this orthodox Anglican identity is *not* clear, often only implicit, and in need of much greater definition.

In order to ultimately assess the specifically Anglican nature of this orthodox Anglicanism, I will offer some definition of Anglicanism by which any Anglican identity may be evaluated. Four types of definitions have been employed to understand Anglican identity: *ecclesial, normative, practical,* and *historical* definitions. After discussing the nature of each of these kinds of definitions, I will offer a model of religious identity that will help to synthesize these definitions of Anglican identity in terms of three stages in the historical development of Anglican identity.

DEFINITIONS OF ANGLICANISM

Although a universally agreed-upon definition of Anglicanism is not possible, some attempt must be made at definition if there is to be any consistent and coherent basis for analysis, action, and communion. If Anglicanism, including orthodox Anglicanism, is to be a useful identity, then it must be possible to offer some basis for knowing what Anglicanism is, why its continued existence is valuable, and who is and is not an Anglican.

Extended definitions of Anglicanism are surprisingly difficult to find, at least in part because it turns out that religious identities are inherently complex. This helps explain the reluctance of Anglicans to define just who they are. In a book titled *Anglican Identities*, Archbishop of Canterbury and celebrated Anglican scholar Rowan Williams overtly forswears "any aim to provide a fresh rallying-point for Anglican identity in these pages."[1] Williams's title itself seems to concede that defining a single Anglican identity may be an impossibility.

Many vague, confusing, and even conflicting definitions of Anglicanism have been offered, a fact that reflects the problem of Anglican identity. Some definitions are so broad and weak that, if they were generally accepted, they would strongly suggest that Anglicanism does not have

---

1. Williams, *Anglican Identities*, 7. Williams does, in fact, provide a "generous" definition of "Anglican," which he refers to as "the sort of Reformed Christian thinking that was done by those (in Britain at first, then far more widely) who were content to settle with a church order grounded in the historic ministry of bishops, priests, and deacons, and with the classical early Christian formulations of doctrine about God and Jesus Christ—the Nicene Creed and the Definition of Chalcedon" (*Anglican Identities*, 2).

a coherent enough identity to effectively discuss an Anglican future. Some say you're an Anglican if you self-identify as one, while others say that because Anglicanism stresses continuity with the universal church it has no separate identity.

The diversity in definitions of Anglicanism and the lack of extended definitions of Anglican identity suggest how confused Anglican identity has become and how difficult it has become to define. In spite of the difficulty in defining Anglicanism, four kinds of definitions of Anglicanism are commonly employed: *ecclesial*, *normative*, *practical*, and *historical* definitions.

Ecclesial Definitions of Anglicanism

Ecclesial or institutional definitions focus on official relationships between churches that claim a shared identity. Ecclesial definitions of Anglicanism most commonly center on equating Anglicanism with the Anglican Communion and thus provide the clearest definitions of Anglicanism, for it is relatively easy to say who is or is not a part of the Anglican Communion. The Anglican Communion is usually defined as the group of churches that are in formal communion with the See of Canterbury and is thus defined primarily in institutional or ecclesial terms, with little definition of theology or practice. The ecclesial unity of the Anglican Communion is maintained not only by the See of Canterbury but also by the other Instruments of Unity: the Lambeth Conferences, the Anglican Consultative Council, and the Primates' Meeting.

This ecclesial definition appears to be (not surprisingly) the basis for Lambeth Conference discussions and resolutions, as well as discussions arising out of the Anglican-Roman Catholic International Commission (ARCIC), which focus on the Anglican Communion as the locus of Anglicanism in the world today. The 1930 Lambeth Conference explicitly defined Anglicanism in this way: "It is part of the Holy Catholic and Apostolic Church. Its centre of unity is the See of Canterbury. *To be Anglican it is necessary to be in communion with that See*" (emphasis added).[2] Some prominent Anglican theologians also employ this ecclesial definition of Anglicanism. Paul Avis

2. "The Virginia Report," 3.32. While "The Virginia Report" quotes the 1930 Lambeth Conference as explicitly saying that "to be Anglican it is necessary to be in communion with that See," I can find no record of this statement in either the Resolutions of the 1930 Lambeth Conference or in the Reports of Committees. Since this statement has been repeated by others and has been incorporated into an important official Anglican Communion paper ("The Virginia Report"), it bears further scrutiny.

provisionally offers the succinct definition: "Anglicanism is the faith, practice, and spirit of the Churches of the Anglican Communion."[3]

While the ecclesial definition of Anglicanism has the virtues of simplicity and brevity and is one that is commonly employed, it has significant limitations. If "Anglican Communion" and "Anglicanism" are coterminous, would this mean that churches not formally in communion with Canterbury but that appear for all intents and purposes to be Anglican (for example, the member churches of the ACNA) should be considered less Anglican than churches in the Anglican Communion whose norms and practices are less clearly those of the Church of England (for example, the Church of South India)?

Even more critical to any definition of Anglicanism that hopes to survive the early part of the twenty-first century is the problem of how to define churches on either side of the growing orthodox/liberal schism. For example, the Global South provinces that are still part of the Anglican Communion are also leading members in GAFCON, of which the ACNA is a member. These orthodox provinces, which constitute the majority of the Anglican Communion, both in terms of the number of provinces and the number of members, clearly consider the ACNA to be fully Anglican, while the See of Canterbury and TEC do not.

The equation of Anglicanism with the Anglican Communion is a fairly recent phenomenon. Did Anglicanism not exist prior to the first Lambeth Conference in 1867, and did the mere creation of that Conference create Anglicanism by fiat? Such questions suggest that it is not sufficient to simply identify Anglicanism with the Anglican Communion and that other kinds of definitions of Anglicanism are necessary to fully describe it.

Normative Definitions of Anglicanism

Normative definitions are based on norms or standards that are deemed to be essential or critical aspects of a religious identity. Such normative definitions of Anglicanism are useful because they provide clear boundaries and make the acts of definition and identification more possible. Historically, as well, Anglicanism has been identified by certain Christian and Anglican norms. Without such normative definitions, Anglicanism, and other religious identities, have less clarity and coherence and are difficult to articulate.

3. Avis, "What is 'Anglicanism'?," 405. See also Holmes, *What is Anglicanism?*, vii, and Presler, "Old and New in Worship and Community," 721.

Any Anglican identity is, first and foremost, a *Christian* identity. The place to start in attempting any definition of Anglicanism is to understand how Anglicans have seen their distinctly *Christian* identity. The Chicago-Lambeth Quadrilateral is commonly used as a basis for understanding Anglican identity, particularly its Christian identity. The first part of the Quadrilateral is an important statement on the Holy Scriptures as "containing all things necessary to salvation," and as being the "rule and ultimate standard of faith;" the second cites the Apostles' and Nicene Creeds as sufficient summaries of Scripture; the third affirms the two sacraments of Baptism and the Lord's Supper; and the fourth affirms the historic episcopate, locally adapted.

However, the Quadrilateral was ecumenically oriented and was not intended to be an internal definition of Anglicanism. Also, those who wrote and approved the Quadrilateral were already committed to the specifically Anglican formularies of the traditional Prayer Book, the Ordinal, and (in most cases) the Articles of Religion. Some have tended to elevate the Quadrilateral to the position of an (if not *the*) Anglican formulary and to interpret it as a free-standing document interpreted apart from the context of the classical Anglican formularies within which it was written and has until recently been understood. By thus elevating the Lambeth Quadrilateral (and also demoting the classic Anglican formularies), some contemporary Anglicans reduce the specific content of Anglicanism in an attempt to allow for ever-increasing diversity. While this development is attractive because it may yield a wide range of interpretations, it is not conducive to a clear Anglican identity and definition.

Anglicanism may be defined in terms of two kinds of formularies: general and special. The general formularies, or *Christian* formularies, are ones that are not specifically Anglican and are thus related to the Lambeth Quadrilateral. These formularies have their basis in the two Testaments of the Bible and include: the creeds, the decrees of the ecumenical councils, the writings of the church fathers, and the common law of the church.

Particular or "Anglican" formularies include: *The Book of Common Prayer* (especially the 1662), the Ordinal, the Thirty-nine Articles, and the canon law of particular Anglican provinces, national churches, and dioceses. In terms of Anglicanism as a whole, it is the Prayer Book, the Ordinal, and the Articles of Religion that many especially see as the Anglican formularies, and their role in establishing and maintaining Anglican identity has been crucial.

Normative definitions are particularly useful and are based on established historical and authoritative norms that provide continuity and a context for other definitions. However, normative definitions require some ecclesial authority to define and defend them, and challenges to some of these historic norms are at the forefront of the crisis in Anglican identity. The struggle between orthodox and liberal understandings of Anglicanism is, to a large degree, a struggle over norms and interpretations of them, which come from competing ecclesial authorities. Because of the authority and stability of normative definitions of Anglicanism, challenges to these definitions have a dramatic ability to threaten a coherent Anglican identity.

Practical Definitions of Anglicanism

A third kind of definition of Anglicanism centers not on structures or norms but on certain characteristics of Anglicanism that might be categorized as "practical," or matters of a particularly Anglican ethos, behavior, and practice. Practical definitions of Anglicanism stand in contrast to normative definitions not only because they focus less on substance and more on practice but also because they are often used to deny or downplay normative definitions. Discussions of these practical definitions include characteristics such as a distinctive theological methodology (as opposed to a distinctive *content*), an ethos of comprehension and toleration, and notions of a dispersed authority. Urban Holmes employs a practical definition of Anglicanism based on a distinctive theological methodology, believing that Anglicanism is a mode of making sense of the experience of God and a particular approach to the construction of reality. He denies that Anglicanism has ever been a confessional church and believes that Anglicans privilege dialectic quest over precision and immediate closure.[4] Often, in describing a uniquely Anglican method of theology as Holmes does, the "three-legged stool" of Scripture, tradition, and reason is invoked.[5]

A second commonly mentioned practical characteristic of Anglican identity is the fact that authority in Anglicanism is a dispersed authority. As delineated by a statement of bishops to the 1948 Lambeth Conference,

4. Holmes, *What is Anglicanism?*, 1, 7.

5. The triad of "Scripture, tradition, and reason" is usually attributed to Richard Hooker, even though it is not clearly stated in his writings. For a discussion of how it is related to a practical definition of Anglicanism, see Avis's discussion in "What is Anglicanism'?," 411–16.

authority is dispersed or distributed among Scripture, tradition, creeds, the ministry of the word and sacraments, the witness of the saints, and the *consensus fidelium*, liturgy being the crucible in which these elements of authority are unified.[6] This notion of dispersed authority is important because depending on how highly these authorities are valued and how they are valued relative to one another, Anglicanism might be described in very different terms; this is especially true if Scripture is seen as only one among many dispersed authorities of equal importance and its normative authority thereby diminished.

A third and crucial practical definition of Anglicanism focuses on the Anglican characteristic of the "comprehension" of differing traditions or spiritualities. Anglican comprehension is a much-debated concept, but most would agree that on some level it is, indeed, characteristic of Anglicanism. Historically, this comprehension has been seen in terms of the way in which Anglicanism embraces both Catholic and Protestant principles, although comprehension has gone through stages of evolving meaning.

Practical definitions of Anglicanism are the weakest and least useful kind of definition, especially if used apart from other kinds of definitions. For example, founding an Anglican identity upon the use of the triad of Scripture, tradition, and reason is not as fruitful as it appears to be. It is not clear that there is anything particularly Anglican about using Scripture as a norm that is to be interpreted by tradition and reason: virtually all Christian traditions could claim to do so. Practical definitions by their very nature also tend to be vague. For example, when the idea of comprehension is enlarged from meaning a comprehension of both Catholic and Protestant principles (a generally useful practical definition) to meaning the kind of comprehension or toleration in which contradictory ideas are all seen as true, then a common, clear identity becomes difficult to maintain, and clear norms are undermined.[7]

Practical definitions, when understood as a characteristic *ethos* of a more substantial identity, may be useful in defining religious identities such as Anglicanism. When the idea of comprehension is used to describe the limits of acceptable diversity, for example, in the variety of Anglican spiritualities comprehended within a normative Anglican identity, it may prove a great asset. However, practical definitions of Anglicanism, whether based

6. "Lambeth Conference 1948," Part II, 84–86.

7. See J. I. Packer's discussion of four kinds of comprehension in *A Kind of Noah's Ark?*, 19–31. See also Sykes, *The Integrity of Anglicanism*.

on theological method, dispersed authority, the ideal of comprehension, or some other aspect, are often used to undermine normative definitions.

Historical Definitions of Anglicanism

A final kind of definition of Anglicanism commonly offered is a historical one, based on the development of the Anglican tradition over time. Some begin with the planting of the church in the British Isles in the first few centuries after Christ and stress the continuity of the church of England with the early, pre-Roman, church, in spite of nearly a millennium of the Church of England falling under the aegis of the Roman Catholic Church. More commonly, many define Anglicanism beginning with the reconstitution of the English church under Henry VIII because at this point the *de facto* distinctiveness of Anglicanism began.

Historically defined, Anglicanism has Catholic and Protestant characteristics that are both present in Anglicanism today. The English church has roots in the catholic faith that was planted in England in the first few centuries after Christ and was reshaped by the English Reformation that reformed the received catholic traditions, by the Evangelical and Catholic Revivals of the eighteenth and nineteenth centuries, and by other historical movements. Any historical definition of Anglicanism must also take into account recent developments,[8] especially the global Anglicanism now inculturated into former British colonies.

The value of historical definitions of Anglicanism is that they help locate Anglicanism in the context of the catholic and apostolic church and also help to highlight the continuity between contemporary and historical Anglicanism. They also facilitate understandings of the connections between and development of the other kinds of definitions in relation to each other. Since religious identities develop over time as the church interacts with culture, and since decisive reshapings of Anglican identity have occurred within the context of particular historical circumstances, a historical component is a crucial aspect of definitions of Anglicanism. Historical definitions of Anglicanism might, therefore, be useful in helping to understand

---

8. This is exactly the approach taken by William Sachs in *The Transformation of Anglicanism*. Sachs also recognizes the importance of certain common features that have provided a sort of historical definition of Anglicanism: English descent, structures of global scope, catholic forms, cultural malleability, and a Reformation heritage (*Transformation of Anglicanism*, 2).

how ecclesial, normative, and practical definitions relate and develop over time, a point which will be developed later in this chapter.

However, historical definitions of Anglicanism are also insufficient by themselves. They are limited in that they can only be *descriptive* of what has happened and cannot by themselves *prescribe* what ought to be or prescribe a means for evaluating what has happened. Every tradition with a varied history must have some principles or norms by which it values various aspects of that history, even if Anglicans often disagree about what principles or norms are most appropriate. A merely historical definition might have the effect of locking Anglicanism into the past, or, conversely, of enslaving it to a particular, contemporary identity in which what currently exists is taken as the definition of what should be. As Avis notes, "The fact remains that the political, social and cultural context can only provide the *occasion* for a church and contribute to the shaping of its outward form: it cannot provide a *definition* of a church or its raison d'etre."[9]

I will not offer a specifically historical definition of Anglicanism: instead, my contribution to a discussion of historical definitions of Anglicans consists of an application of my model of religious identity to Anglicanism in three stages of Anglican identity.

A MODEL OF RELIGIOUS IDENTITY

Each of these four kinds of definitions is useful in its place, and yet each is by itself insufficient to account for the complexity of Anglican (or any Christian) identity. Part of our difficulty in defining Anglicanism is we employ incomplete conceptions of religious identities, including that of Anglicanism. If we could integrate all four of these kinds of definitions into a larger model of understanding religious identity, then a more complete definition of Anglicanism, and one that is capable of explaining more of the complexities and ambiguities within Anglicanism, will emerge.

I am proposing just such a model of religious identity that will prove useful in more completely defining and explaining Anglican identity and that will hopefully apply to other religious identities.[10] In this model, Angli-

---

9. Avis, "What is 'Anglicanism'?," 406.

10. When I defended my PhD thesis at Lancaster University, a Muslim scholar sat in as a neutral observer. She remarked that my model of religious identity would be very useful to a discussion of Islam as well.

can identity is established and maintained by the interplay between ecclesial authority, norms, and practical elements of religion.

Chapters 3–5 will analyze each of these three elements or kinds of definitions of Anglicanism. Historical definitions will not be analyzed in their own chapter: instead, an understanding of Anglican identity based on the other definitions as they have related to each other over a three-stage historical development will be included in this chapter. Chapters 3–5 will also contain aspects of historical development as necessary.

Each of these three elements—ecclesial authority, norms, and practical elements—is important in creating and maintaining a religious identity, such as Anglicanism. A full description of identity will, therefore, take all three into account, and so definitions of Anglicanism that focus only on being in communion with Canterbury (ecclesial definitions), or only on the Bible, the Prayer Book, and the Articles (normative definitions), or only on a theological method or certain ideals such as comprehension (practical definitions) will be incomplete. These three elements are also related to other models for understanding ecclesial identity, such as Robert Paul's discussion of three authorities, the church, the Bible, and the Spirit,[11] which are related to "ecclesial authority," "norms," and "practical elements," respectively. J. Robert Wright also argues that in the history of Christianity in the West, three chief answers to the question of authority have been given, all of which have had some followers within the Anglican tradition. Those authorities are the institutional church, Scripture, and the individual testimony of the Holy Spirit,[12] which also correspond in general to "ecclesial authority," "norms," and "practical elements." Another confirmation of the three-fold nature of religious identity comes from the phrase "doctrine, discipline, and worship," a phrase commonly used by Anglicans to express their identity. "Doctrine" corresponds to normative identity; "discipline" to ecclesial identity; and "worship" to practical identity.

While the practical elements or ethos of a religious group are an important factor in religious identity, they are more difficult to identify in their interaction with authority and norms. Without denying the importance of practical definitions, I will present a simplified model of religious identity that may help in defining Anglicanism primarily in terms of the interplay between ecclesial authority and norms throughout Anglican history.

11. Paul, *Church in Search of Its Self*, 40–47.
12. Wright, "Sources and Structures of Authority."

In its simplest terms, religious identities are created and maintained most clearly when strong ecclesial authority and clear norms are present. In the absence of a strong religious authority, diversity is the natural state of things. When the religious activity of a society is unregulated, it will tend to be very pluralistic, but when the state uses coercive force to regulate religious activity, religious monopolies are more likely. Whenever there is a strong authority willing to act strongly, diversity will be limited to some degree, and religious identity will be more clearly preserved. This strong authority that employs coercive force to regulate the religious economy often comes from the state, but an ecclesiastical authority, such as the Roman Catholic Church of the medieval period, may also act to limit religious diversity.[13]

The role of ecclesial authority in establishing and maintaining religious identities is accompanied and supported by the religious norms that interact with this authority. Often, these norms are theological in nature, although in Anglicanism the liturgical norm of the Prayer Book has a critical importance that is not present in many other Christian churches. Preserving core teachings that undergo little change is critical to the long-term vitality of churches. Such core teachings generate high levels of member commitment and tight social networks and preserve the religious capital accrued and valued by existing members. When these core teachings are inimitable, they help to retain members and prevent schisms. When, therefore, religious organizations revise core teachings, they threaten organizational vitality.[14]

Confirmation of this thesis comes from studies of the Protestant Reformation. The polar tendencies of an individualist religion of the heart and an individualist religion of the head had to be held together in Protestantism by either the authority of the state or by a strong doctrine of the church with a firm ecclesiastical discipline, or else Protestantism would divide and swing between these two theological extremes.[15] Significantly for any study of orthodox Anglicanism, orthodox Anglican Philip Turner states that

13. I am indebted especially to the work of Rodney Stark for these insights. See Stark and Finke, *Acts of Faith*, 193–99, as well as Stark and Bainbridge, *Future of Religion*, 99–125.

14. Roger Finke, "Innovative Returns to Tradition," 20–23.

15. Paul, *Church in Search of Its Self*, 53n.

"authority, as classically understood, exists to strengthen and further the common beliefs and practices that give a people identity."[16]

Studies of denominational identity also suggest that religious identity is related to the relationship between authority and norms. Roozen and Nieman believe that any adequate understanding of denominations must include the relationship between organization and theology,[17] that is, "ecclesial authority" and "norms." Roozen concludes that groups which tend to be more theologically diffuse and preclude a definitive theological assessment will experience continued political contestation because of the lack of consensus. Furthermore, accountability and discipline in such groups is too weak to mitigate the corrosive potential of individualism and voluntarism. Strength of identity generally leads to greater unity and less fragmentation. This strength of identity exists when the characteristics of a church are explicit and widely shared; invoke commitment and group loyalty and cohesion; have consequences discernible in the church's strategies for action; and provide distinguishable boundaries.[18]

This model of religious identity has great power to explain important distortions of Christian identities: norms without ecclesial identity will tend to become contested, fragmented, and heretical; ecclesial authority without clear norms will tend to become arbitrary and tyrannical; and behaviors and practices without an ecclesial identity and norms will tend to become moralistic and then relativistic.

A brief review of the history of Anglican identity, in terms of this model of ecclesial authority and norms, will suggest that a strong authority that enforces clear norms will produce a strong and clear identity, while any reduction of the strength of either ecclesial authority or norms is likely to lead to a weaker and less clear identity. This, in turn, suggests that a large part of the contemporary Anglican identity crisis may be due to a failure of Anglicanism to identify a strong ecclesial authority to succeed the English state, as well as to the weakening of traditional Anglican norms.

16. Radner and Turner, *The Fate of Communion*, 7. Turner's comment is especially significant because *Fate of Communion* is probably the best articulation of the Communion Conservative position that will be discussed later in this chapter.

17. Roozen and Nieman, "Introduction," 9.

18. Roozen, "National Denominational Structures' Engagement," 591–604.

A HISTORY OF ANGLICAN IDENTITY

This integrated and nuanced model of religious identity has the virtue of helping to explain the complex nature of Anglican identity as it has developed over time (thus highlighting the importance of the historical element in definitions of Anglicanism) and helping confirm the idea that a more complete definition of Anglicanism should take into account ecclesial authority, norms, and practical definitions as they interact over time. Such a model will also highlight the complexity of the present Anglican identity that has proven so difficult to define and which is now relatively weak.

The historical evolution of Anglican identity may be seen as having taken place in roughly three stages, each of which can be summarized primarily in terms of the relationship between ecclesial authority and norms, while also taking into account some of the important new developments of each stage which may be considered elements of a practical identity. The first stage lasted from 1533 to 1833; the second stage from 1833 to the middle of the twentieth century; and the third stage from the middle of the twentieth century until the present. These stages can only serve as crude markers of what are more complex phenomena, and it is not, ultimately, possible to present them in terms of a precise chronology. In reality, the stages overlap, and within all of the stages multiple identities emerged side by side, even if the newly emerging identities were often not recognized until a later time.

My own opinion is that Anglicanism is an ecclesial identity that can be traced back to the early centuries after Christ when Christianity originally came to the British Isles. A major, initial stage of Anglicanism that predates 1533 by more than a millennium lasted from the early centuries after Christ until Augustine of Canterbury was sent by Gregory the Great to England in 597. This earliest Anglican identity was British, Celtic, and Anglo-Saxon. After 597 (and especially after the Synod of Whitby in 664), a second early stage of Anglicanism began, one in which the English Church increasingly came under domination by the Roman Catholic Church, even while continuing to assert varying degrees of independence. Each of these two earlier stages, in turn, could be subdivided into further stages. In spite of my belief that an authentically British/English Church existed long before Henry VIII's "Great Matter," I've chosen to begin my study of Anglican identity in 1533 because a definitive Anglican identity was forged in the sixteenth century, one which is still especially relevant to a discussion of contemporary Anglican identity.

The First Stage of Anglican Identity

In the first stage of Anglican identity, (roughly 1533 to 1833), a strong *authority* and clear *norms* were asserted in the sixteenth and seventeenth centuries and maintained in the eighteenth and nineteenth centuries, largely under the influence of the establishment of the Church of England by the state. Therefore, Anglican *identity* was also fairly clear and strong. Beginning in 1533, Henry VIII's aspirations changed the relationship of the church to the state, not only in freeing the Church of England from papal influence but also by placing the English church to a larger degree under the authority of the Crown. The two go together, for once the authority of the Roman Catholic Church was removed, some other authority had to be found. This authority, so crucial to understanding Anglican identity, was, to a very large degree, the English church as dependent on and in some ways coordinate with the English state, initially the Crown but with the role of Parliament increasing over time. The Henrician Revolution, therefore, had an important political component (or ecclesial authority), and although it initially left the beliefs and practices of the English Church relatively untouched, it allowed for further ecclesiastical change to be enacted by political authority. While the full implications for the *identity* of the Church of England were not immediately clear, the *authority* of the Church of England was clearly changed from that of the Pope and magisterium to that of the state and the religious authorities it authorized and sponsored.

Although the brief reign of Edward VI involved no real change in the *authority* of the Church of England from that of Henry's reign, the change in *identity* that began in Henry's reign began to take a different shape, the direction of which became more clear with the rapid and extensive doctrinal and liturgical changes or change in Anglican norms that took place in Edward's reign. Scholars may dispute the exact nature of Anglican identity under Edward, but they agree that under his reign Archbishop of Canterbury Thomas Cranmer enacted changes that had important implications for Anglican identity. The changes in Anglican identity were most saliently portrayed in Cranmer's Prayer Books of 1549 and 1552, as well as in the Forty-two Articles of 1553. After a brief return to Roman Catholicism under Mary Tudor (1553–1558), in which the *identity, authority,* and *norms* of the Church of England officially reverted to Roman Catholicism, Elizabeth I returned the *identity, authority,* and *norms* essentially to what they had been under Edward. The authority was as an established church that was directly under the authority of the Crown (and later

Parliament). Cranmer's 1552 Prayer Book was restored in 1559 with only minor revisions as an Anglican norm, and the Thirty-nine Articles took their definitive form in 1571.

The *identity* that was established by the end of Elizabeth's reign has often been categorized as a Reformed Catholic one: the Church of England claimed to be a catholic church that kept the apostolic and catholic faith while reforming the perceived errors and abuses that had accumulated in the Roman Catholic Church of the late medieval period. Under the political establishment of the Church of England, whose *identity* was a kind of Reformed Catholicism and whose *authority* was the established church under the state, the specifically Anglican *norms* of the Prayer Book and Articles were established and acted as the primary markers of this Reformed Catholic identity. While some debate exists about how strongly Protestant the English Reformation and Elizabethan Settlement were in their reformation of certain traditions, scholars generally agree that Cranmer and others were also attempting to retain many of the catholic traditions of the church (as opposed to the more radical reforms of Puritans and Anabaptists).

The concept of Anglicanism as a Reformed Catholicism is still an important one: a 1948 Lambeth Conference report stated that the Prayer Book is the embodiment of the Reformed Catholic character of Anglicanism and that the English Reformers were not trying to make a new church but were continuing the one that had existed before.[19] Henry Chadwick is a representative of a long line of distinguished scholars who see the Prayer Book and Articles as having a Reformed Catholic character when he states that "most of the substance of the Articles may be labeled Reformed Catholicism."[20]

In light of the consistent appeal of many Anglican Reformers and of Anglican divines of the seventeenth century to the church fathers and the catholic faith, it seems reasonable to assign a Reformed Catholic character to the Anglicanism of this period, especially in the seventeenth century.[21] Although even in this first stage Anglican identity was rendered relatively clear because of the clear authority of the state and the normative formularies it produced, Anglican identity was still a complex mixture of

19. "The Anglican Communion," Lambeth Conference 1948, 83.

20. Chadwick, "Tradition, Fathers, and Councils," 93.

21. See Quantin, *The Church of England*, who presents abundant evidence of the shift toward a greater emphasis on the church fathers and catholicity in the seventeenth century, when compared to the sixteenth-century Anglican divines and Reformers.

different identities, not the least of which were its Protestant and Catholic identities. The actual complexity of even this relatively clear identity is suggested by the fact that from the reign of Henry VIII until 1688 we may discern, in fact, *six* time periods and that the English Reformation lasted not forty years but 160 years.[22]

One notable movement within Anglicanism at this time, which can be considered an aspect of practical Anglican identity, was the Evangelical Revival which took place in the mid to later eighteenth century. Emphases of the Evangelical Revival which were woven into the tapestry of Anglican identity include: a renewed emphasis on Scripture; the importance of personal conversion narratives; sermons (sometimes over the sacraments); and individual piety (sometimes over the corporate church). The Evangelical Revival brought with it an emphasis on private and public morality, a missionary zeal to reach the lost peoples of the world, and a passion to abolish the sin of slavery.

The Second Stage of Anglican Identity

In the second stage of Anglican identity (roughly from 1833 to the mid-twentieth century), as the Church of England planted churches in English colonies, *authority* began to weaken while *norms* continued to remain relatively strong for a period. *Identity* remained relatively clear, even though some of the foundations for a weaker identity were in place. Once the Protestant Church in the United States of America (PECUSA)[23] was created in the late eighteenth century as an ecclesiastical entity legally and officially separate from the Church of England, Anglicanism began to enter what might be called its second stage, a stage which roughly lasted from the mid-eighteenth century until perhaps the 1960s and the multiplication of new Anglican provinces. When the Church of England was the only ecclesiastical entity within "Anglicanism," it made no sense to speak of "Anglicanism" but only of the Church of England or *ecclesia Anglicana*. With the expansion of Anglicanism beyond the Church of England, some other way of comprehending the Church of England in relation to her former colonies was made necessary. In terms of ecclesial *authority* within Anglicanism as a whole, in

22. Zahl, *Protestant Face of Anglicanism*, 12–27.

23. I will be referring primarily to PECUSA as the exemplar of the changes in the second stage of Anglicanism, although the Scottish Episcopal Church was also in existence at this time.

this second stage a new understanding of authority had to emerge because the Church of England, in its established relationship with the state, could no longer serve as the ecclesiastical authority for PECUSA, for example. In this second stage, before the Anglican Communion was officially created, there was no clear authority for Anglicanism as a whole, but only separate authorities within the Church of England and PECUSA, what later came to be seen as separate provinces within an Anglican Communion.

During this second stage, especially as the Lambeth Conference developed without any juridical authority, provincial autonomy became the norm. The implications of this weak Communion-wide authority would not be seen clearly until the third stage, and yet the foundation was set in this second stage. In essence, as Anglicanism was transformed from being the Church of England to being a relationship between churches in continuity with the Church of England, authority was weakening, even while identity appeared to remain relatively unchanged.

Without a common authority, it might appear likely that separate Anglican provinces such as PECUSA would diversify and diverge relatively rapidly, and yet the case of PECUSA seems to suggest that if a common *identity* is sought, especially as embodied in common *norms*, diversity might still be contained for a time. PECUSA's desire to retain a common identity with the Church of England is clear from the Preface to the original 1789 *Book of Common Prayer* of PECUSA, which contains the following statement, also printed in subsequent revisions: "This Church is far from intending to depart from the Church of England in any essential point of doctrine, discipline, or worship."[24] This desire to retain continuity with the Church of England produced a resolution in 1814 in PECUSA's General Convention that affirmed continuity with the Church of England and stated that aside from a civil distinction the two churches were in fact the same body that shared the same doctrine, discipline, and worship.[25]

Although it was under a separate ecclesiastical authority, PECUSA saw its identity in terms of continuity with the Church of England, which saw itself in terms of continuity with the ancient, catholic, apostolic church. The High Churchmen in the early nineteenth century believed that the United Church of England and Ireland with its colonial

24. "Preface," *Book of Common Prayer* (1789). A 1786 Resolution of PECUSA's General Convention also stated its resolution to maintain the same essential articles of faith and discipline as the Church of England.

25. Radner, "Conciliarity and the American Evasion," in Radner and Turner, *Fate of Communion*, 232.

appendages, the Scottish Episcopal Church, and PECUSA all belonged to each other, even before these three churches were technically in communion with one another (interchangeability of ministers was established in 1840). The idea that the three churches belonged together grew gradually, and yet there was still no common, collective name for them. Terms such as "The Reformed Catholic Church" and "The Reformed Episcopal Church" were used by some and continued in use until 1867, but it was the term "Anglican Communion," first used in 1851 but not coming into more prominent usage until 1867, which prevailed in the end. The term "Anglicanism" itself, suggesting an identity that was not identical with the Church of England, was first used in 1838 by John Henry Newman, as the Oxford Movement attempted to establish the Church of England on a new basis other than that of an established church.

This common identity of the Church of England and PECUSA was not only a general attempt to claim a continuity of identity but also included the retention of Anglican *norms*: the Prayer Book in a form close to the original, the Thirty-nine Articles (restored to PECUSA in 1801), the Ordinal, the episcopacy, the creeds and first four ecumenical councils, and, in a looser way, the witness of the patristic era. The retention of the Prayer Book and the Articles especially marked PECUSA's desire to retain the Reformed Catholic identity it had inherited from the Church of England, and, in fact, wherever the traditional Prayer Book and Articles are clearly retained as norms they may be seen as boundary markers that help establish and maintain some kind of a Reformed Catholic identity. The role of the Prayer Book in particular, as a kind of surrogate authority for Anglicanism has been noted by many.[26]

In this second stage of Anglican identity, the Church of England began to predicate itself on an authority different from that of the state authority that had been accepted since the time of Cranmer. This shift in authority may be characterized as a change in paradigm from an Erastian one to an apostolic one. Although the influence of the state in the life of the Church of England continued, the success of the Oxford Movement (initiated in 1833), with its anti-Erastian stance and desire to establish the Church of England upon the foundation of its catholic and apostolic nature, resulted in this new apostolic paradigm becoming more influential. The pre-existing Reformed Catholic identity of Anglicanism potentially fit with this apostolic

26. Sykes, *The Integrity of Anglicanism*, 45–46, 96; Bennett, "Preface to Crockford's Clerical Directory," 197–98; Gibson, "Future Role of Liturgy," 17, 20.

paradigm, even if the details of authority in such a paradigm needed to be worked out. Radner and Turner note, "As the Anglican Communion grew, conformity to the Doctrine and Discipline of the Church of England was transformed into 'uniformity with the "Primitive Church"' of the first four centuries as explicated in the *Book of Common Prayer* shared throughout the globe."[27] Partially for this reason, the Prayer Book continued to act as a strong authority in this second stage. This transformation might be seen as lying on the cusp of the second and third stages of Anglican identity, for it represents another step away from an identity that is in organic continuity with the Church of England. It thus became possible to think of Anglicanism in terms of primitivism, as a direct return to the early church, without necessarily having an organic continuity with the Church of England itself. This conception of being Anglican without being English came to fruition in the third stage of development.

Also during this second stage, the Anglicanism that was planted in the still dependent English colonies was frequently a different Anglican identity from that which existed in the Church of England or PECUSA. For example, the Anglican spirituality planted and sustained in East Africa, as represented by Uganda, was primarily a revivalistic Evangelical Anglican spirituality, and Ugandan Anglicans have probably never seen themselves as Reformed Catholics: the catholic spirituality is relatively absent in some provinces such as the Church of Uganda. This different Anglican identity was not always evident until the influence of the Church of England was reduced and communications developed to the point that the identity of global Anglicanism began to be better known. The transforming effect of the colonial Anglican churches, planted in stage two, upon the identity of Anglicanism would not be seen fully until the later part of stage three and the emergence of a post-colonial Anglicanism more clearly differentiated from the Church of England.

This second stage, then, witnessed not only the emergence of PECUSA, with a relatively large degree of continuity with the Church of England, but also the development of a greater pan-Anglicanism, represented by the Lambeth Conferences, and the planting of colonial and mission churches whose influence on Anglican identity would not be felt until a much later date. Since Anglicanism, to the degree that it was even seen as "Anglicanism," was seen primarily through the eyes of the English and American churches, a greater degree of continuity and uniformity was assumed than

27. Radner and Turner, *Fate of Communion*, 152.

actually existed in this second stage, an assumption that often still exists today. In short, Anglican identity in this second stage was still relatively clear and strong norms were preserved, even as authority became more ambiguous and identity was changing in unnoticed ways.

Along with the development of colonial Anglican churches in this second stage, two other significant movements acted in practical ways to transform the character of Anglican identity. The first was the Oxford Movement, usually dated from Keble's 1833 Assize Sermon, which trumpeted the dangers of the English church being governed by the English state at a time when non-Anglicans in Parliament enforced binding legislation concerning the life of the church. For this reason, the Tractarians (named after *The Tracts for The Times* published by the Oxford Movement leaders) sought to establish the Church of England, and, therefore, Anglican identity on the basis of an apostolic, rather than an Erastian, model. The Oxford Movement has sometimes been called The Catholic Revival, and it changed the ethos of the Church of England in dramatic ways. At its heart, the Oxford Movement was a return to both the patristic consensus and the Prayer Book rule of life, which, in various ways, had fallen into disuse by the beginning of the nineteenth century. Among the contributions of the Oxford Movement to a practical Anglican identity are such accomplishments as: greater frequency of the celebration of the Holy Communion; a restoration of the Daily Office as a daily celebration; liturgical experimentation; more ornate ceremonial; the practice of sacramental confession; the founding of theological colleges; the renewal of the monastic life; a revival and interest in architecture and other arts; a revival of patristic literature; an emphasis on a poetic and sacramental worldview in contrast to rationalism and liberalism; and a renewal of hymnody from past ages. The Oxford Movement prepared the way for the emergence of an Anglo-Catholic spirituality, which has now become a part of Anglican identity.

A second important movement in the second stage of Anglican identity was a growing liberal strand of Anglicanism. In previous centuries, Anglicans who were willing to depart from traditional theology in various ways were called Latitudinarians. In the nineteenth century, a Broad Church identity emerged, which exalted the place of human reason, often over and against the Scriptures or church tradition, as the final arbiter of truth. During this same century, Darwin's *Origin of the Species* provoked a challenge to traditional Christian theology, while German biblical criticism made its way into England and helped undermine confidence in the authority and trustworthiness of the Christian Bible. By the twentieth century, this Broad Church Anglican identity had morphed into the liberalism that has proven so challenging to Anglican identity in the twenty-first century.

The Third Stage of Anglican Identity

In the third and current stage (roughly from the mid-twentieth century to the present), as English colonies gained their independence, both *authority* and *norms* became relatively weak; therefore, *identity* has become relatively weak. This third stage has actually co-existed with the first-stage identity of Anglicanism as the Reformed Catholicism of the Church of England and the second-stage identities of continuity with the Church of England and the less well-recognized and still developing identity of a global Anglicanism that was often more Evangelical than Catholic. In one sense, the Anglican Communion came into being with the Lambeth Conferences in 1867, and so the roots of stage three go back at least that far. Owen Chadwick believes that when the Lambeth Conference was created, it created a consciousness of the Anglican Communion, and this consciousness of the Anglican Communion produced a desire to embody it in instruments.[28] As colonies gained their independence and the number of provinces and members within the Anglican Communion grew, the idea that Anglicanism was, in essence, the Anglican Communion gained strength. In fact, the insistence on referring to Canterbury in provincial constitutions is relatively new. The idea of a worldwide Communion and of Canterbury as the primary instrument of unity are developments of the past sixty years, coinciding with the new autonomy of previously colonial churches. The relatively recent origins of the majority of Anglican provinces helps partially explain the slow emergence of an understanding of Anglicanism as diverse, global, and defined by the Anglican Communion. Of the thirty-nine Anglican provinces, only ten were in existence before 1947. Twenty-two of the thirty-nine provinces were created since 1969, and ten of them since 1988. The ideal of being a global Communion characterized by a high degree of interconnectedness and mutual awareness may be as recent as the 1990s: this is especially true for orthodox Anglicans in the West who re-discovered their Global South Anglican brothers and sisters as a result of the 1998 Lambeth Conference.

This *identity* of Anglicanism as those churches in communion with the See of Canterbury, or the Anglican Communion, has in many ways become

28. Chadwick, "Introduction," xiii.

the dominant Anglican identity that marks what is a third stage of Anglican identity, even while the previous identities also continue to exist. In this third stage of Anglican identity, the ecclesial authority of Anglicanism is weak: provincial autonomy, in practice, trumps the moral or advisory authority of the four Instruments of Unity of the Anglican Communion. There is no authority to check the diversity between provinces, a problem acutely identified by TEC's consecration of Gene Robinson in defiance of all four Instruments of Unity and the pleading of Anglican leaders worldwide.

The *norms* by which Anglicanism, in its identity as the Anglican Communion, identifies itself are also relatively weak. At the Anglican Communion level, there are no formularies that all provinces must accept, although the four parts of the Lambeth Quadrilateral are generally asserted as being essential: instead, clear and strong norms have been replaced with an emphasis on processes and vague relationships. Instead of the Prayer Book and Articles, the Anglican Communion norms appear to be such things as the ideals of communion (*koinonia*), mutual respect for provincial autonomy, subsidiarity, and interdependence. The great emphasis currently placed on the Instruments of Unity is at least in part a compensation for the relegation of the Prayer Book (with its unifying power) to one option among many. A significant fact of this third stage of Anglican identity, then, is that even as an ecclesial definition of Anglicanism was becoming dominant (Anglicanism as the Anglican Communion), both ecclesial authority and the norms that supported and worked with such authority were weakening. This key dynamic is crucial for understanding some of the reasons why many orthodox Anglicans believe there is an Anglican identity crisis.

The identity of Anglicanism is continuing to shift away from the idea of continuity with the ancient church through continuity with the Church of England. It is not just the doctrine, discipline, and worship of the Church of England from which Anglicanism is now distancing itself (especially by distancing itself from the Articles and Prayer Book) but also an identity that is self-professedly based on the Church of England. Colonial provinces have now officially changed their identities from being "The Church of England" in a particular country to simply being "The Church" of that country. The Anglican Church in Canada did not change from its original name of the Church of England in Canada until 1958, while the Anglican Church of Australia was the Church of England in Australia until 1981.

The "Anglo-Saxon captivity" of Anglicanism is also a concern for many, and the new provinces continue to express a desire to inculturate in ways separate from their English roots. While communion with Canterbury is important to many current definitions of Anglicanism, dissatisfaction with the speed and clarity with which the See of Canterbury has responded to the current crisis over homosexuality and biblical authority makes many orthodox Anglicans question the continuing importance and value of an Anglican identity based on communion with Canterbury.[29]

Significant aspects of practical Anglican identity that have emerged during this time include, especially, the independence of former British colonies that have now formed independent Anglican churches, free to in-culturate and adapt their own forms of Anglican spiritualities. At the same time, liberalism has gained ascendency in the Western Anglican provinces, such as TEC, the ACC, and the Church of England. In response to this, GAFCON and ACNA have emerged.

In summary, a normative Anglican identity of a Reformed Catholi-cism emerged in the sixteenth century, enforced by the English state and marked by the norms of the Prayer Book and Articles and an English ethos (stage one). In stage two, the identity evolved to a continuity with the Church of England and the ancient church based on a continuing Reformed Catholic identity and common norms that are not enforced at the Communion level, accompanied by the competing Anglican identities of the emerging colonies and the notion of Anglicanism as the Anglican Communion. This identity, in turn, became an identity founded upon being in communion with the See of Canterbury as the definition of be-ing Anglican but with no strong authority at the Communion-wide level and few common norms (stage three). This overview of Anglican identity, seen in terms of the historical interaction of ecclesial authority and norms, provides some confirmation for the idea that Anglican identity has been created and maintained to some degree by the interaction of ecclesial au-thority and norms over time. It also provides a basis for understanding the complexity of Anglican identity and the relatively weak and unclear nature of Anglican identity at present.

While I have presented these three stages as linear and progressive, in reality they are overlapping identities that have coexisted in complex ways: this is more clearly the case at present. Anglican identity is less like a single document that has been erased and replaced with another

---

29. The Church of Nigeria is an example of this response, having changed the terms of communion with itself from a common communion with Canterbury to a common identity based on the 1662 Prayer Book and Articles.

document and more like a palimpsest on which a succession of still extant documents has been written. The fact that all stages with their differentiated identities coexist and interact is possibly one of the reasons that not many clear definitions of Anglicanism have been offered, despite the widespread recognition of an Anglican identity crisis and the ongoing orthodox Anglican realignment.

Anglicans, including orthodox Anglicans, have an identity crisis to a large degree because there is a weak authority and unclear norms and now pre-existing, competing, and multiple, sometimes incompatible, identities. In the absence of strong authority and norms, diversity in Anglicanism is increasing and making the establishment of any clear identity difficult, a fact that often has not been adequately recognized.

It is possible that Anglicanism is witnessing a fourth stage of Anglican identity and one that represents a final break with continuity with the Church of England and any clearly distinguishable Anglican identity. In this fourth stage, Anglicanism may become a diverse federation or network of postcolonial churches whose relationships to the doctrine, discipline, and worship of the Church of England, as well as to each other, will also be diverse and not easily categorized. If, as Kevin Ward believes, "the growing sense of a worldwide Anglican identity coincided with the age of high imperialism,"[30] the disintegration of this colonial imperialism suggests that this fourth stage may represent a "post-Anglican" Anglicanism in which Anglican identity has little necessary connection with the Church of England and little, collective, global coherence.

This point has special relevance to orthodox Anglicans who, although they are articulating a more clearly orthodox identity, are still a part of this complex and often ambiguous Anglican identity. Orthodox Anglicans not only have the same challenges in understanding Anglican identity that Anglicans in general have but are also active participants in the creation of what may be a "post-Anglican" Anglicanism.

The three stages of Anglican identity may be summarized in this way:

Stage I: 1533–1833—Erastian Reformed Catholicism, with strong authority and strong norms

Stage II: 1833–1960s—the development of colonial, global relationships, with continuing authority and norms that were relatively strong

---

30. Ward, *History of Global Anglicanism*, 300.

Stage III: 1960s–present—the emergence of a global Anglican Communion with a corresponding increase in diversity and a weakening of both authority and norms

ANGLICANISM DEFINED

I've spoken about the typical Anglican avoidance of defining Anglicanism due to its complex and ambiguous nature and built the foundation for a more nuanced and comprehensive definition. Now that I've articulated a complex model of Anglican identity, I'm in a position to offer my best attempt at a definition of Anglicanism. Recognizing the full weight of the truism that "fools rush in where angels dare to tread," here it is: "Anglicanism is the life of the catholic church that was planted in England in the first few centuries after Christ; reshaped decisively by the English Reformation that reformed the received catholic traditions and also by the Evangelical and Catholic Revivals and other historical movements of the Spirit; and that has now been inculturated into independent, global churches."

THE STATE OF ORTHODOX ANGLICAN IDENTITY

What, then, is the present state of orthodox Anglican identity within the context of these larger three stages of Anglicanism and the definition I've offered?

The orthodox Anglican realignment that is underway, especially the convergence into an identifiably orthodox Anglicanism, is predicated on a relatively clear and coherent orthodox Anglican identity. What would constitute such a relatively clear and coherent orthodox Anglican identity? At a minimum, it should be possible for orthodox Anglicans to say with some degree of clarity and certainty who is an orthodox Anglican and who is not and to articulate some criteria by which it is possible to judge whether or not one is an Anglican. While orthodox Anglicans are making a relatively clear distinction about Anglican orthodoxy, based on views of the creeds, the Bible, and biblical sexual morality, they are finding it more difficult to articulate an orthodox *Anglicanism*. To articulate a relatively clear and coherent orthodox Anglican identity, orthodox Anglicans should be able to reach some general consensus about the nature of orthodox Anglicanism in terms of ecclesial, normative, and practical definitions. Chapters 3–5 will present evidence that orthodox Anglicans are finding it difficult to articulate such an orthodox Anglican identity in a clear and coherent way, even though they seek just such an identity.

Orthodox Anglicans are producing two kinds of identity: a stricter kind of clear and coherent identity that they desire and that may be realized to some degree, and a looser, more diverse kind of identity that will actually be lived out to a larger degree. The tension between these two views is captured in Robert Schreiter's work, *The New Catholicity: Theology Between the Global and the Local*. Schreiter discusses the construction of religious identity in terms of two models of culture, what he terms "*integrated* concepts of culture" and "*globalized* concepts of culture." According to Schreiter, "*integrated* concepts of culture depict culture as patterned systems in which the various elements are coordinated in such a fashion as to create a unified whole."[31] This patterned nature provides a sameness that gives a sense of identity to its participants and provides a feeling of security or "feeling at home." The *integrated* model is patterned after traditional societies that are relatively self-enclosed, self-sufficient, and governed by rule-bound tradition. It serves as a firm basis for the values a group desires to uphold and speaks of a wholeness that stands against the fragmentation of society and the competitive pressures of capitalism, evokes an image of communion, and brings a sense of coherence to diverse elements. However, the *integrated* concept of culture excludes what cannot be assimilated or integrated and gives the impression of more solidity than is actually the case.[32] It should also be noted that this *integrated* concept of culture is related to a relatively limited, homogenized, and *integrated* Anglican identity as conceived in terms of the Church of England, particularly as shaped by the state-influenced identity established in the sixteenth and seventeenth centuries.

The degree of diversity, ambiguity, and messiness now present within orthodox Anglicanism, and within the Anglican Communion, suggests that an alternative conception of religious identity is also necessary. The truth that identity is only sought in times of instability, conflict, and change helps explain why the anxiety about identity is a ubiquitous pursuit in the twenty-first century. One of the reasons, therefore, why a clear orthodox Anglican

31. Schreiter, *The New Catholicity*, 47–48. Because I will make repeated use of Schreiter's terms throughout the thesis and because "globalized" may also have meanings associated with globalization, I will italicize *globalized* whenever it has reference to Schreiter's "globalized concept of culture." For the sake of consistency, I will also italicize *integrated* when used in Schreiter's sense.

32. Schreiter, *The New Catholicity*, 47–51.

identity is being sought by orthodox Anglicans is because of the changes and challenges to received ideals of Anglican identity that have emerged from the diversity represented by liberal Anglicanism (widely recognized by orthodox Anglicans) but also by Anglicanism as a whole, including orthodox Anglicanism (not so widely recognized by orthodox Anglicans).

Schreiter contrasts the "*integrated* concept of culture" with what he calls the "*globalized* concept of culture." In the *globalized* concept of culture, culture is something to be constructed and is a ground of contest in relations. Identity is viewed as fragmentary or multiple, constructed, and imagined, and change is assumed to be the normal state of affairs. Global-local encounters often produce a disorienting mixture, or *tiempos mixtos*, in which the premodern, the modern, and the postmodern exist together in the same place. These *tiempos mixtos* create incompatible, coexistent logics,[33] what may, at times, seem like an apt description of contemporary Anglicanism.

Nancy Ammerman also believes there are two sides to religious identity, what she variously calls "structured" and "emergent," "constructed" and "constrained," and "fluidity" and "constraint." In her view, while continuity of identity clearly prevails in religions, at the same time, a complex society continually challenges that continuity. The task of creating an identity is made challenging by the pluralization of contexts and the diversity of authority and power present.[34] Confirmation of the complex and dynamic nature of religious identities, such as orthodox Anglicanism, comes from Ammerman when she writes, "Understanding religious identities will require that we listen for stories in all their dynamic complexity, situating them in multiple relational and institutional contexts in which contemporary people live their lives."[35] What Anglicans are experiencing is, therefore, a microcosm of the postmodern world in which individuals and churches deeply desire and achieve fixed identities while at the same time having to both construct those identities and protect them from the erosive influences of pluralizing and destabilizing external forces.

The theme of unity in diversity, exemplified by the American political slogan *E. pluribus unum*, is exceedingly important in understanding identities, including religious identities.[36] Too much unity or conformity in

---

33. Schreiter, *The New Catholicity*, 53–58.

34. Ammerman, "Religious Identities," 207–24.

35. Ammerman, "Religious Identities," 224.

36. I'm conscious of the trinitarian dimensions of this theme of unity in diversity.

religion is often the result of coercion and is characteristic of sects. Too much diversity, on the other hand, threatens clear and meaningful identities. In contemporary Anglicanism, including orthodox Anglicanism, the question is whether or not the still increasing diversity, in the absence of strong and clear authority and norms, will yield a clear and coherent identity.

The remainder of the book will support the idea that while orthodox Anglicans are assuming and seeking a more *integrated* identity (in terms of ecclesial, normative, and practical definitions), they will actually live out an identity that is, to a large degree, a *globalized* one.

While this will prove discomforting to many, it may also be a source of relief. Religious identities are inherently complex and messy, even when the identity is rendered relatively clear by strong authority and norms. This is certainly true of the Anglicanism that emerged from the English Reformation with both Catholic and Protestant principles, an uneasy marriage which has yielded not only contests and confusion but also creativity and comprehension. The epiphany that Anglicanism is an inherently complex identity can actually be liberating for Christians struggling with ecclesial and even personal identities: the fact that there was no pure Golden Age of the church in the past to which the contemporary church can never hope to attain may be a welcome relief to some.

Another writing project of mine is to unravel a trinitarian spirituality that runs through the Christian religion, a spirituality in which three strands of religious identity (ecclesial, normative, and practical) are united in a whole life in Christ.

Chapter 3 ——————————

Ecclesial Orthodox Anglicanism

INTRODUCTION

BECAUSE ANGLICANISM STILL TENDS on many levels to be identified with the Anglican Communion, the status of the Anglican Communion is crucial in attempting to determine any contemporary Anglican identity, including a specifically orthodox one. Although orthodox Anglicans have already responded to the deficiencies of the Anglican Communion by creating both GAFCON and the ACNA, for the most part, they still desire to be a part of the Anglican Communion. Furthermore, GAFCON and ACNA have both inherited and created ecclesial difficulties of their own. The strength of the ecclesial structures of the present Anglican Communion, as well as those of GAFCON, is, therefore, a key to evaluating any future orthodox Anglican Communion.

The ordination of homosexuals is one innovation that orthodox Anglicans are willing to deal with in some fashion, but the difficulty in efforts to discipline provinces that have gone beyond desired limits of diversity highlights not only the problems in the current Anglican Communion but also potential problems for a future orthodox Anglican communion or federation. Orthodox Anglicans may assume that a more clearly orthodox Anglican communion will unite orthodox Anglicans. But how strong and coherent will the ecclesial identity be of the specifically orthodox Anglican communion or alternative ecclesial identity that will result from the institutional or ecclesial realignment that is part of the ongoing realignment within orthodox Anglicanism?

The present bonds of communion are too weak to serve as a strong and clear basis for a future orthodox Anglican identity. Orthodox Anglicans desire to articulate more clear and coherent structures for a specifically orthodox Anglican identity but are in the process of achieving an orthodox Anglicanism that, while structurally stronger in some ways, will continue to be messy, fragmentary, and network-like in nature and resemble a *globalized* and less *integrated* orthodox Anglican identity. In fact, orthodox Anglicans have already created new orthodox Anglican ecclesial bodies: GAFCON at the global level and the ACNA in North America. As we will see, these two bodies are also experiencing difficulties in terms of their ecclesial identities.

A BRIEF HISTORY OF
THE ANGLICAN COMMUNION

A closer look at the development of the Anglican Communion, in particular, is needed if it is likely that it may be used as the starting point for an ecclesial definition of any future orthodox Anglicanism and in order to understand why some orthodox Anglicans are willing to depart from it.

So long as Anglicanism was confined to the Church of England and the colonial churches directly dependent on the Church of England, the concept of an Anglican Communion was not a necessity. A major adjustment that Anglicanism had to make on its way to being transformed into the Anglican Communion, therefore, came with the formation of the Protestant Episcopal Church in the United States of America (PECUSA) after the American Revolutionary War. While the new American church remained heavily influenced by English principles and traditions, the new national American church was endowed with the authority to order its own doctrine, ministry, and liturgy. However, the emergence of the Anglican Communion, resulting from the independence of other former British colonies, caused Gareth Bennett to ask the question: "What, apart from their English descent, did hold together these autonomous bodies, each of which had assumed full power to alter its doctrinal formularies, change its practice of ministry and, if it chose, unite itself with some non-Anglican church?"[1]

The nineteenth century saw the further development of Anglicanism toward being the Anglican Communion as colonial churches began to evolve synodical governments and became independent, and as more

1. Bennett, "Preface to Crockford's Clerical Directory," 193.

provinces, regional and national in nature, gradually began to emerge. As the Anglican Communion began to grow and a desire to have closer ties between its members also began to grow, the idea for the first Lambeth Conference was proposed. Anglicans generally agreed that some means should be established by which decisions affecting all provinces should be made with the representation of all. While some initially conceived of the Lambeth Conferences as essentially conciliar, the next best thing to a general council of the whole church, the Lambeth Conferences have never had any binding authority over the autonomy of Anglican provinces.

The first Lambeth Conference in 1867 provided what amounted to guidelines for a true Communion to exist when it stated that "Unity and Faith in Discipline will be best maintained among the several branches of the Anglican Communion by due and canonical subordination of the Synods of the several branches to the higher authority of a Synod or Synods above them."[2] This provision for a continuity of the "faith in discipline" implies a Communion-wide synod with juridical authority that has, in fact, never existed. The 1867 Lambeth Conference also stated that the binding of the colonial churches to the Church of England required that those churches receive without alteration the standards of faith and doctrine of the Church of England and furthermore that if any adaptations were made, they must be subjected to an Anglican Communion synod at a higher level.

However, since the Anglican Communion has had no strong authority, it could not enforce its earlier desire to have its members maintain the standards of the Church of England. The new autonomy of former colonial churches that had now gained independence also meant that ecclesial authority in Anglicanism could no longer be a simple matter of churches following the authority, norms, and ethos of the Church of England. In this way, from its beginning, the Anglican Communion had both weak authority and norms, and any identity built on it is likely to be a relatively weak one.

Because of this lack of Communion-wide authority and because of the lack of Communion norms and a means of discipline, the present Anglican Communion is, in actuality, a federation and not a communion. The Encyclical Letter of the 1930 Lambeth Conference stated that "this communion is a commonwealth of Churches without a central constitution: it is a federation without a federal government."[3] Archbishop Jensen of Sydney,

2. "Resolution IV," 1867 Lambeth Conference, in *The Six Lambeth Conferences*, 54.

3. "Encyclical Letter," 1930 Lambeth Conference, in *The Lambeth Conferences, 1867–1948*, 155.

Australia, an influential orthodox Evangelical leader, agrees that the Anglican Communion is a federation of churches, saying, "Why not accept that we are a federation (or 'commonwealth') of largely autonomous churches?"[4]

Today, the Anglican Communion is defined as those churches in communion with the See of Canterbury, a communion that is facilitated and cemented by the four Instruments of Unity: the Archbishop of Canterbury, the Lambeth Conferences, the Primates' Meeting, and the Anglican Consultative Council. The Anglican Communion consists of thirty-nine autocephalous provinces, which are mostly national churches, although some are regional in nature.

THE STRENGTH OF THE PRESENT ECCLESIAL BONDS

The first way to gauge the strength and coherence of a future ecclesial orthodox Anglican identity is to examine the strength of the bonds of unity in the present Anglican Communion. Many orthodox Anglicans affirm the basic nature and shape of the present Communion, and even members of GAFCON wish to remain within the Anglican Communion. In fact, the emergence of GAFCON as a kind of parallel ecclesial structure only makes sense within the context of the present Anglican Communion. Therefore, the place to begin an assessment of the strength and coherence of any ecclesial orthodox Anglican identity is the present structures of the Anglican Communion.

How strong are the ecclesial bonds of unity in the present Anglican Communion?

The 2004 Windsor Report, officially called "The Lambeth Commission on Communion," was the Lambeth Commission's official report to the Anglican Communion, which offered a way forward after TEC's consecration of Gene Robinson. In particular, the Commission was to report on the legal and theological implications flowing from the American and Canadian churches' 2003 decisions, the canonical understandings of communion, impaired and broken communion, and the ways in which provinces may relate when one province is unable to maintain fullness of communion with another part of the Communion.

The primates, the majority of whom are usually considered orthodox, responded to the Windsor Report this way:

4. Jensen, "The Windsor Report is Bound to Fail."

> We believe that the Windsor Report offers in its Sections A & B an authentic description of the life of the Anglican Communion, and the principles by which its life is governed and sustained. While we believe that many elements of this account offer a picture of what is ideal, rather than what is currently actually experienced, we accept the description offered in Sections A & B of the Windsor Report as the way in which we would like to see the life of the Anglican Communion developed, as we respond in faithful discipleship to Christ.[5]

The Windsor Report had the sanction and support of the highest levels of authority in the Anglican Communion, including the most important orthodox Anglican leaders: the orthodox primates. Even those orthodox Anglicans who were critical of the report generally accepted its description of how the Anglican Communion presently works. The Windsor Report discusses four bonds of union that it believes still hold the Anglican Communion together: Scripture, the episcopate, the Instruments of Unity, and the synodical life of the Communion. In order to evaluate the coherence and viability of any ecclesial orthodox Anglicanism, these four remaining bonds of unity must each be discussed in some detail.

Scripture

Scripture is the first bond of unity discussed by the Windsor Report and is the highest authority in Anglicanism, but a detailed discussion of it will be deferred until chapter 4, since it is a part of the normative identity of Anglicanism.

The Episcopate

The second bond of communion presented by the Windsor Report is the role of the episcopate. The Windsor Report claims that "the unity of the Anglican Communion is both expressed and put into effect among other things through the *episcopate*" and further states that bishops represent the universal church to the local and *vice versa*.[6] Historically, Anglicans

---

5. "Anglican Communion Primates' Meeting Communique, February 2005," https://www.anglicannews.org/news/2005/02/the-anglican-communion-primates-meeting-communique,-february-2005.aspx.

6. "Windsor Report," 30–31.

have seen bishops as the locus of unity, with their dioceses being the fundamental units of church administration and local eucharistic ministry. Bishops, therefore, have a role that connects the local level with the universal and have the ability to express the unity in diversity that the Anglican Communion defines itself as having.

However, a single bishop by himself cannot truly act as an instrument of unity above the diocesan level: this requires that he act in unity with other bishops, a concept related to the term *collegiality*. The Windsor Report speaks of autonomy in terms of "autonomy-in-communion," that is, an autonomy of provinces, dioceses, or bishops that stands in relation to others and which therefore has an obligation to others: "the very nature of autonomy itself obliges each church to have regard to the common good of the global Anglican community and the Church universal."[7] *Collegiality* has been defined by the Anglican Consultative Council as "the process by which corporate leadership in the Church is exercised, whether between bishops as chief pastors in a Province, or between a Bishop and his clergy, or between Bishop, the clergy, and the laity in a diocese."[8] Collegiality applies to such instruments as the Lambeth Conferences and the Primates' Meeting and is closely related to *conciliarity* (corporate leadership that involves bishops, clergy, and laity), which may be seen in the Anglican Consultative Council.[9] The Windsor Report, in fact, has little to say directly about the power of bishops as a bond of union, probably because such power can only be exercised at a higher level, such as the Instruments of Unity.

If bishops in TEC (or other provinces) act autonomously in a way that disrupts or threatens to break the communion of the Anglican Communion, and the province of which they are a part acts autonomously either to condone or ignore such an action, what power within the Communion has the authority to discipline or otherwise rein in the problematic diocese and province? Clearly, it cannot be a single bishop, either from within that province or from another province. The bond of affection that the Windsor Report discusses as "the episcopate," therefore, becomes in reality, the bond of union created by the Instruments of Unity that provide a role for a collegial episcopate: the Primates' Meeting and Anglican Consultative Council.

7. "Windsor Report," 36.
8. White, "Collegiality and Conciliarity," 202.
9. White, "Collegiality and Conciliarity," 202.

The Instruments of Unity

After discussing the role of the episcopate in creating a common Anglican bond, the Windsor Report proceeds to discuss the four Instruments of Unity: the Archbishop of Canterbury, the Lambeth Conferences, the Anglican Consultative Council (ACC), and the Primates' Meeting. The Instruments of Unity are not symmetrical in their authority. Some appear to have more influence than others, and the Primates' Meeting seems to be gaining more power, especially among orthodox Anglicans. In addition, as the Windsor Report states, the nature of the moral authority of the instruments needs to be more clearly articulated, and there is at present "no clear demarcation indicating which responsibilities fall to which instrument."[10]

How strongly do the present Instruments of Unity work to maintain a clear Anglican identity in the face of increasing diversity and innovation?

The Archbishop of Canterbury

The Windsor Report begins its discussion of the Instruments of Unity with a discussion of the Archbishop of Canterbury, noting that he is the chief pastor in the Anglican Communion[11] and has been both in his person and office the pivotal instrument and focus of unity and a touchstone of what it means to be Anglican.[12] The Archbishop of Canterbury convenes the Primates' Meeting and the Lambeth Conferences and is ex officio the President of the Anglican Consultative Council: he is, therefore, at the center of the four Instruments of Unity. Perhaps most importantly, the Archbishop of Canterbury is the one who invites churches to be part of the Anglican Communion, and so he has a *political* authority to determine the bounds of the Communion.

All of this suggests a strong role for the Archbishop of Canterbury in maintaining common bonds within the Anglican Communion. However, the particular role of the Archbishop of Canterbury as a force or bond of unity appears to be waning and is already probably not as strong as some might believe or the Windsor Report suggests it is.

The authority of the Archbishop of Canterbury within the entire Anglican Communion is ill-defined. The 1998 Lambeth Conference

10. "Windsor Report," 44.

11. "Windsor Report," 31.

12. "Windsor Report," 41.

"reaffirms the role of the Archbishop of Canterbury as a personal sign of our unity and communion,"[13] but says no more than this. Although the Archbishop of Canterbury is considered to have some degree of "primacy," a report of the 1908 Lambeth Conference states, "No supremacy of the See of Canterbury over Primatial or Metropolitan Sees outside England is either practicable or desirable."[14] The primacy of the Archbishop of Canterbury is a symbolic primacy and not a primacy of jurisdiction, and is personal, and not ecclesial or administrative, in nature. The Archbishop of Canterbury, therefore, has no legal authority to make binding or enforceable decisions for the entire Anglican Communion.

Nowhere, then, is the authority of the Archbishop of Canterbury stated to be a legal or juridical authority, and the Archbishop of Canterbury has no jurisdiction outside England. At the Communion level, the Archbishop of Canterbury has little power to bind Anglicans together and is not able to bind together Anglicans who have continuing significant differences. If, for example, a liberal province such as TEC or the Anglican Church of Canada (ACC) desires "to walk apart" by consecrating a homosexual bishop, the Archbishop of Canterbury has no formal power or authority to prevent this, although he could choose not to invite these provinces to the next Lambeth Conference. In fact, when Archbishop of Canterbury Rowan Williams issued invitations to Lambeth 2008, he invited the ACC bishops and all of the bishops from TEC, with the exception of Gene Robinson. The present Archbishop of Canterbury, Justin Welby, has, likewise, invited bishops from both TEC and the ACC, as well as bishops in same-sex marriages and partnerships. GAFCON primates have interpreted this as inherently violating the Lambeth 1998 Resolution 10.1, which affirmed traditional, biblical understandings of human sexuality.

In spite of the current crisis and the perceived need by many orthodox Anglicans for greater juridical and Communion-wide authority to reside somewhere in the Communion, there appears to be little or no interest by orthodox Anglicans in giving the Archbishop of Canterbury enhanced responsibility. The Windsor Report itself stated, "We do not favour the accumulation of formal power by the Instruments of Unity, or the establishment of any kind of central 'curia' for the Communion."[15] Orthodox Anglicans endorsed this statement and participated in the creation of it.

13. "Resolution III.6" in *Called to be a Faithful Church*, 34–35.

14. "Report No. 10," 1908 Lambeth Conference, in *The Six Lambeth Conferences*, 418.

15. "Windsor Report," 44.

The authority of the Archbishop of Canterbury is further undermined by the issue of civil partnerships: England's Civil Partnership Act of 2005 puts the Church of England in a precarious position, and the resulting House of Bishops Pastoral Letter permits civil partnerships among its clergy. Archbishop Akinola of Nigeria called for the suspension of the Church of England from the Anglican Communion, and other orthodox primates also indicated that the issue of civil partnerships is likely to further undermine the authority of both the Church of England and the Archbishop of Canterbury. Since that time, the Church of England has permitted openly homosexual priests to be ordained, and in 2016 the Bishop of Grantham, Nicholas Chamberlain, became the first bishop in the Church of England to announce that he is a practicing homosexual.

For these reasons, it is becoming less and less likely that the office of the Archbishop of Canterbury will offer a strong bond of unity such as the Windsor Report appears to suggest.

The Lambeth Conferences

The second Instrument of Unity is the Lambeth Conferences. The Lambeth Conferences have the potential to be what a single bishop, and even the Archbishop of Canterbury, is not: a broad Anglican authority at the highest level that is collegial and involves the bishops as the locus of unity. Since the original goal of the Lambeth Conferences was to provide a voice for all members of the Anglican Communion, in keeping with the principle that what affects all should be decided by all, the Lambeth Conferences are potentially suited for service as a strong force for unity within the Anglican Communion. In fact, at Lambeth 1998 it was clear that the voice of the entire Anglican Communion, and not just that of the older, wealthier, and Western Anglican provinces, was being heard.

While the strength of this voice has acted to provide "moral" authority to the will of the majority of the Anglican Communion, the fact remains that the Lambeth Conferences have no power or authority to make decisions that are binding on the constituent provinces of the Communion. While originally the Canadians conceived of the Lambeth Conference as essentially conciliar, in reality, the Lambeth Conferences have never had any binding authority over the autonomy of the Anglican provinces.

The 1948 Lambeth Conference concluded that former Lambeth Conferences "have wisely rejected proposals for a formal primacy of

Canterbury, for an Appellate Tribunal, and for giving the Conference the status of a legislative synod."[16] The 1998 Lambeth Conference, at which the voice of the orthodox majority was forcefully heard on some issues, could only say of its own role in the Anglican Communion that it reaffirmed "the role of the decennial Lambeth Conference and of extraordinary Anglican Congresses as called, together with inter-provincial gatherings and cross-provincial diocesan partnerships, as collegial and communal signs of the unity of our Communion."[17] Despite the potential for the Lambeth Conferences to be a strong bond for ecclesial Anglicanism, dioceses and provinces are truly autonomous in that their decisions are binding and have a legal authority in a way that the Lambeth Conferences, in spite of their representation of a larger part of the church and Communion, do not. The Lambeth Conferences themselves, from the first one in 1867 to the one in 1998 (the 2008 Lambeth Conference produced no resolutions), have asserted and re-asserted their understanding that provinces are autonomous, with only vague restrictions on this autonomy.

The weakness of such provincial autonomy, in spite of the 1948 Lambeth Conference's glowing affirmation of the virtues of this system, has become apparent as a consequence of the actions of TEC and the Anglican Church of Canada (ACC). The 1998 Lambeth Conference passed, by an overwhelming majority, a resolution that clearly affirmed the traditional biblical view of human sexuality, Resolution I.10, and yet the Conference has been powerless to enforce its resolutions. The provincial autonomy of TEC and the ACC clearly takes precedence over the moral authority of the Lambeth Conferences.

Like the Archbishop of Canterbury, the Lambeth Conference at present has no strong power to unite, and there are no clear signs of interest in giving it juridical authority. The fact that the Lambeth Conference meets only once every ten years also makes it an authority that is not well suited to deal with crises that arise within the Communion, and some other authority in the Communion would have to act during the intervening years between conferences to encourage provinces to comply.

Both TEC and the ACC will be present at Lambeth 2020 (and even same-sex clergy and bishops), which, along with the inaction of official Anglican meetings and panels of reference, amply demonstrates the inability of the Lambeth Conference to act as a strong authority for Anglican identity.

16. 1948 Lambeth Conference, Part II, in *The Lambeth Conferences, 1867–1948*, 84.

17. "Resolution III.6.e" in *Called to be a Faithful Church*, 35.

The Primates' Meeting

The third Instrument of Unity is the Primates' Meeting, which was established by the 1978 Lambeth Conference and which has been held with increasing frequency since the 2003 actions of TEC and the ACC. The 1998 Lambeth Conference reaffirmed the 1988 Lambeth Conference's statement about the Primates' Meeting, which "urges that encouragement be given to a developing collegial role for the Primates' Meeting under the presidency of the Archbishop of Canterbury, so that the Primates' Meeting is able to exercise an enhanced responsibility in offering guidance on doctrinal, moral and pastoral matters."[18] The 1998 Lambeth Conference additionally asked "that the Primates' Meeting, under the presidency of the Archbishop of Canterbury, include among its responsibilities positive encouragement to mission, intervention in cases of exceptional emergency which are incapable of internal resolution within provinces, and giving of guidelines on the limits of Anglican diversity in submission to the sovereign authority of Holy Scripture and in loyalty to our Anglican tradition and formularies."[19]

The phrase "enhanced responsibility" has become a crucial one in understanding the developing role of the primates: if there is any Communion-wide authority that might possibly become more than "moral" or "spiritual" in nature, it is likely to be the Primates' Meeting, if for no other reason than that at this time more orthodox Anglicans seem willing to seek it.

However, there are already apparent limitations on this "enhanced responsibility" for the primates. First, Lambeth 1998 merely *requested* that the primates provide *guidelines* for limits on diversity. Even assuming that the primates act upon this, guidelines themselves are not an articulation of actual limits. Second, if limits were to be established, who would have the authority to establish them, and who would have the authority to enforce them? As far as enhanced responsibility goes, whether setting guidelines on diversity or intervening in dioceses or provinces, Lambeth 1998 had no authority other than an advisory or moral authority to authorize the primates to take "enhanced responsibility."

Lambeth 1998 also recommends that the primates intervene in "cases of exceptional emergency." In fact, some primates have intervened vigorously in parishes in TEC, providing alternative episcopal oversight in a large number of cases. Although some of the orthodox primates have taken

---

18. "Resolution III.6.a" in *Called to be a Faithful Church*, 34.
19. "Resolution III.6.b" in *Called to be a Faithful Church*, 34.

it upon themselves to intervene, a move many orthodox Anglicans applaud, the Windsor Report uses nearly identical language in its condemnation of such intervention as it uses for the divisive innovations of TEC and the ACC,[20] and such moves have proven contentious within the Anglican Communion, even among orthodox Anglicans. Such authority to intervene may exist; however, if it does, it does so in terms that are not clearly laid out in the present Anglican Communion. Once again the present structures of the Anglican Communion are too weak to prevent increasing diversity and innovation, and any orthodox realignment that allows for the crossing of geographical boundaries would, therefore, require a change from the structures of the present Communion.[21]

The Windsor Report states that the Primates' Meeting has refused to acknowledge anything more than a consultative and advisory authority for itself.[22] In spite of the desire of many orthodox Anglicans for the primates, in particular, to exercise discipline in dealing with TEC and the ACC, the primates, in their February 2005 Communiqué, steadfastly refused to enact any formal discipline. Instead, they merely *requested* that TEC and the ACC voluntarily withdraw their members from the Anglican Consultative Council for the period leading up to the next Lambeth Conference and that their fellow primates "use their best influence to persuade their brothers and sisters to exercise a moratorium on public Rites of Blessing for Same-sex unions and on the consecration of any bishop living in a sexual relationship outside Christian marriage."[23] Enhanced responsibility was advocated most immediately after the consecration of Gene Robinson, but with the creation of GAFCON, it seems as if a move to enhance the responsibility of the Primates' Meeting is no longer an active solution.

The one action which the Anglican Communion has been able to muster with regard to the innovations of TEC came as a result of the

20. "The Windsor Report," 53–54, asks for "regret" from TEC for their actions and a "moratorium" on consecrating homosexual bishops; it also asks for "regret" and a "moratorium" from those who have intervened (59).

21. Most of this primatial intervention has ceased with the creation of ACNA and its many choices of orthodox Anglican jurisdictions for orthodox Anglican churches to affiliate with.

22. "Windsor Report," 44. Part of the task of the Windsor Report was to explore a possible greater role for the primates.

23. "Anglican Communion Primates' Meeting Communique, February 2005," https://www.anglicannews.org/news/2005/02/the-anglican-communion-primates-meeting-communique,-february-2005.aspx.

Primates' Meeting in 2016. At that meeting a communique was issued which asked that for three years TEC "will not take part in decision making on any issues pertaining to doctrine or polity." However, shortly after this request, members of TEC were allowed to take place in a meeting on polity and doctrine, although, apparently, they were not given a vote. GAFCON interpreted this as sophistry and manipulation, proving that even such minimal requests will be contested. Regardless, TEC, the ACC, and openly homosexual priests and bishops have been invited to Lambeth 2020, so it appears as if the moratorium produced no lasting change in either TEC or its relation to the Anglican Communion. Some have even speculated that the next Lambeth Conference, originally slated for 2018 (it meets every ten years and met last in 2008) was delayed so as to occur after the three-year "suspension."

The Anglican Consultative Council

The fourth Instrument of Unity, the Anglican Consultative Council (ACC), is probably the least understood of the four Instruments of Unity. Formed in 1968, as least partially to give voice to the laity, the ACC's constitution defines its purpose as being "to advise on inter-Anglican, provincial and diocesan relationships."[24] Since the purpose of the ACC is clearly an advisory and communicative role, it is difficult to see how it is likely to serve as a very strong ecclesial bond for the Anglican Communion. This is true especially since it does not have the advantage of the historical and singular focus of the Archbishop of Canterbury or the collegial episcopate of the Lambeth Conferences or Primates' Meeting. While it may facilitate communication, the Anglican Consultative Council has been, in some ways, the Instrument of Unity that has been looked to least for leadership. Among orthodox Anglicans, as well, the ACC is the least-trusted of the Instruments of Unity, at least partially because it is sometimes considered the most liberal.

Because the ACC is not commonly spoken of as a strong force for leadership or unity in the Anglican Communion, because its role is least understood, and because it is in part distrusted by orthodox Anglicans, it will not be considered in any more detail. The ACC has the same limitations on its authority as the other Instruments of Unity, and since there is

24. "Windsor Report," 43n. Further information on the role of the Anglican Consultative Council may be found here: https://www.anglicancommunion.org/structures/instruments-of-communion/acc.aspx.

nothing to suggest that its responsibility will be enhanced, it is probably the least likely of the Instruments of Unity to be a strong force for unity.

Each of the four Instruments of Unity asked TEC not to consecrate Robinson as a bishop, and each was powerless to prevent TEC from acting autonomously. Sixteen years later (as this is written), the Instruments of Unity have been unwilling or unable to discipline TEC. The Instruments of Unity, as presently constituted, have not been a sufficiently strong bond of union in the Anglican Communion, and, therefore, will not provide a strong and clear basis for an ecclesial orthodox Anglicanism.

Synodical Life

The fourth bond of unity within the Anglican Communion which the Windsor Report discusses is what it terms *synodality*, or the "synodical life of the Church as the practical means of living together under Scripture, and with discernment and reception as the modes in which the Communion operates in relation to new proposals and the emergence of differences."[25] Synodality is considered by the Windsor Report to be walking together and discovering the nature of unity and communion by listening to as many voices as possible. It is closely related to a discussion of *reception*, as a testing of new ideas, which is done within the context of the *consensus fidelium*, or "common mind of the believers."[26] Anglicans at all levels typically make decisions in synods with the representation of bishops, clergy, and laity.

Synodality is characteristic of the Anglican Communion, according to Resolutions 4, 5, and 8 from the 1867 Lambeth Conference and Resolution 24 from the 1897 Lambeth Conference. Resolution 24 of the 1867 Lambeth Conference, the first Lambeth Conference, states that "in the opinion of this Conference, unity in faith and discipline will be best maintained among the several branches of the Anglican Communion by due and canonical subordination of the synods of the several branches to the higher authority of a synod or synods above them."[27]

The real question is: "How does synodality work in the Anglican Communion?" Synodality on the diocesan level is fairly well understood in Anglicanism because it is common for the bishop to govern a diocese in the context of a synod in which bishops, clergy, and laity are all represented

25. "Windsor Report," 33–34.
26. "Windsor Report," 32–33.
27. "Resolution IV," 1867 Lambeth Conference, in *The Six Lambeth Conferences*, 54.

and in which the bishop and synod together have actual juridical authority. However, at the Communion level, the concept of synodality has not received adequate discussion.

The starting point for understanding synodality at the Communion level is the provincial autonomy that the Communion has consistently asserted and which has been a presupposition for all Anglican Communion discussions since the beginning of the Conferences in 1867. The Encyclical Letter of the 1878 Lambeth Conference states that "the duly certified action of every national or particular Church, and of each ecclesiastical Province (or Diocese not included in a Province), in the exercise of its own discipline, should be respected by all the other Churches, and by their individual members."[28]

Provincial autonomy, however, without any limits on it, could potentially lead to chaos and division, and so in theory provincial autonomy is mitigated by the principle of *communion*, which the Windsor Report believes is the fundamental limit on autonomy.[29] The Windsor Report describes this as "autonomy in communion," "autonomy only in relation to others," and "freedom in relation."[30] Earlier Lambeth Conferences also placed certain theoretical limits on the autonomy of provinces: the 1930 Lambeth Conference affirmed a provincial autonomy based upon a common faith and order.

In particular, the Windsor Report discusses the principle of *subsidiarity* as a check on the potential problems of an unchecked provincial autonomy. *Subsidiarity* is the principle that matters should be decided as close to the local level as possible and finds its counterpart in the "ancient canonical principle that what touches all should be decided by all,"[31] a concept which the Windsor Report introduces but does not adequately apply. Both sides of subsidiarity are expressed well in the 1998 Lambeth Conference when it states, "This Conference affirms the principle of 'subsidiarity,' articulated in chapter 4, The Virginia Report, which provides that 'a central authority should have a subsidiary function, performing only those tasks

28. "Encyclical Letter of 1878," in *The Six Lambeth Conferences*, 84. See also "Resolution 48," 1930 Lambeth Conference, in *The Lambeth Conferences, 1867–1948*, 173; and "Resolution 21.3," 1978 Lambeth Conference, in Coleman, *Resolutions*, 186.

29. "Windsor Report," 36.

30. "Windsor Report," 35–36.

31. "Windsor Report," 27.

which cannot be performed at a more immediate or local level,' provided that these tasks can be adequately performed at such levels."[32]

The problem with synodality in the Anglican Communion as a whole, however, is that there is no entity that acts synodically at the Communion level. The primates and Lambeth Conferences do, in fact, meet collegially, and the Anglican Consultative Council meets synodically in some sense,[33] and yet none of these have legal authority at the Communion level such as exists in dioceses or provinces. There is, therefore, a mismatch between what synodality at the diocesan and provincial levels mean and what synodality means at the Communion level. The "canonical subordination of the synods of the several branches to the higher authority of a synod or synods above them" which the 1867 Lambeth Conference spoke of does not actually exist in the current Anglican Communion. In this sense, then, subsidiarity also fails because no entity in the Anglican Communion has the authority to make decisions for all at the Communion level in the way that synods have authority to make binding decisions within dioceses or provinces. Furthermore, there are no provincial laws that deal with inter-Anglican relations. The Anglican Communion's assertions and declarations of provincial autonomy seem to be clear and forceful, while the Communion's counterbalancing interprovincial communion and synodality are ill-defined and weak.

The preceding discussion strongly suggests that the present Anglican Communion, with its weak bonds of unity, is unable to act forcefully to prevent innovations. This includes not only innovations that may threaten an orthodox identity of Anglicanism, such as the ordination of homosexuals, but also others that may threaten a specifically Anglican identity such as the disuse of the Prayer Book or Articles as Anglican norms. Many orthodox Anglicans are willing to maintain the structures of the present Communion and thus maintain the present weakness in Communion-wide authority. However, to the degree that a future ecclesial orthodox Anglican identity replicates the structures and authority of the present Anglican Communion, it will be unlikely to be able to establish and maintain a distinctly orthodox Anglican identity.

The former Archbishop of Canterbury Robert Runcie's words set forth the challenge as forcefully as any:

32. "Resolution III.3" in *Called to Be a Faithful Church*, 33.

33. The ACC is the only one of the four Instruments of Unity that includes lay representation.

> Let me put it in starkly simple terms: do we really *want* unity within the Anglican Communion? Is our worldwide family of Christians worth bonding together? . . . But we have reached the stage in the growth of the Communion when we must begin to make radical choices, or growth will imperceptibly turn to decay. *I believe the choice between independence and interdependence, already set before us as a Communion in embryo twenty-five years ago, is quite simply the choice between unity or gradual fragmentation.*[34] (Emphasis added.)

To create a clearer and more coherent Communion would require a substantial change from the terms of the present Communion.

TWO ORTHODOX ANGLICAN ECCLESIAL VISIONS

The present Anglican Communion, then, has a number of significant problems that will be transmitted to any future orthodox Anglican communion, unless such a communion is founded upon a new set of principles, because it is actually a federation with relatively weak bonds in which provincial autonomy prevails. Is there another option for orthodox Anglicans, besides simply inheriting and perhaps adapting the terms of the present Communion, and would any other ecclesial identity be more effective?

There are, in essence, two visions that orthodox Anglicans have articulated in their desire to find a way forward, represented by two kinds of orthodox Anglicans that have been called "Communion Conservatives" and "Federal Conservatives." In a 2006 article that appears to be the origin of this typology, Graham Kings describes four Anglican groups that see the future of Anglicanism differently.[35] The differences occur based on two important intersecting fault lines: first, the issue of same-sex relations and, second, attitudes towards the Anglican Communion as represented by the Windsor Report and "Windsor Process." Kings calls these four groups Communion Liberals, Federal Liberals, Communion Conservatives, and Federal Conservatives.[36] The distinction between liberals and conservatives,

---

34. "Windsor Report," 32. Runcie's prophetic words were spoken in 1988.

35. Kings, "Shechem, Corinth, and Columbus." Kings himself states that he is working on ideas first presented by the Bishop of Exeter and Andrew Goddard.

36. The first fault line (same-sex relations) is a matter of normative identity, while the second (attitudes towards the Anglican Communion) is a matter of ecclesial identity.

in this case, is over the issue of same-sex relations, with liberals in favor of such relations and conservatives opposed.

Communion Conservatives and Federal Conservatives are the two identities in this typology that are relevant to this book with its focus on the future of orthodox Anglicans, and they represent two distinct visions for the future of the Anglican Communion.

Communion Conservatives favor maintaining the structures of the present Anglican Communion, and, therefore, their vision will replicate the problems of the present Communion. On the other hand, Federal Conservatives desire to change the structures of the present Communion but in the process of changing these structures are creating their own set of challenges to a clear and coherent ecclesial identity.

THE COMMUNION CONSERVATIVE VISION

Communion Conservatives see Anglicanism primarily in terms of communion with the See of Canterbury. The Communion Conservative vision involves making use of the current structures and mechanisms that exist in the Anglican Communion to deal with the issue of unacceptable diversity, and Communion Conservatives are content to follow the "Windsor process," or blueprint for Communion-wide action put into motion by the 2004 Windsor Report. Communion Conservatives want to allow for a "strategy of time" to be able to deal with the issue of autonomous provinces (TEC and the ACC) which have chosen to step outside the identified boundaries of what the entire Communion has deemed acceptable diversity.

Radner and Turner's *The Fate of Communion* is one of the most extensive and thoughtful discussions of the vision of Communion Conservatives, although in some ways it is now out of date. Perhaps the most helpful sentence in that book is one that may serve as a summary of the solution Radner and Turner offer to the twin problems of authority and identity: "A conciliar economy holds that the meaning of the Bible is perspicuous when sought in the middle of common practice, prayer, and worship."[37] This conciliar vision is fleshed out by Radner and Turner throughout the book in terms of a tension between "ecclesial integrity" that is represented by fidelity to the apostolic witness and "tolerable diversity" within this fundamental integrity. Another way of seeing this ecclesial integrity is in terms of the authority of "Scripture in communion," while diversity (not

37. Radner and Turner, *Fate of Communion*, 6.

necessarily tolerable diversity) is represented by the pluralistic impulse towards local autonomy. Disputes affecting ecclesial integrity and tolerable diversity take place in the midst of a scripturally formed people who hear the Bible in the midst of an ordered worship and prayer. These disputes are carried out by means of a protracted, free, and open theological debate, within a wider conciliar economy that places limits on autonomy.[38] Radner and Turner do not adequately address the question of how such a conciliar economy actually acts to limit diversity or autonomy, but it is important to note that they are wrestling with the issue of how to limit diversity as a means of preserving identity.

Since interpretations in Scripture are contested, how will this "Scripture in communion" resolve disputes, and what are the proper means of employing the process of "reception" of innovations? Radner and Turner claim that the proper means are none of the following: the exercise of ecclesial authority; rationalization of canon law; reference to creeds, confessions, and formularies; or vague notions of a "core doctrine." Instead, the reading of the Bible in the ordered fellowship of prayer and worship is the foundation for all else—common prayer, eucharistic celebration, communal instruction, common practice, and ecclesial integrity and tolerable diversity.[39] Authority, therefore, arises out of *communion* and not *magisterium*, and the first order of business is the nurture and protection of the *koinonia* or communion of the church.[40]

It is clear, then, why the notion of communion is integral to Radner and Turner's strategy as Communion Conservatives, and it is not surprising, then, that they have patience with the present Anglican Communion, its bodies, and its processes. More than that, they find that the Windsor Report "provides a credible way for the Anglican Communion to remain a communion rather than devolve into a federation of churches. Further, it suggests a credible way for the non-Roman churches throughout the world to respond to the potentially church-dividing tensions. . . ."[41] They are critical, therefore, of those provinces that have already pronounced a break in communion with TEC, for this represents a denial of the principle of mutual subjection that the primates (and the Windsor Report itself) have affirmed, and such provinces have taken independent action and not waited

---

38. Radner and Turner, *Fate of Communion*, 113–17.

39. Radner and Turner, *Fate of Communion*, 118–19.

40. Radner and Turner, *Fate of Communion*, 149.

41. Radner and Turner, *Fate of Communion*, 199.

until a common mind had been reached.[42] The forging of links to primates and other regions in the Communion as a means of achieving orthodoxy by detachment from the local ecclesial reality of TEC is condemned by the Communion Conservatives because the structure that is likely to result from this theology and strategy may be more like a federation than a communion with its closer, united ties.[43]

Thus, Communion Conservatives are content to work within the present structures of the Anglican Communion and to follow the principles outlined by the Windsor Report as a blueprint for the process of dealing with undesirable innovations.

However, since the Communion Conservative vision involves accepting the structures and processes of the present Anglican Communion, this vision also involves accepting and replicating the problems with ecclesial authority that were discussed earlier in this chapter. There is at present no Communion-wide authority, at least in the juridical sense, and provincial autonomy is stronger than any countervailing Communion-wide authority. The moral authority that exists in the Instruments of Unity has not proven effective in restraining TEC or the ACC. While Communion Conservatives sometimes argue for some form of discipline, it is not clear under any Communion Conservative plan how a Communion with no authority will, within a reasonable period of time, develop that authority, or if it will at all.

For example, the Communiqué from the Primates' Meeting in Tanzania in February 2007 requested that TEC make an unequivocal common covenant that their bishops will not authorize any rites for the blessing of same-sex unions or consent to a candidate for episcopal orders who is living in a same-sex union. The primates gave TEC a deadline to comply with this request and stated that if these requests were not honored that the Anglican Communion would remain damaged at best, a fact that has consequences for the full participation of TEC in the life of the Communion. This Communiqué might, therefore, indicate a way in which the Communion Conservative vision could enact discipline within the present structures.

However, it appears as if very shortly after the Communiqué was released TEC signaled that it would not honor such requests, as the primates intended them. Archbishop Venables wrote,

---

42. Radner and Turner, *Fate of Communion*, 9.

43. Such thinking, of course, fails to realize that the present Anglican Communion is itself a federation and not a true communion, as I have discussed earlier.

> We gave much time to producing a Communiqué which was unambiguous and straightforward. Tragically, in the Presiding Bishop's remarks to the Church Center community just two days after the close of the meeting she misguidedly argues that there was agreement and understanding among the Primates that blessings of same-sex couples could continue as "pastoral care" as long as there was no official published liturgy for it. That assertion quite scandalously demonstrates the very concern that the Communiqué addresses in identifying this situation.[44]

Taken in its strongest sense, the response from the Anglican Communion might be construed as meaning that if TEC refused to comply, it would no longer be considered a part of the Anglican Communion. If TEC thus refuses to comply, and the Anglican Communion "excommunicates" TEC, a somewhat clear solution to the problem of TEC's liberalism (from the orthodox Anglican perspective) might become a reality. The Anglican Communion as presently constituted would be preserved (with the exception of TEC) and would make clear to its provinces that any further consecration of homosexual bishops or authorization of same-sex rites would result in a similar discipline. In this way, the present Anglican Communion could become a more clearly orthodox Communion and might set a precedent for how to deal with liberalism or other undesirable diversity.

While such a scenario seems fairly clear, many problems would remain. Would, for example, other liberal provinces accept the exclusion of TEC without making some other ecclesial arrangements, including possibly leaving the Anglican Communion itself? Would the discipline of the Anglican Communion extend to the ordination of homosexual priests as well (and not only bishops)? Given the difficulties the Church of England itself is beginning to experience concerning same-sex unions, what would the Anglican Communion do if the Church of England blessed such unions?

It is now extremely unlikely that the Anglican Communion will discipline TEC in any meaningful way. As previously discussed, the only discipline the Anglican Communion has enacted since 2003 was to "disinvite" TEC representatives from voting in meetings where doctrine and polity were being decided. However, the three-year moratorium is now up, and TEC is free to participate fully in the life of the Communion. Since 2003, the following events have occurred, all of which convincingly demonstrate that the Communion Conservative strategy is no longer a

---

44. "Pastoral Letter from Gregory Venables," http://www.theroadtoemmaus.org/RdLb/32Ang/Ang/DarEsSalaam-Venbles.htm.

viable option for dealing with the diversity, innovation, and autonomy of liberal Anglicans such as TEC.

1. TEC has authorized official same-sex rites as part of the doctrine, discipline, and worship of its church.

2. TEC voted in its 2018 General Council to mandate that all dioceses make provision for allowing same-sex marriage rites: only eight bishops were not in favor, and only one of these has refused the compromise that was offered.

3. Both TEC and the ACC were invited and will be present at Lambeth 2020.

4. Same-sex clergy and bishops have been invited to Lambeth 2020, which is not only a refusal to discipline but actually an innovation, since this is the first time such an invitation has been issued.

5. The Church of England has permitted openly homosexual priests to be ordained.

6. The Church of England has allowed an openly homosexual man to serve as bishop.

None of these actions resulted in any discipline; none of them has changed the nature or course of the Anglican Communion. It's nearly impossible to imagine a scenario by which, as the Communion Conservatives in TEC desire, TEC may be reformed in a more orthodox direction. The number of orthodox bishops in TEC has declined from forty-two to somewhere between one and eight in just fifteen years. How will more orthodox Anglican bishops ever be consecrated in TEC if the approval of homosexual ordination and same-sex rites is a litmus test in TEC? Furthermore, the clergy and laity votes in favor of same-sex unions constituted a super majority. Humanly speaking, no viable mechanism for reform seems open. Making reform within TEC even less likely is the fact that the vast majority of the staunchly and zealously orthodox Episcopalians have left TEC since 2003, to go either to orthodox Anglican churches in the ACNA or else to leave the Episcopal tradition entirely.

Communion Conservatives have one additional difficulty that Federal Conservatives do not have, and that is in identifying other orthodox Anglicans outside of the Anglican Communion. If, for example, "Anglican Communion" and "Anglicanism" are coterminous, then Communion Conservatives have the great difficulty of accepting the Anglican identity of liberal Anglicans who have denied the authority of Scripture in their view and yet refusing to acknowledge an Anglican identity for orthodox Anglicans who happen not to be a part of the present Anglican Communion. Already there are groups such as member churches in the ACNA that are self-professedly orthodox Anglicans (and hold the Articles and the Prayer Book as norms) and yet are not in communion with Canterbury. The assumption that only one church in a geographical area may be in communion with Canterbury would seem to imply that in this ecclesial definition such churches are not Anglican. That the relationship of such groups to Anglicanism is a question in need of an answer was recognized by the 1998 Lambeth Conference, which stated that it believed "that important questions are posed by the emergence of groups who call themselves 'continuing Anglican Churches' which have separated from the Anglican Communion in recent years."[45]

The Communion Conservative vision, therefore, is highly unlikely to provide a clear and coherent ecclesial identity for orthodox Anglicans because in accepting the structure and processes of the present Communion, they are also accepting the problems that exist in the present Communion: weak authority, unclear norms, and lack of discipline.

What seemed like a longshot in 2003 now looks like an impossibility. The Communion Conservative strategy looks to be dead.

THE FEDERAL CONSERVATIVE VISION

The other vision for an ecclesial identity for orthodox Anglicans is that of Federal Conservatives. As defined by Kings, Federal Conservatives are orthodox Anglicans who "do not consider highly the ecclesiology of the Windsor Report and especially its warnings against trans-provincial interventions."[46] In contrast to Communion Conservatives, Federal Conservatives seek three things that are lacking in the Anglican Communion as presently constituted: clear norms, appropriate discipline when necessary, and the authority necessary to safeguard norms and apply discipline. These represent the ecclesial and normative identities of Anglicanism that we have been discussing.

---

45. "Resolution IV.11.a," in *The Lambeth Conference Resolutions Archive from 1998.*
46. Kings, "Shechem, Corinth, and Columbus."

Since these three are presently lacking in the Anglican Communion, Federal Conservatives have responded in vigorous ways, most notably in the formation of both GAFCON and the ACNA.

In general, Federal Conservatives expected the primates, especially the primates of the Global South, to take the "enhanced responsibility" that the 1998 Lambeth Conference recommended for them and to use that authority to enact the Federal Conservative vision. The Federal Conservative vision could be put into effect if a strong enough authority on the Federal Conservative side took strong action and was supported by a significant number of orthodox Anglican churches in the Global South and North America. In keeping with the theory of religious identity described in chapter 2, such a strong authority is likely to be necessary to re-assert a strong and clear identity with clear norms.

The Formation of GAFCON and the ACNA

What the Federal Conservatives actually did was to create the ecclesial bodies known as GAFCON (Global Anglican Future Conference) and the ACNA (Anglican Church in North America). The future of the Federal Conservative vision is intimately bound to the future of GAFCON and the ACNA, which together now form by far the most significant orthodox Anglican ecclesial bodies. Some orthodox Anglican churches, for example, those in the US known as the Continuing churches, should also be considered orthodox Anglicans, but due to their Anglo-Catholic principles (primarily, but not exclusively, the issue of women's ordination), they have opted not to become members of the ACNA. However, they are a small minority of orthodox Anglicans both in the US and globally.

GAFCON was established in 2008 when some of the orthodox Global South primates convened to decide what orthodox Anglicans worldwide should do in response to the liberalism of TEC and the unwillingness or inability of the Anglican Communion to enact any measure of discipline. The major accomplishment of the first GAFCON, strategically held one month before the 2008 Lambeth Conference, was the issuing of the crucial Jerusalem Declaration, as well as a prefatory "Statement on the Global Anglican Future" that is part of "The Complete Jerusalem Statement." This Statement pronounced that GAFCON hereby:

1. launch the GAFCON movement as a fellowship of confessing Anglicans

2. publish the Jerusalem Declaration as the basis of the fellowship

3. encourage GAFCON Primates to form a Council.[47]

So significant and authoritative are the Jerusalem Statement and the founding purposes of GAFCON that the "Statement on the Global Anglican Future" is worth quoting at length. The Statement proclaims that GAFCON was established due to a three-fold crisis.

> The first fact is the acceptance and promotion within the provinces of the Anglican Communion of a different 'gospel' (cf. Galatians 1:6–8) which is contrary to the apostolic gospel. This false gospel undermines the authority of God's Word written and the uniqueness of Jesus Christ as the author of salvation from sin, death and judgement. Many of its proponents claim that all religions offer equal access to God and that Jesus is only a way, not the way, the truth and the life. It promotes a variety of sexual preferences and immoral behaviour as a universal human right. It claims God's blessing for same-sex unions over against the biblical teaching on holy matrimony. In 2003 this false gospel led to the consecration of a bishop living in a homosexual relationship.
>
> The second fact is the declaration by provincial bodies in the Global South that they are out of communion with bishops and churches that promote this false gospel. These declarations have resulted in a realignment whereby faithful Anglican Christians have left existing territorial parishes, dioceses and provinces in certain Western churches and become members of other dioceses and provinces, all within the Anglican Communion. These actions have also led to the appointment of new Anglican bishops set over geographic areas already occupied by other Anglican bishops. A major realignment has occurred and will continue to unfold.
>
> The third fact is the manifest failure of the Communion Instruments to exercise discipline in the face of overt heterodoxy. The Episcopal Church USA and the Anglican Church of Canada, in proclaiming this false gospel, have consistently defied the 1998 Lambeth statement of biblical moral principle (Resolution 1.10). Despite numerous meetings and reports to and from the 'Instruments of Unity,' no effective action has been taken, and the bishops of these unrepentant churches are welcomed to Lambeth 2008. To make matters worse, there has been a failure to honour

47. GAFCON, "Jerusalem Statement."

promises of discipline, the authority of the Primates' Meeting has been undermined and the Lambeth Conference has been structured so as to avoid any hard decisions. We can only come to the devastating conclusion that 'we are a global Communion with a colonial structure'.[48]

Ecclesiastically, GAFCON defines itself as "a fellowship of Anglicans, including provinces, dioceses, churches, missionary jurisdictions, parachurch organisations and individual Anglican Christians whose goal is to reform, heal and revitalise the Anglican Communion and expand its mission to the world."[49] Normatively, GAFCON defines itself this way: "The doctrine of the Church is grounded in the Holy Scriptures and in such teachings of the ancient Fathers and Councils of the Church as are agreeable to the said Scriptures. In particular, such doctrine is to be found in the Thirty-nine Articles of Religion, the Book of Common Prayer and the Ordinal."[50]

Ecclesiastically, GAFCON is a *conference*, and not a communion. As with the Anglican Communion, there is currently no juridical authority to limit diversity within GAFCON members, in spite of the orthodox nature of the fellowship. GAFCON is led by a Council of Primates who steer the various meetings of GAFCON, but this Council has no authority (other than moral persuasion and a general collegiality) to coerce or discipline any member who does not abide by the common mind of GAFCON. GAFCON also has no constitution or canons. It is in the process of becoming more like a communion of churches and has established nine networks to facilitate a common life, but the ecclesial bonds of GAFCON, at least officially, are as weak as those of the Anglican Communion. While so far, a common orthodox identity being asserted against the liberalism of TEC (especially on matters of human sexuality) has created a great deal of unity, as has a decade of good will and a common orthodox vision, the inherent ecclesial structures of GAFCON do not provide for a stronger authority than the present Anglican Communion.

GAFCON has another inherent ecclesial difficulty: the majority of members of GAFCON are also currently members of the Anglican Communion. It's not immediately clear if this ambiguous, split identity can be maintained indefinitely, or if so what the nature of it would be. If, for

48. GAFCON, "Jerusalem Statement."
49. GAFCON, "Jerusalem Statement."
50. GAFCON, "Jerusalem Statement."

example (as is extremely likely), TEC and other liberal Anglican churches decide to continue their innovations even beyond what they have already enacted, will this provoke GAFCON members to leave the Communion? If not, then doesn't the continued presence of GAFCON primates and provinces in the Anglican Communion constitute an implicit acceptance of the status quo, and what is the purpose of the Communion from an orthodox perspective? If GAFCON provinces do leave the Anglican Communion, then what authoritative ecclesial authority does GAFCON have to offer in its place to keep the remaining orthodox Anglican churches together and without further innovation? GAFCON's hope and assumption, based on the 2018 GAFCON meeting, is that the liberal churches of the present Communion will wither and that the Communion can be changed from within. However, this "inside" strategy sounds similar to the strategy of the Communion Conservatives, who desire to work within the Communion, and not to leave it. GAFCON 2018 stated: "People asked if we were meeting in Jerusalem to declare a break with Canterbury. The answer was emphatically 'No.'"[51]

The most important statement made by GAFCON 2018 was this, taken from their "Letter to the Churches":

> In light of the recommendations of the Synodical Council, we respectfully urge the Archbishop of Canterbury
> to invite as full members to Lambeth 2020 bishops of the Province of the Anglican Church in North America and the Province of the Anglican Church in Brazil and
> not to invite bishops of those Provinces which have endorsed by word or deed sexual practices which are in contradiction to the teaching of Scripture and Resolution I.10 of the 1998 Lambeth Conference, unless they have repented of their actions and reversed their decisions.
> In the event that this does not occur, we urge Gafcon members to decline the invitation to attend Lambeth 2020 and all other meetings of the Instruments of Communion.[52]

It will be interesting to see if all members of GAFCON will honor this request, since the ACNA has not been invited to Lambeth 2020, but TEC and the ACC have, both in violation of what GAFCON has urged.

---

51. GAFCON, "Jerusalem 2018—Introduction."
52. GAFCON, "Letter to the Churches."

While GAFCON is the primary Federal Conservative response at the international level to the liberal innovations of TEC and the inability of the Anglican Communion to discipline TEC, the ACNA is the primary response to this situation in North America. The ACNA emerged out of the messy orthodox Anglican realignment after TEC's consecration of Gene Robinson in 2003. Some churches sought and found alternative oversight from Global South primates and provinces (such as the Anglican Mission in America or AMiA); some entire dioceses left TEC and remained autonomous entities (such as the former Episcopal dioceses of Pittsburgh, Fort Worth, and others); and some desired to establish a larger federation of orthodox Anglican churches in North America.

In a 2004 letter to the Archbishop of Canterbury, six orthodox Anglican groups (the Common Cause Partners), representing four orthodox Anglican churches in the US, pledged a commitment to make common cause for the gospel of Jesus Christ and for a united, missionary, and orthodox Anglicanism in North America. In 2009, the Common Cause Partners, along with other orthodox Anglican bodies, formed the ACNA, which happened in response to the call from GAFCON 2008 for an orthodox Anglican province in North America. The Global South primates desired a united orthodox Anglican province that would make the common task of ministry much easier than if there were dozens of autonomous churches and also facilitate the goal of the recognition of the new province by the Anglican Communion. GAFCON 2018 said:

> We recognise the desirability of territorial jurisdiction for provinces and dioceses of the Anglican Communion, except in those areas where churches and leaders are denying the orthodox faith or are preventing its spread, and in a few areas for which overlapping jurisdictions are beneficial for historical or cultural reasons.
>
> We thank God for the courageous actions of those Primates and provinces who have offered orthodox oversight to churches under false leadership, especially in North and South America.
>
> We believe this is a critical moment when the Primates' Council will need to put in place structures to lead and support the church. In particular, we believe the time is now ripe for the formation of a province in North America for the federation currently known as Common Cause Partnership to be recognised by the Primates' Council.[53]

---

53. GAFCON, "Final Statement."

The ACNA is comprised of approximately thirty dioceses, which include 132,000 Anglicans in 1,004, as of 2019. It describes its ecclesial structure this way:

> The Anglican Church in North America is a voluntary association of dioceses, and its structure is based upon the principle of subsidiarity, which recognizes that the bulk of ministry happens at the congregational level. A diocese serves to support the ministry of its congregations, and the Province only undertakes those tasks that a congregation or diocese is not in the best position to facilitate. This means that the provincial structure is intentionally lean.[54]

An important ecclesial link exists between GAFCON and the ACNA, for both represent the Federal Conservative vision of orthodox Anglican ecclesial identity, and GAFCON called for the formation of the ACNA. The ACNA describes its relation to GAFCON and international orthodox Anglicanism in this way:

> The Anglican Church in North America is in full communion with the GAFCON Provinces of Nigeria, Kenya, Uganda, Rwanda, Congo, South America, and Sudan and South Sudan. This recognition continues to grow in momentum with the Anglican Church in North America being made a full partner province of the Global South, an official structure of the Anglican Communion. In addition, individual dioceses including Sydney Australia, and Northwest Australia, have recently established formal relationships with the North American Province.[55]

Due to the voluntary nature of the ACNA, and the fact that each ecclesial body retains its own autonomy, the ecclesial authority of the ACNA is, like the Anglican Communion and GAFCON, relatively weak. There is no apparent mechanism for disciplining any of its constituent members, and dioceses and churches are free to withdraw at any time. Unlike GAFCON, the ACNA does have its own constitution and canons.

In terms of its normative Anglican identity, the ACNA has articulated very similar norms to GAFCON. These include the Bible as the inspired Word of God, and final authority and unchangeable standard for Christian faith and life; the episcopate; the three creeds; the first four Councils; the 1662 Prayer Book and Ordinal, and the Thirty-nine Articles.[56]

54. ACNA, "Fact Sheet."
55. ACNA, "Fact Sheet."
56. ACNA, "Theological Statement."

While the Federal Conservative vision may, therefore, desire to introduce stronger and clearer ecclesial authority, norms, and discipline, it is also likely to introduce significant new challenges to a clear and coherent orthodox Anglican identity. Among the issues Federal Conservatives will face are those regarding authority, scope and unity, and norms.

The question of authority remains for GAFCON. By what authority do the GAFCON primates act apart from the Archbishop of Canterbury and the other primates with whom they are still in communion? The Anglican Communion consists of thirty-nine provinces, and, excepting TEC and the ACC, thirty-seven are still in communion with the Global South provinces. Will the Global South primates act apart from the other primates? An additional question is how unified is the orthodox Global South, only part of which is in GAFCON? Parts of the Global South may be more centrist than they appear. In spite of the apparently united front presented by the Global South in their strongly-worded 2006 Kigali Statement, three primates backed away from that statement shortly after it was released. While a coalition of six to twelve Global South primates formed a bloc that pushed for the expulsion of TEC at the 2007 Primates' Meeting, only six refused to take communion with TEC's Presiding Bishop Schori, and the boundaries of the various voting blocs among the primates are apparently somewhat fluid. Additionally, many Global South provinces are dependent on finances from liberal Western provinces such as TEC, and many familial bonds with liberal Western provinces have been developed over decades, bonds which many Global South provinces are loath to give up.

A significant question for the entire Federal Conservative vision involves the future relationship of GAFCON to the Church of England. Given the growing liberalism of the Church of England, which seems destined to accept and enforce the same innovations as TEC, will GAFCON declare itself out of communion with Canterbury? This would seem logically necessary at some point, but the concept of Anglicanism without the Church of England would have crucial consequences for the identity of Anglicanism. Communion Conservatives have expressed their concerns that if a Federal Conservative vision prevails, the Anglican Communion will cease to be a communion. It would become a federation of churches linked by weakening historical relations and pragmatic considerations. At worst, it would continue to fragment into groups in various degrees of communion with one another.

Such issues challenge the clarity and coherence of the orthodox Anglican realignment. The Federal Conservatives' vision might potentially solve the problem of theological realignment and produce a relatively common theological basis for orthodox Anglicans, but perhaps at the expense of not including all orthodox Anglicans and thus jeopardizing a united realignment and one that is geographically clear. Convergence, the third aspect of the orthodox realignment, would, therefore, remain a problem and might actually be rendered more problematic.

OTHER ECCLESIAL DIFFICULTIES

Communion and Federal Conservatives both face three additional challenges to establishing an orthodox Anglican ecclesial identity: the issue of women's ordination, the network-like nature of their emerging ecclesial identity, and the possible emergence of a "post-Anglican" Anglican identity.

Women's Ordination

The ecclesial identity of orthodox Anglicanism has already been compromised by the ordination of women, which has led to a state of imperfect or broken communion. The process by which women's ordination entered into the Anglican Communion (and thereby GAFCON and the ACNA) suggests an inherent problem in the present Communion that is likely to be perpetuated not only in the Anglican Communion but also in GAFCON and the ACNA.

Anglicans of all varieties are concerned about the possible fracture of the present Anglican Communion. However, to a certain degree, the Anglican Communion is (and has been for a few decades) a Communion that is divided. While the liberal actions of TEC and the ACC have been the presenting issue since 2003, the Anglican Communion is already divided over the issue of women's ordination. This division is not just a division of opinion but also, at times, a real and ecclesial division. Many of the Anglican provinces have declared themselves out of communion or in impaired communion with TEC and the ACC over issues of human sexuality. However, it is already the case that *orthodox* dioceses and provinces are living in a communion that is impaired: since the advent of women's ordination in the Communion, there is no longer an interchangeability of ministers and the sacraments they minister.

This impaired or broken communion exists not only in the Anglican Communion in general but also *among orthodox Anglicans*: some orthodox parishes, dioceses, and provinces do not recognize the validity of the ordination of women in other orthodox parishes, dioceses, and provinces.

Why is women's ordination so divisive for Anglicans? Catholic Anglicans, especially, are opposed to women's ordination for reasons related to ecclesiology, the sacraments, and ministry. If the sacraments are "generally necessary for salvation," as the Catechism in the traditional Prayer Books teaches, and if the sacramental validity of women priests is in question, then the stakes for Catholic Anglicans are, in fact, very serious. If women cannot be validly ordained, then there is no assurance of sacramental validity when women administer the sacraments. Catholic Anglicans also see women's ordination as a violation of biblical teaching, as well as the apostolic traditions of the church.

Another major reason the issue of women's ordination is so divisive, even among orthodox Anglicans, is that it goes to the heart of the issue of authority. Women's ordination presents challenges for a coherent authority in three ways: first, the question of whether or not those ordaining women had the authority (and not merely the power) to ordain; second, the challenge to this authority by those who object and will not submit to the ruling of a church or synod on this issue; and third, the exact status of the authority of the ordained women when this authority is not accepted by all.

With women bishops the "three planes" on which a bishop is the person who maintains church unity no longer intersect. Regarding the first plane, a woman bishop may not be able to act in the episcopal role as the president of the eucharistic community since some of her people are unable to accept the validity of her ministry. In this way, the primary pastoral role is damaged. The second plane, in which the bishop unites the church to the universal church, is also damaged because a woman bishop cannot be universally recognized, even among orthodox Anglicans. The third plane, continuity of time, is also damaged by women bishops because of questions about the ability of a woman bishop to maintain continuity in her own person and to participate in handing down this recognized continuity.[57]

Women's ordination has already proven divisive at a number of levels. In 2005 in the Church of England, for example, 350 parishes barred the Archbishop of Canterbury from conducting communion services in them because of his support for women's ordination, and when women priests

---

57. White, *Authority and Anglicanism*, 80–81.

were first ordained in 1992, approximately four hundred Church of England priests converted to Roman Catholicism. The power of the consecration of women bishops to divide the Anglican Communion even further is evidenced by the 2005 decision of the Church of England's General Synod to allow for women bishops, an action that provoked the threat of up to eight hundred clergy, including a number of bishops, leaving the Church of England if women were consecrated as bishops.

The divisiveness of women's ordination is a factor not only in Anglicanism in general but also among orthodox Anglicans. Both GAFCON and the ACNA are composed of some member churches who ordain women and some who do not. This means that within each of these orthodox Anglican ecclesial bodies a state of impaired or broken communion already exists. In both GAFCON and the ACNA, there is no interchangeability of ministers, and in both those Anglicans who not consider the ordination of women valid cannot partake of the Holy Communion in good conscience when a female clergy is celebrating.

In 2017, the ACNA Task Force on Holy Orders presented its conclusions to the ACNA bishops for their consideration. That report provides a "Chart on Women's Ordination in the Anglican Provinces," from which we can gauge which Anglican provinces ordain women to which offices. Six of the Global South provinces ordain women to none of the three offices; two provinces in the Global South and an additional one in GAFCON ordain only female deacons; four provinces in the Global South, four more in GAFCON, and one other province ordain both female priests and deacons; and four provinces in the Global South, four in GAFCON, and eleven others ordain women to all three offices. While this summary represents only a moment in time, the trend throughout Anglican provinces as a whole is toward ordaining women to more offices, and not towards reducing women's ordination.[58]

The ACNA is also divided over the issue of women's ordination, with some constituent churches ordaining women and others not: the majority do not. Initially, many understood the ACNA to have promised a moratorium on the practice, while the issue of women's ordination was being decided. However, after existing now for more than a decade, the issue of women's ordination remains unresolved, and no clear and vigorous action has been taken. The 2017 report of the Task Force on Holy Orders was never intended to decide the issue: that authority resides with the ACNA

---

58. ACNA, "Chart on Women's Ordination," 256.

bishops in council. When the ACNA bishops released their response to the Task Force report, the statement was interpreted by those within the ACNA in very different ways. For the time being, the ACNA clearly intends to allow for women's ordination; however, the longer it is permitted, the more it is likely to take root in the ACNA and the more likely that any decision against women's ordination will be perceived as a betrayal by those who favor the practice.

The problems with impaired and broken communion become even more pronounced when the ecumenical mission of Anglicanism is considered. It is part of the Anglican heritage and identity that Anglicanism considers itself to be a bridge church that may help facilitate the reunification of Roman Catholic, Eastern Orthodox, and Protestant Christians.[59] However, this ecumenical mission is jeopardized by Anglicans' ordination of women, and, therefore, the divisiveness that women's ordination has brought within the Anglican Communion has been brought to Anglicanism's ecumenical relationships as well.

The Windsor Report, which has been held in high esteem by Communion Conservatives and which included orthodox Anglicans among its drafters, was clearly concerned about the ecumenical implications of TEC and the ACC's actions. It stated that "condemnation has come from the Russian Orthodox and Oriental Orthodox churches, as well as a statement from the Roman Catholic church that such moves create 'new and serious difficulties' to ecumenical relationships."[60] However, the same kind of condemnation from Anglicanism's ecumenical partners was given when women began to be ordained in the Anglican Communion. At the 1976 Anglican-Orthodox Conference, the Orthodox Churches warned, "If the Anglican Churches proceed to the ordination of women to the priesthood and episcopate, this will create a very serious obstacle to the development of our relations in the future."[61] Pope John Paul II wrote that "the ordination of women to the priesthood in some provinces of the Anglican Communion, together with the recognition of the right of individual provinces to proceed with the ordination of women to the episcopacy, appears to

59. See, for example, Archbishop of Canterbury Fisher's "Encyclical Letter" to the 1948 Lambeth Conference, in *The Lambeth Conferences, 1867–1948*.

60. "Windsor Report," 18.

61. Bridge, *Women and the Apostolic Ministry?*, 95.

pre-empt [ARCIC-II's] study and effectively block the path to the mutual recognition of ministries."[62]

Orthodox Anglican proponents of women's ordination are concerned about the ecumenical implications of the consecration of Robinson, as well as the implications of this action for Anglican unity; however, orthodox Anglicans have not always acknowledged that the ordination of women has already created the same kind of ecumenical obstacles and problems for Anglican unity as has the consecration of Robinson. The problems of impaired internal communion and impaired ecumenical unity are present among orthodox Anglicans, and not only the Anglican Communion as a whole, and cut across the Communion and Federal Conservative categories, since there are both proponents and opponents of women's ordination in both groups.

The problems that women's ordination presents for ecclesial Anglicanism are not limited to the substance of the issue itself but also involve questions about the process, *a process that many orthodox Anglicans seem content to retain and which has implications for how orthodox Anglicans may deal with other innovations.* In spite of the serious damage to the ecumenical mission of Anglicanism that women's ordination has done and the state of broken and impaired communion it has created within Anglicanism, the Windsor Report holds up the process by which women's ordination was permitted in the Anglican Communion as a model for how innovations should be received.[63]

The process by which women's ordination has been accepted in the Anglican Communion is the process of *reception*, by which innovations in Anglican provinces are tested at the Communion level. *The Grindrod Report* of 1988 first articulated the process of reception and foresaw reception as a long-range and far-reaching process by the whole church. It stated that until the "process of reception is reasonably settled the issue of the ordination of women to the episcopate, as indeed the ordination of women to the presbyterate, would remain open to discussion."[64] Furthermore, *The Grindrod Report* stated that even if a province autonomously proceeded to consecrate a woman bishop that the "decision would still have to be tested in the universal Church."[65] According to *The Grindrod Report*, the process

62. Butler, "The Ordination of Women," 108.
63. "Windsor Report," 14–16.
64. Toon, *Reforming Forwards?*, 13.
65. Toon, *Reforming Forwards?*, 13.

of reception is to involve official responses by the synods and councils of the church at the highest levels of authority. The church as a whole should receive synodical decisions; however, the authority of those exercising leadership in this process is neither a formal nor an imposed authority.

The credibility of reception as a process that is acknowledged to be a provisional, lengthy, and catholic process is undermined, however, by the actual way women's ordination has been received; by the rapid expansion of the number of women who have been ordained; by the consecration of women as bishops; and by the continuing authority of provincial autonomy.

The process by which women were first ordained in the Anglican Communion (before the term "reception" was used) does not provide a sound foundation for the testing and possible limiting of innovations. The first woman ordained to the presbyterate in the Anglican Communion, Florence Li Tim Oi in 1944, was ordained despite official opposition from the Anglican Communion. The 1948 Lambeth Conference clearly refused to permit such an experiment. It not only referred back to the Lambeth Conference 1930 that stated that the Anglican branch of the catholic church could not ordain women to the presbyterate but also added that "such an experiment would be against that [Anglican] tradition and order and would gravely affect the internal and external relations of the Anglican Communion."[66] Despite censure and pressure from the 1948 Lambeth Conference, Bishop Hall of Hong Kong did not require Tim Oi to renounce her ordination, one of the first signs that the Anglican Communion would be impotent in the face of the innovations of autonomous provinces.

Before the 1978 Lambeth Conference could more clearly address the issue, Hong Kong, Canada, the United States, and New Zealand had all ordained women to the priesthood, and eight other provinces had accepted the ordination of women in principle. Partially in response to the acceptance of women's ordination by some provinces, Lambeth 1978 recognized "the autonomy of each of its member Churches, acknowledging the legal right of each Church to make its own decisions about the appropriateness of admitting women to Holy Orders."[67] Thus, in some ways, it appears that historically the process of reception has been to follow the innovations of individual provinces and then gradually relinquish stronger Communion-wide language barring such innovations.

66. "Resolutions 113–15," 1948 Lambeth Conference, in Coleman, *Resolutions*, 119–20.

67. "Resolution 21," 1978 Lambeth Conference, in Coleman, *Resolutions*, 186–87.

The speed at which the ordination of women has proceeded also undermines the process of reception. The Lambeth Conference Resolutions of 1920, 1930, and 1948 that were clearly against the ordination of women above the office of deaconess gave way to the 1968 Resolution that declared the issue inconclusive and the 1978 Resolution that each province had the liberty to decide the issue for itself. In TEC, women's ordination was received with great rapidity. The 1967 General Convention allowed women to serve as lay readers; the 1970 General Convention allowed women to be seated as delegates and also allowed for women to be ordained to the diaconate; the 1976 General Convention permitted women to be ordained to the presbyterate; and by 1989 TEC had its first female bishop.

The extent to which women's ordination has been accepted is closely related to its speed and also makes a true process of reception, in which the innovation is at some point potentially disallowed, less likely. The extensive ordination of women suggests a premature conclusion to what is supposed to be a lengthy and ecumenical process. Once a large number of women has been ordained and integrated into parochial, diocesan, provincial, and Communion life, it is unlikely that Anglican churches would then decree the orders and ministry of such women invalid.

The fact that Anglicans have now consecrated women as bishops also reveals that reception is not a process that has worked well in testing innovations. Since Anglicans have preserved three distinct orders of ministry, there could be no justification for any province or the entire Communion to permit the consecration of women to the episcopate in a process of reception unless the "long process" of the reception of women presbyters was already completed. Officially, the ordination of women priests is still in the process of reception. However, as Peter Toon asks, "*On what reasonable grounds is it possible to think of moving ahead to the consecration of women when the very fact of the ordination of women as presbyters and their deployment in parishes is still a matter of an open process of reception for testing and discernment . . . ?*" (emphasis added).[68]

The process of reception is one more illustration of the problems that provincial autonomy creates for authority in the Anglican Communion. In spite of the fact that the process of reception is to be submitted to the larger church, there is no official authority at the Communion-wide level by which the Anglican Communion could prohibit the ordination of women or legislate a hiatus. No council, such as reception is supposed

68. Toon, *Reforming Forwards?*, 50.

to require, is available in the Anglican Communion as a whole to judge on the issue of women's ordination in the way that provincial authorities are able to initiate such innovations. The inevitable logic of reception, in the framework of provincial autonomy, is that women's ordination will be received with little or no chance of repeal. *This same dynamic is in effect for all possible innovations: provinces (and sometimes dioceses) have the authority to innovate, but the Anglican Communion has little or no authority to prevent such innovations.*

Both GAFCON and the ACNA emerged out of the present Anglican Communion, which has permitted women's ordination. Likewise, the vast majority of those within the ACNA who favor women's ordination are those who came out of TEC recently. The twin innovations of the ordination of homosexuals and the ordination of women occurred within the same context of the culture of TEC (and the wider Anglican Communion) from the 1960s to the 2000s. Both GAFCON and the ACNA, therefore, are very likely more influenced than they realize by the Anglican Communion and TEC, both in their perspective on women's ordination and in the process by which it is approved.

Bishop Robert Duncan, the first Archbishop of the ACNA and a supporter of women's ordination, stated that there were "two integrities" at work and that a century of the process of reception would sort the issue out.[69] Although the ACNA has not commonly employed the term "reception" for the process by which it discerns the validity of women's ordination, its process is virtually the same as that of reception used by the wider Anglican Communion, both with regard to women's ordination and also to homosexual ordination and same-sex rites. When it comes to women's ordination, GAFCON and the ACNA are replicating the experience of the Anglican Communion and seem likely to continue to permit and expand the ordination of women. One critical difference should be emphasized: while GAFCON now assumes the ordination of women and is no longer in a process of reception, the ACNA does not consider the acceptance of women's ordination a foregone conclusion, in spite of the difficulties already discussed.

The women's ordination issue is only one representative of the central dynamic now at work in Anglicanism: provincial autonomy with few, if any, Communion-wide brakes on provincial innovations. The participation of many orthodox Anglicans in promoting women's ordination and

69. Duncan, "The Future of Anglicanism."

the process of reception suggest that orthodox Anglicans will continue to allow and even initiate innovations they do not perceive as threatening to the fundamentals of their orthodox identity.

Networks

Another challenge to a clear and coherent ecclesial identity that orthodox Anglicans are facing is the fact that orthodox churches and groups continue to develop in ways that resemble neither a communion nor a federation but an even looser structure that might be called a *network*. Networks, as a looser form of corporate relationship than communion or even federation, are an increasingly common aspect of postmodern culture. Manuel Castells identifies a network as a series of interconnected nodes. He believes that networks are open structures that are able to expand without limits and integrate new nodes as long as these new nodes share the same communication code. Network-based social structures are highly dynamic, open systems that are susceptible to innovation without threatening their balance. The morphology of such networks is a source of a dramatic reorganization of power relationships, and the switches connecting the networks become privileged instruments of power.[70] In the new network culture, structural oppositions unravel, and the political balance of power disappears. The network culture consists of spreading webs that link, relate, and entangle their members in multiple, mutating, and mutually defining connections in which no one is really in control. Such descriptions of networks help to explain the increasingly complex and mutating ecclesial connections that exist among orthodox Anglican primates, churches, coalitions, think tanks, and other entities.

Some see diocesan boundaries as being fictions. In certain countries, Anglican dioceses are more clusters of congregations in particular localities rather than units of carefully organized missions and parishes that cover the whole land. Peter Jensen Archbishop of Sydney, Australia, and until recently the General Secretary of GAFCON, also believes that the Anglican Communion that is emerging is "already more like a web of interconnected pieces than a unitary whole" and that "the present crisis has dramatically increased this network appearance."[71]

---

70. Castells, *Rise of the Network Society*, 470–71.

71. Jensen, "The Windsor Report is Bound to Fail."

The idea of a networked church is supported by the fact that in the Anglican dioceses in Nigeria a diocesan bishop represents an average of 227,000 members, while in Uganda the number is 280,000. The size of these dioceses makes it likely that the coherence of such dioceses is likely much less than in typical Western dioceses and that the role of the bishop and the understanding of his authority is likely to be different than what is assumed in the West. The nature of diocesan life and the relationship between churches in Africa is not well-known, and it may be that the Anglican structures, diocesan and otherwise, that are taken for granted in a Western context may not be the reality of Anglican churches in other parts of the world.

Little has been studied about the African Anglicanism that has been so crucial in the renewed orthodoxy within the Anglican Communion, but it is possible that the way some provinces and dioceses within African Anglicanism operate also suggests the likelihood of a network model for any orthodox Anglican Communion. For example, Simon Chiwanga, a bishop in the province of Tanzania (considered orthodox), discusses the *mhudumu* or organic model of episcopacy, which abandons the hierarchical understanding of ministry and substitutes a model where ministry is more shared. In this model, which Chiwanga describes as a shift from an "episcocentric" model of leadership to a "polycentric" model, the ministry of the church, in fact, begins to look more like a network.[72]

The experience of orthodox Anglicans worldwide suggests that networks are already in operation and will continue to be central to any future orthodox Anglican Communion. The situation in the United States, probably the best-known situation, is instructive. It is, perhaps, not coincidental that the orthodox dioceses still in TEC that sought recognition by the entire Communion, and which eventually developed into the ACNA, referred to themselves as the Anglican Communion Network (ACN), or just "the Network."

One specific example of the new networked orthodox Anglicanism is The Anglican Mission in America (AmiA). The AmiA organized itself according to non-geographical boundaries and has "affinity bishops" in which individual parishes select which bishop they will serve under. The degree of choice that exists, as opposed to the historical "givenness" of dioceses and episcopal authority, is also represented by the choices individual orthodox parishes have made to come under the jurisdiction of Nigeria,

---

72. Chiwanga, "Beyond the Monarch/Chief," 297–317.

Kenya, Rwanda, and several other provinces or dioceses. Miranda Hassett's work, in particular, has highlighted the ways in which orthodox Anglicans in the US and orthodox Anglicans in Africa have developed an intricate network of relationships.[73]

The ACNA has actually reined in some of the networked nature of orthodox Anglicanism in North America. Yet, given the voluntary nature of membership in the ACNA and the fact that any definitive decision concerning the issue of women's ordination will almost certainly cause sizable minorities of Anglicans to leave ACNA, a relatively loosely held ecclesial identity is likely to continue in ACNA. As mentioned above, GAFCON is at present a conference with networked relationships, and does not yet arise even to the level of a federation of churches.

"Post-Anglican" Anglicanism

Regardless of which direction the ecclesial identity of orthodox Anglicanism takes, it is possible that orthodox Anglicanism (and Anglicanism in general) is entering a fourth stage of ecclesial identity. This fourth stage of identity will be a federation or network of postcolonial churches whose relationships to the doctrine, discipline, and worship of the Church of England, as well as to each other, will also be diverse and not easily categorized. In fact, orthodox Anglicans may especially be at the forefront of helping to forge new Anglican identities in a number of ways. At present, the Anglican Communion has been a focal point of ecclesial definitions of Anglican identity. But with the Communion's inability to articulate and defend any core identity and with the waning importance given to the Anglican Communion by orthodox Anglicans in both GAFCON and the ACNA, the Communion seems a vain hope for being a unifying ecclesial force.

The Anglican Communion did not even become especially important as the ecclesial definition of Anglicanism until approximately the last sixty years. Asian Anglicans have a long history of seeing themselves not so much as Anglicans or churches in communion with Canterbury but simply as parts of the Holy, Catholic Church. Michael Poon, a keen observer of global Anglicanism, desires what may be categorized as a "post-Anglican" Anglicanism, writing that "it is interesting that whenever I suggest that 'Holy

---

73. Hassett, "Episcopal Dissidents, African Allies." Hassett has revised her PhD dissertation into a book, *Anglican Communion in Crisis*, but I have used her dissertation instead since it contained information left out of the book.

Catholic Church' would provide a better alternative to 'Anglican' in describing our Communion, the lively conversations would almost immediately end! I had become a plague to the *Anglo*-cans!"[74]

This "post-Anglican" Anglicanism that is becoming part of the emerging fourth stage in Anglican identity is already reflected within the Anglican Communion itself in ways that relatively few have acknowledged. The creation of the Church of South India in 1947 marked only the beginning of a new era of the multiplication of new Anglican provinces. What is especially interesting about the Church of South India is that even though it is a "united" church, composed of not only Anglicans but also Presbyterians, Methodists, Congregationalists, and others, it is officially part of the Anglican Communion. What unites the Church of South India is essentially the Lambeth Quadrilateral: its website states, "Episcopacy is thus combined with synodical government, and the church explicitly recognizes that Episcopal, Presbyterian, and congregational elements are all necessary for the church's life. The Scriptures are the ultimate standard of faith and practice. The historic creeds are accepted as interpreting the biblical faith, and the sacraments of baptism and the Lord's Supper are recognized as of binding obligation."[75] The Church of South India is only one of four such united churches that are provinces in the Anglican Communion, the others being the Church of North India, the Church of Pakistan, and the Church of Bangladesh.

Other churches that are not part of the Anglican Communion are, nevertheless, in communion with it. Bishops from churches in communion with Anglicans, such as those from Lutheran, Old Catholic, Mar Thoma, Philippine Independent, and United Churches, were members of the 1998 Lambeth Conference, and those from the United Churches in South Asia (for example, the Church of South India) were given full voice and vote.

The enormous growth of Anglicanism in the orthodox Global South, coupled with a newfound awareness of the existence and importance of Global South Anglicans, has also contributed to an understanding of the ecclesial identity of Anglicanism that has less to do with the Church of England or the See of Canterbury than has been the case in the past. Increasingly, orthodox Anglicans feel an allegiance to Global South Anglican leaders more than they do to the Archbishop of Canterbury or the

74. Poon, "Deliver Us from 'Corporate Perversion.'"

75. Church of South India International Resource Center, http://www.csimichigan. org/ChurchofSouthIndia.html.

Anglican Communion. This complex, messy, and network-like relationship between the orthodox Anglicans in North American and the Global South leaders and provinces is also helping to create a new ecclesial Anglican identity that is relatively weak.

While orthodox Anglicans will have difficulty establishing a clear and coherent ecclesial identity, it is possible that they may succeed in establishing a relatively clear and coherent normative identity. Chapter 4 will assess the clarity and coherence of the normative identity orthodox Anglicans are already developing.

Chapter 4 ⸻

Normative Orthodox Anglicanism

INTRODUCTION

WHILE THE ECCLESIAL IDENTITY of orthodox Anglicanism is problematic in several ways, orthodox Anglicans might be able to more firmly establish normative definitions. Normative definitions of orthodox Anglicanism are a reflection of the theological realignment that orthodox Anglicans have initiated and which is predicated on a clear and coherent identity. In actuality, ecclesial and normative definitions of Anglicanism must work closely together and cannot be fully separated. The ecclesial identity of orthodox Anglicanism would be more easily established and maintained if clear norms were established; these norms would be more faithfully preserved if the ecclesial authority in an orthodox Anglican communion acted to use and preserve them.

Historically, Anglicanism has been held together not only by a shared communion with the See of Canterbury (ecclesial Anglicanism) but also by the common doctrine, discipline, and worship (normative Anglicanism) proceeding from the English Church that has formed a strong bond of union for the members of the Anglican Communion. These common norms are the theological and liturgical standards to which Anglicans have historically been bound and which have helped shape and determine Anglican identity.

The new Anglican provinces have historically retained these norms of the Church of England to a large degree as they sought to maintain continuity with the doctrine, discipline, and worship of the Church of England. Both the Preface to the original 1789 *Book of Common Prayer* of the Protestant Episcopal Church in the United States (PECUSA) and the original Constitution of PECUSA clearly asserted that PECUSA desired to continue in the common life of the Church of England. The 1948 Lambeth Conference asserted that the communion of Anglican Communion members was based upon a common faith and order. The 1998 Lambeth Conference also recognized the continuing role of Anglican tradition and norms when it recommended that the primates be given enhanced responsibility to provide "guidelines on the limits of Anglican diversity in submission to the sovereign authority of Holy Scripture and *in loyalty to our Anglican tradition and formularies*"[1] (emphasis added).

Thus, being Anglican has historically meant not just a current being in *communion* with but also a being in *continuity* with this common life on which the present Anglican Communion has been based.

Among the various aspects of this common life are the elements of the Lambeth Quadrilateral: the belief in Scripture as the highest authority, belief in the historic creeds, the two dominical sacraments, and the episcopacy as locally adapted. While the Lambeth Quadrilateral expresses general Christian norms, Anglicanism has historically adhered to certain specifically Anglican norms as well. Other Christian norms include the decrees of the General Councils and, generally, the consensus of the writings of the church fathers as the record of the mind of the church in reading Scripture. Most importantly, in terms of specifically Anglican norms, are the Thirty-nine Articles, the *Book of Common Prayer*, and the Ordinal, which are widely recognized as the three essential historical Anglican formularies.

Any specifically orthodox Anglicanism will only emerge if orthodox Anglican leaders desire to preserve historic Anglican belief and practice against certain innovations that they view as illegitimate. It is clear that there is a powerful orthodox consensus that such innovations as the consecration of homosexual bishops and the blessings of same-sex unions are outside of Christian and Anglican orthodoxy. Such an argument is made primarily on the basis of biblical injunctions against homosexuality. What is not clear, however, is whether or not there are specific *Anglican* norms, beyond a general commitment to Scripture as the highest authority, that will mark the future of orthodox Anglican identity and on the basis of which orthodox Anglicans may more fully realign and converge. Among the various norms that might be established, three stand out both

---

1. "Resolution III.6.b" in *Called to be a Faithful Church*, 34.

historically and in current discussions: Scripture, the Thirty-nine Articles, and the *Book of Common Prayer*.

SCRIPTURE AND ITS INTERPRETATION

The first norm that orthodox Anglicans are turning to as a foundation for defining orthodox Anglicanism is Scripture. In spite of a shared belief in the supreme authority of Scripture for orthodox Anglicanism, orthodox Anglicans continue to allow for an increasing diversity of interpretations of Scripture that to a substantial degree undermines a clear and coherent identity. This is especially true because of the different views orthodox Anglicans have regarding the role of tradition in interpreting Scripture. Given the orthodox Anglican claim that TEC's innovations demand discipline because they violate the norm of Scripture, the orthodox Anglican use of Scripture is all-important in examining a normative orthodox Anglican identity and will have vast implications for the future of orthodox Anglicanism.

The ecclesial bonds of unity as presented by the Windsor Report were assessed in chapter 3; however, a discussion of the first of the bonds listed by the Windsor Report, Scripture, has been deferred until this chapter because of its normative nature. Scripture has been held by Anglicans to be their supreme authority, and, therefore, the first step in understanding orthodox Anglican norms is to understand the normative place of Scripture in orthodox Anglicanism. The appeal to Scripture as the supreme authority in Anglicanism is generally acknowledged and is evident in many of the most important Anglican documents.

The Windsor Report contains an important summary of the Anglican understanding of Scripture:

> Within Anglicanism, scripture has always been recognized as the Church's supreme authority, and as such ought to be seen as a focus and means of unity. The emphasis on scripture grew not least from the insistence of the early Anglican reformers on the importance of the Bible and the Fathers over against what they saw as illegitimate mediaeval developments; it was part of their appeal to ancient undivided Christian faith and life. . . . The Bible has always been at the centre of Anglican belief and life.[2]

---

2. "Windsor Report," 27.

The Orthodox Anglican Re-Affirmation of Scripture

Orthodox Anglicans consider Scripture to be clear enough to serve as the basis for the essential doctrines of the faith, to guide behavior, and to be the touchstone of what separates orthodoxy from heterodoxy. It is precisely because of the supreme authority of Scripture in Anglicanism that Gene Robinson's consecration and same-sex rites have been met with such vehement opposition by orthodox Anglicans. It is, therefore, likely that a future orthodox Anglican Communion, of whatever sort, will preserve a clearly orthodox identity, as seen in terms of the authority of Scripture and the authoritative nature of traditional biblical teaching on sexual morality.

One of the most important questions regarding Scripture for the *Anglican* identity of orthodox Anglicanism, however, is whether or not an appeal to Scripture is a coherent enough principle to unite orthodox Anglicans. In other words, will an appeal to Scripture enable orthodox Anglicans to preserve a specifically *Anglican* identity, or will orthodox Anglicanism assume a more general Christian orthodox identity whose specifically Anglican character will not be clearly maintained?

Orthodox Anglicans, despite their differences, have discovered a renewed unity in response to the challenge of liberal Anglicanism in the Western Anglican provinces such as TEC and the ACC. This unity is based, above all else, on a common regard for the authority and teaching of Scripture that constitutes a primary part of a common Anglican orthodoxy. As we saw earlier, when we looked at GAFCON's founding, the Global South primates established GAFCON because certain provinces were preaching a different gospel which undermined the authority of the written Word of God, a false gospel that included a denial of Scripture's teaching on marriage and homosexuality.

On certain issues, such as the articles of the creeds or shared biblical standards of sexual morality, orthodox Anglicans are united to a very large degree. However, since orthodox Anglicans often have different ecclesiologies and views of ministry, sacraments, and other issues, an orthodox hermeneutic beyond a general appeal to Scripture is necessary. What limits on biblical interpretation have orthodox Anglicans historically employed, in what contexts have the Scriptures been read, and are these limits and contexts still norms on which orthodox Anglicans agree? The answer to these related questions will answer, to a large degree, the question of the strength and coherence of a normative orthodox Anglicanism based on Scripture.

The Role of Tradition in Orthodox Anglicanism

Historically, Anglicans have turned to the notion of tradition and reason as the primary frameworks in which Scripture is interpreted. While reason remains an important interpretive tool for orthodox Anglicans, orthodox Anglican leaders today generally seem to have no disagreement over the use of reason, appreciating it as a useful but not autonomous aid to interpretation and concerned about its autonomous use by liberal Anglicans. The submission of the Anglican Communion Institute (ACI) to the Windsor Report process, "Communion and Discipline," is typical of the orthodox understanding of reason when it states, "*reason* within Anglicanism referred to that theological grounding in creation which enabled the Christian to read the Bible and to apprehend its plain sense, guided by the Holy Spirit, within the life of the Church and obedient to its teaching (*Tradition*). It was not, of course, tied to any notion of human rights and market diversity."[3] Similar statements affirming the proper place of reason but being careful to distinguish between improper or "liberal" uses of reason are fairly common and consistent among orthodox Anglicans.

Tradition is a more contentious authority for orthodox Anglicans, a fact that helps explain the diversity of orthodox Anglican interpretations of Scripture. While tradition has played a crucial role in Anglican interpretations of Scripture, some Anglicans have weakened or denied this appeal to tradition in a way that creates problems for a clear and coherent orthodox appeal to Scripture because without a continued appeal to tradition it is more likely that diversity will continue to increase within orthodox Anglicanism. This tradition consists of a variety of sources, but beyond the highest authority of Scripture, Anglicans have especially valued both the creeds and the first four to seven ecumenical councils as normative interpretations of Scripture. Although more diffuse than either the creeds or the councils, Anglicans have frequently turned to the writings of the patristic era as a normative guide to the meaning of Scripture where it is not immediately clear. In addition, both the Thirty-nine Articles and the *Book of Common Prayer* have been seen as Anglican norms that ought to be employed in order to guide Anglican understanding of Scripture. There appears to be little dispute among Anglicans about the use of either the creeds or the first four councils as Anglican norms, and the place of both the Articles and the Prayer Book will be considered in detail later in this chapter.

3. "Communion and Discipline," 18.

The differences in orthodox Anglican interpretations of Scripture are, therefore, exemplified by their differences in regard for the testimony of the church fathers and the early church tradition as the context in which the Bible should be interpreted. The position of key Anglicans in the sixteenth and seventeenth centuries towards the church fathers was generally very favorable, a point relatively well established. The sixteenth-century English Reformers made extensive use of the church fathers in their controversies with the Roman Catholic Church. While there is some dispute about the strength of their appeal and their methodology, the seventeenth-century Anglican divines, in large part, made greater use of the Fathers as the basis for Anglican theology, especially in contrast to Puritan hermeneutics and arguments that were being employed.[4]

The early history of the Prayer Book also makes clear the early Anglican belief that the church fathers provided crucial support that the Church of England's beliefs and practices preserved the catholic faith and were in submission to the teaching of Scripture. The 1552 Act of Uniformity speaks of the Prayer Book as "a very godly order, agreeable to the Word of God and the primitive Church." The Thirty-nine Articles also uphold the patristic consensus of tradition as one of the things they were designed to protect. As Evangelical Anglicans Packer and Beckwith argue, the Articles identify the faith they confess with the faith of the Fathers and are convinced that "the road which they fence is, in fact, the highroad of catholicity, from which the Romans and Anabaptists alike had gone astray."[5] Especially important is the statement by Canon A5 of the Church of England itself, which states that "the doctrine of the Church of England is grounded in the Holy Scriptures, and in such teachings of the ancient Fathers and Councils of the Church as are agreeable to the said Scriptures."

Often, however, some Evangelical Anglicans, who now comprise the majority of orthodox Anglicans,[6] have not valued the historic practices of

---

4. On this point, Quantin's *The Church of England and Christian Antiquity* is authoritative.

5. Packer and Beckwith, *Thirty-Nine Articles*, 50.

6. Barrett and Johnson state that of the eighty million Anglicans in 2000, thirty million were Evangelical, while another seventeen million were Charismatic, a related orthodox Anglican spirituality. Barrett and Johnson, *World Christian Trends*, 271. The majority of orthodox Anglican leaders worldwide are Evangelical. The Church of Uganda, for example, is one of the most populous Anglican provinces and is dominated by an Evangelical spirituality. Nigeria, the most populous province after England, is also heavily Evangelical, as are many of the Global South provinces.

the church or the church fathers as authoritative interpreters of the Bible as highly as have Anglicans historically. This key shift in the use of tradition helps account for some of the diversity among orthodox Anglicans and suggests that such diversity is likely to continue increasing because some Evangelicals feel freer to innovate in areas where the use of tradition has historically limited diversity. While at the beginning of the nineteenth century High Churchman and Evangelicals with a high view of the church and sacraments were close in many ways, as a result of the polarizing influence of the Oxford Movement, Evangelicals not only distanced themselves progressively from the Tractarians but also from the church fathers, to whom the Tractarians turned for support of their beliefs. Evangelicals often reacted negatively to this emphasis on the church fathers, reversing the Tractarians' belief that it should be the ancient church, and not the Reformers, who should be the ultimate expounder of the meaning of the church. As a result of the Tractarians' emphasis on the church fathers, Evangelicals now identified themselves more closely with the Reformers than with the church fathers. Eventually, Evangelicals often replaced a reliance upon the church fathers with a reliance upon *sola scriptura* with private judgment.

One example of an influential orthodox Anglican who minimizes the role of tradition in interpreting Scripture is Paul Zahl, who was Dean of Trinity School for Ministry (TSM) from 2003–2007. TSM is a critical orthodox Anglican institution since it is the largest Anglican seminary in North America and the only one with a specifically Evangelical (and also Charismatic) ethos. In *The Protestant Face of Anglicanism*, Zahl states his belief that "the Protestant element within Anglicanism is less comfortable with tradition, partly because tradition persistently holds up the Christian Church as intermediating between Scripture and humanity, while Protestants believe no intermediary is necessary."[7] Zahl's argument against the role of tradition appears as well in his *A Short Systematic Theology*. In "Thesis 23," Zahl states that "in theology without constraints, tradition, on the one hand, and church, on the other, always play secondary roles."[8] For Zahl, "tradition is always secondary to the gospel of blood atonement and to the freedom of reason created from it. Human traditions are a crazy weave of outdated circumstances, past idiosyncrasies, unexamined

---

7. Zahl, *Protestant Face of Anglicanism*, 82.
8. Zahl, *Short Systematic Theology*, 86.

ideas that have somehow over time accumulated the weight of authority, and passed-down 'wisdoms.'"[9]

The diversity of orthodox Anglican interpretations of Scripture that results from different evaluations of the importance of tradition is demonstrated by the issue of women's ordination. While both orthodox Anglicans who support and those who oppose women's ordination base their arguments on an appeal to the Bible, their respective interpretations of the biblical evidence concerning women's ordination lead them to opposite conclusions. A naked appeal to Scripture, without some understanding of the need for authoritative principles of interpretation or authoritative interpreters, is not sufficient for orthodox Anglicans to settle important issues in any coherent way. Although certainly other interpretative principles are at work, the attitudes of orthodox Anglicans towards tradition is often decisive.

An illustration of two different attitudes towards tradition in guiding a biblical interpretation of women's ordination may be seen in the papers written by two professors of TSM. In "Why Godly Women Can Have A True Calling to the Ordained Ministry," Peter Moore, former Dean of TSM, argues for women's ordination, while in "Women, Ordination, and the Bible" Rod Whitacre argues against it. Moore argues that the ordination of women is not only compatible with Scripture but actually called for, in light of the development of scriptural thought. Moore acknowledges that the ordination of women is not supported by specific biblical texts but instead argues that women's ordination is consistent with the development of the roles and ministries of women found in Scripture. He briefly refers to "traditionalist" interpretations of women's ordination but makes no reference to tradition as a guide for his own interpretation, substituting instead the concept of "development," which he uses to argue against the traditional view that disallows women's ordination.[10]

Whitacre, like Moore, uses the Bible as the primary evidence to argue his case; however, his interpretive principle is clearly different. In contrast to Moore, Whitacre makes use of tradition as an interpreter of Scripture. In discussing the teachings of St. Paul on women, Whitacre cites a large number of early church fathers who forbade women to speak or teach. Whitacre further states that if we were true to our Anglican heritage and looked to the ancient undivided church for guidance in interpreting Scripture, we would not have nearly the confusion we now have. Valuing the importance

9. Zahl, *Short Systematic Theology*, 86.

10. Moore, "Godly Women."

of tradition to orthodox Anglican interpretations of Scripture, Whitacre adds, "Given the clarity of Scripture, and the confirming clarity of Tradition, the acceptance of this innovation by the Episcopal Church jeopardizes its relation to historic Anglicanism."[11]

More recently, "The Holy Orders Task Force Final Report" was issued by the ACNA in 2017 to allow High Church, Evangelical, and Charismatic adherents to offer their assessment of the validity of women's ordination. Although the issue of tradition is not highlighted in the presentation, the presentation of the ecclesiology of each of the three reveals very different biblical hermeneutics at work. While the High Church position offered presents a fairly standard Anglican presentation of ecclesiology in keeping with the Prayer Book, for example, the Evangelical position offered places the emphasis on the Word over the sacraments, which are subordinated to the Word and seen as being "visible words." In addition, the Evangelical position denies that infants are regenerate at baptism (in spite of clear language of regeneration in all traditional Prayer Books), and seemingly denies any special status to ordained clergy, arguing that church order was not instituted from the beginning.[12]

The Evangelical explanation of The Report favorably quotes Michael Green: "We have reserved absolution and celebration jealously to that elite status of professional priests (as if one strand within the priestly body of Christ was more priestly than another). The contrast with the New Testament could hardly be more complete."[13] The Report also positively quotes leading Evangelical John Stott: "do not hesitate to say that to interpret the Church in terms of a privileged clerical caste or hierarchical structure is to destroy the New Testament doctrine of the Church."[14] This teaching undermines not only tradition but Anglican tradition, which assumes, especially in the Prayer Book, that only bishops or priests can absolve or celebrate communion. In addition, it overthrows the Anglican tradition

---

11. Whitacre, "Women, Ordination, and the Bible." This version of Whitacre's article seems not to be available online currently. However, a related 2014 article by Whitacre, "Reasons for Questioning Women's Ordination in the Light of Scripture," is available here: http://www.tsm.edu/wp-content/uploads/Whitacre%20-%20Women's%20ordination%20-%2028Aug2014.pdf. I've retained my references to Whitacre's original article because it provides a striking contrast between two contemporaneous Anglican professors at the same seminary but who argue from different perspectives.

12. Fairfield, "Anglican Evangelical Tradition," 93–100.

13. Fairfield, "Anglican Evangelical Tradition," 95.

14. Fairfield, "Anglican Evangelical Tradition," 95.

that the three-fold office was instituted from the beginning, at the same time that the church was created: Christ appointed apostles, and St. Paul ordained elders everywhere he planted churches.

The issue of hermeneutics is highlighted when the Evangelical presentation expresses that the authoritative witness and normative interpreter of Jesus is not the heirs of the apostles but the New Testament itself. This understanding neglects the fact that interpretations of the New Testament are highly contested (for example, between TEC and the ACNA) and that some individual or ecclesial authority is always necessary to interpret the Scriptures.

The logical conclusion of this Evangelical demotion of church tradition is that if priests are not serving at an altar or acting in any sacrificial capacity and are only ministering the Word; if ordination confers no special status on clergy; and if the task of priests is pastoral and homiletic but not sacramental: then women can, indeed, be ordained. The point is not just that orthodox Anglicans in the ACNA differ over the issue of women's ordination but that they have fundamentally different hermeneutics by which to interpret Scripture. It's unlikely that these important hermeneutical disagreements will be limited to the issue of women's ordination; instead, they are likely to spill over into other issues involving the nature of the church, the sacraments, holy orders, and ministry. If ordination is not essential to the church and confers no special status to the clergy, it might allow for women's ordination, but only at the expense of making ordination largely unnecessary and of allowing for other innovations.

The Evangelical Anglicanism represented by the diocese of Sydney, Australia suggests the kinds of innovations in Anglican tradition that some Evangelical Anglicans are likely to introduce on the basis of an appeal to the Bible apart from tradition. One of the most important of the innovations Sydney Anglicanism has flirted with is lay celebration of Holy Communion. Historically, Anglicans have kept the tradition of the church on reserving celebration of the Holy Communion for the ordained clergy, a tradition in keeping with a catholic and patristic interpretation of the Bible's teaching on sacraments and ministry and one accepted by virtually all Anglicans until very recently. The willingness of Sydney Anglicans to approve lay celebration, therefore, represents a different reading of Scripture than the historical Anglican one, a difference based largely on the willingness of Sydney Anglicans to reject tradition as a primary interpretive tool. Harry Goodhew, former Archbishop of Sydney, argued against Sydney proceeding with lay presidency because it was a major deviation from tradition. Goodhew, who said he had no objections to lay presidency himself, opposed the move because, as with the ordination of women, there was not an Anglican consensus on the matter. He further conceded that if the diocese of Sydney allowed for lay presidency it would be more difficult for Sydney Anglicans to oppose the ordination of non-celibate homosexuals or blessing of same-sex unions.[15] It appears that Sydney has backed away from lay presidency for the time being.

Evangelical arguments for lay presidency often take a form similar to that offered by David Day,[16] who begins his argument by noting that Scripture says nothing on the subject, indicating that it is not a particularly important subject. Having said this, Day acknowledges that the rule that only bishops and presbyters may preside is extremely ancient and that there is not much support for his position from tradition. Arguing that tradition is changeable, Day offers women's ordination as an example, saying that "a Church which has seen the admission of women to the ordained priesthood can hardly treat traditions as unchangeable."[17] Day concludes his argument by an appeal to pragmatism, complaining that the alternatives to lay presidency, such as denying weekly communion to congregations without a priest or importing a priest with no pastoral relationship to the congregation, solve nothing and do not honor the gospel.[18]

Day's Evangelical argument is an important model for possible Evangelical innovations. Such an Evangelical argument begins with Scripture but interprets Scripture apart from tradition and even interprets against a clear and ancient tradition that opposes a particular innovation such as lay presidency. In fact, the practice of lay presidency is not only contrary to two thousand years of catholic tradition but also involves an interpretation of Scripture that is contrary to the 1662 Prayer Book, which assumes the necessity of priests as presidents at the Holy Communion. Day's appeal for lay presidency on the basis of the prior innovation of women's ordination is logical but demonstrates how in employing such a hermeneutic one innovation is likely to act as a precedent for others. Although presently those in favor of lay presidency are a clear minority, some Sydney Anglicans are

15. Harris, "Lay Presidency Heats Up."

16. Day is a former principal of St. John's, Durham, an Evangelical theological college in England.

17. Day, "Ministry of the Laity," 109.

18. Day, "Ministry of the Laity," 114–15.

hoping to begin a larger movement by relying on the same principle of pioneering autonomous innovation that led to the ordination of women in the Anglican Communion. Thus, by arguing from the silence of Scripture, against tradition, and from a pragmatic standpoint, a hermeneutic held by some orthodox Evangelicals is likely to continue to introduce innovations and greater diversity into orthodox Anglican identity.

Orthodox Anglicans all hold to the supreme authority of Scripture and are united in many of the essentials of the faith but disagree on a range of other important issues, such as women's ordination and lay presidency. The primary difference in interpretation is the reduction of the place of tradition (including the tradition as embodied in the Prayer Book) by Evangelical Anglicans, in particular. This reading of Scripture apart from tradition has allowed for innovations in Anglicanism that have increased diversity and helped to erode a clear identity, and are likely to continue to do so.

Although interpretations of Scripture among orthodox Anglicans are likely, therefore, to become increasingly divergent, orthodox Anglicans may still appeal to two powerful traditional Anglican norms to rein in the increasing diversity in biblical interpretation and provide a common life, norms, and identity: the Thirty-nine Articles and the Prayer Book. These two have historically acted as Anglican norms and parts of Anglican tradition that have not only set limits on biblical interpretation but have also acted with Scripture as referents to the larger apostolic and catholic faith.

THE THIRTY-NINE ARTICLES

The Thirty-nine Articles as an Anglican Norm

Although the Articles and the Prayer Book function in different ways, each is seen by orthodox Anglicans as normative ways of receiving the catholic tradition and interpreting Scripture and may, therefore, provide critical boundaries for orthodox Anglican interpretations of Scripture, as they have in the past.

The Thirty-nine Articles commonly have been acknowledged as one of the three specifically Anglican formularies, along with the Prayer Book and the Ordinal. They were written to steer a middle course for the Church of England, in which the extremes of Anabaptism on the one hand and Roman Catholicism on the other were excluded. The purpose of the Articles is evidenced by their subtitle, which, in part, reads: "for the avoiding of diversities of opinions and for the establishing of consent touching true religion." The historic use of the Thirty-nine Articles demonstrates the fact that the Thirty-nine Articles were designed and used as a theological norm for the Church of England and are, therefore, an important Anglican norm for any Anglicanism that desires continuity with the Church of England's doctrine, discipline, and worship.

Subscription to the Articles by the clergy was mandated as early as 1552 by Edward VI. A form of subscription for all clergy was required by Parliament in 1571, and the Canons of 1604 required that all of the Articles be accepted at ordination and that all ministers acknowledge that the Articles are all agreeable to the Word of God. Some form of subscription has been in effect in the Church of England from 1552 until the present day. The current normative status of the Articles in the Church of England is indicated by Canon A5, which states that the doctrine of the Church of England "is to be found in the Thirty-nine Articles of Religion, *The Book of Common Prayer*, and the Ordinal."[19]

This normative character was perpetuated in The Protestant Episcopal Church of the United States (PECUSA), established after the American Revolutionary War, when it adopted the Articles with minor revisions in 1801. Of this action Bishop White, the presiding bishop at the time, wrote:

> The object kept in view, in all the consultations held, and the determinations formed, was the perpetuating of the Episcopal Church, on the ground of the general principles which she had inherited from the Church of England; and of not departing from them, except so far as either local circumstances required, or some very important cause rendered proper. To those acquainted with the system of the Church of England, it must be evident that the object here stated was accomplished on the ratification of the Articles.[20]

The Turn to the Articles

Orthodox Anglicans might plausibly use the Thirty-nine Articles to articulate a clear and coherent orthodox Anglican identity in order to limit diversity and help to assist in a specifically orthodox Anglican interpretation of Scripture. Orthodox Anglican leaders have, in fact, moved to resuscitate

---

19. Church of England, "Canon A5," https://www.churchofengland.org/more/policy-and-thinking/canons-church-england/section-a#b2.

20. Schaff, *Creeds of Christendom*, 654.

the authority of the Articles as an Anglican norm: this is especially true for Federal Conservatives.

Both GAFCON and the ACNA have made the Thirty-nine Articles a part of their founding identity. GAFCON claims that it is bound together by the 2008 Jerusalem Statement and Declaration, part of which states: "We uphold the Thirty-nine Articles as containing the true doctrine of the Church agreeing with God's Word and as authoritative for Anglicans today."[21] Likewise, the ACNA has affirmed the Jerusalem Statement but also states: "We receive the Thirty-Nine Articles of Religion of 1571, taken in their literal and grammatical sense, as expressing the Anglican response to certain doctrinal issues controverted at that time, and as expressing the fundamental principles of authentic Anglican belief."[22]

The Constitution of the Church of Nigeria, the most populous Anglican province, until recently defined itself as a church in communion with other churches in communion with the See of Canterbury. But Nigeria represents orthodox Anglican provinces that have turned more specifically to a normative identity, and one based on the Articles, to define itself. In response to the growing liberalism within the Communion, and even the Church of England itself, the Church of Nigeria amended its Constitution to read: "The Church of Nigeria . . . shall be in full communion with all Anglican Churches Dioceses and Provinces that hold and maintain the Historic Faith, Doctrine, Sacrament and Discipline of the one Holy, Catholic, and Apostolic Church as the Lord has commanded in His holy word and as the same are received as taught in the *Book of Common Prayer* and the ordinal of 1662 and in the Thirty-nine Articles of Religion."[23]

The importance of this change lies not only in the Church of Nigeria's continuing to distance itself from liberal Anglicanism but even more so in its willingness to establish the terms of Anglican communion not on ecclesial definitions of Anglicanism ("being in communion with the See of Canterbury") but on normative definitions of Anglicanism, especially Scripture, the Thirty-nine Articles, and the 1662 Prayer Book.

The call for a return to the Thirty-nine Articles as a clear Anglican norm is, in many ways, a sign that orthodox Anglicans may be able to establish or maintain a coherent orthodox Anglican identity. There are clear benefits

---

21. GAFCON, "Jerusalem Statement."

22. ACNA, "Theological Statement."

23. "Church of Nigeria Redefines Anglican Communion," https://virtueonline.org/church-nigeria-redefines-anglican-communion.

of such a move, especially if they couple it with a move to enforce biblical orthodoxy and maintain common doctrine and worship through an appeal to the Prayer Book. In the first place, a call for a return to the Articles makes clear that Anglicanism has a particular identity that can be defined, since there are specifically Anglican norms, especially theological ones, which can be referenced. This is critical, if orthodox Anglicanism is to maintain an identity beyond a more general orthodox Christian identity.

Second, the studied minimalism of the Articles, although *prescribing* both a biblical orthodoxy and certain applications of this biblical ortho- doxy, as well as *proscribing* the extremes of both Roman Catholicism and Anabaptism/Puritanism, allows for a traditional Anglican ideal of compre- hension that is both catholic and reformed while leaving many less impor- tant things either undefined or minimally defined. Thus, the Articles may preserve a limited form of comprehension without allowing the diversity of an ever-expanding comprehension effectively to obscure a clear orthodox Anglican identity.

A third advantage of a return to the Articles is that the hermeneuti- cal difficulties of a naked appeal to the authority of Scripture may, in part, be remedied by an appeal to the Articles as authoritative interpreters of Scripture on the issues they address. While there are many doctrines and practices that the Articles do not address, having them as an additional authority would retard continuing innovation among Anglicans to some degree, as well as provide one means of abjudicating between differing in- terpretations of Scripture made by orthodox Anglicans.

As N. T. Wright concludes, writing for the Doctrine Commission of the Church of England, "If we let the Articles sink even further into obscu- rity, and make no attempt to fill the vacuum which they leave, we shall have abandoned those controls, those boundary-markers . . . through which the Anglican Settlement of the sixteenth century achieved its identity . . ."[24]

Difficulties with the Turn to the Articles

However, the appeal to the Articles may not be as simple or clear as some orthodox Anglicans hope for, and there are significant practical obstacles to the Articles being so clearly re-adopted as a firm orthodox Anglican norm.

The first problem orthodox Anglicans might encounter in appealing to the Articles to re-establish orthodox Anglican norms is the question of

24. Wright, "Doctrine Declared," 140.

how strictly the Articles will be enforced at various levels of ecclesial orthodox Anglicanism. It is one thing to establish the Articles constitutionally or
canonically as a norm but another thing actually to enforce such a norm
in any meaningful way. This point confirms the importance of ecclesial
authority and norms working together to establish and maintain religious
identities. Although such meaningful enforcement is certainly possible, the
recent history of subscription suggests that the appeal to the Articles as a
norm may not be as strong in practice as it appears in theory. The history
of subscription to the Articles in the Church of England is a good example
of how seemingly strong standards may, in practice, become relatively inef-
fectual. Since the sixteenth century, the Church of England has required its
clergy to subscribe to the Thirty-nine Articles, and the Church of England
itself has retained the Articles as a norm, as evidenced by Canon A5 (cited
earlier) and Canon A2 of its canons, which states that "the Thirty-nine Articles are agreeable to the Word of God and may be assented unto with a
good conscience by all members of the Church of England."[25]

However, the force of subscription to the Articles, and its role in providing a clear norm, may be undermined in several ways. In spite of the legal
requirement for subscription, the Church of England has had many clergy
who have not adhered to the Articles in any strong way. Even in the 1860s,
when the orthodoxy of most clergy could be more generally assumed, pressure to change the form of assent was exerted by those who feared that
overscrupulousness was holding back worthy candidates. Although the
significance of the change of the formula of subscription in 1865 has been
debated, the effect appears to be that many who could not subscribe to the
Articles in detail could now give their assent. The idea of a "general assent"
that did not require agreement with every detail became a very influential
one in subsequent decades. Likewise, the Preface and Declaration of Assent
introduced in 1975 seem to have been devised so that assent could be made
with a good conscience by those not in full agreement with the Articles.
Three causes have led to a lower and looser view of subscription to the
Articles in the Church of England: the alteration in the form of subscription, the excessive latitude of interpretation claimed by subscribers, and the
minimization of the act of subscription.

A crucial question for orthodox Anglicans who desire to return to
subscription to the Thirty-nine Articles as a clear Anglican norm, then, is

25. Church of England, "Canon A2," https://www.churchofengland.org/more/
policy-and-thinking/canons-church-england/section-a#b2.

"How strictly will they require subscription by the clergy?" For example, will the orthodox Anglicans who desire subscription of the clergy be willing to require a strict teaching of the Articles at orthodox seminaries? A new difficulty inherent in subscription, with the increasing turn in Anglicanism to synodical government, is the relationship of the laity to the Articles. Subscription in the past has only applied to clergy, and not to laity, and so the new authority of the laity, through their synodical representation, would also have to be limited by some kind of subscription to the Articles, if a turn to the Articles were to be effective. Such a move, on the face of things, appears unlikely, given the degree of difficulty involved in maintaining even clergy subscription. It is not yet clear whether or not orthodox Anglicans will enforce a stricter subscription, but the trend towards loose subscription will probably prove difficult to reverse. A second problem that compounds the first one is the latitude of interpretation of the Articles that already exists within orthodox Anglicanism. This is a crucial problem because the issue of diversity threatening to overwhelm a clear core Anglican identity, most recently highlighted by the diversity of liberalism, is one that orthodox Anglicans themselves are facing. The question of hermeneutics, so important in interpreting the ultimate Anglican authority of Scripture, is important as well in interpreting the Articles.

Since the time of John Henry Newman's infamous "Tract XC," the latitude of interpretations of the Thirty-nine Articles has grown, along with a more general comprehensiveness within Anglicanism. Anglicans have commonly believed that the Articles should be read in continuity with their original authors' intentions and by using grammatical, historical, and literary methods to discover this fundamental meaning. In fact, "His Majesty's Declaration," affixed to the beginning of the Articles, states "that no man hereafter shall either print, or preach, to draw the Article aside any way, but shall submit to it in the plain and full meaning thereof: and shall not put his own sense or comment to be the meaning of the Article, but shall take it in the literal and grammatical sense."[26]

Newman, however, wrote, "It is a duty which we owe both the Catholic Church and our own, to take the reformed confessions in the most Catholic sense they will admit; *we have no duties toward the framers*"[27] (emphasis added). To the degree that orthodox Anglicans follow Newman in interpreting the Articles in non-natural and individual ways, apart from their

26. Packer and Beckwith, *Thirty-Nine Articles*, 6.
27. Newman, "Tract XC."

historical context, they will continue to undermine the ability of a return to the Articles to act as a potent and clear orthodox Anglican norm.

Anglo-Catholic groups, in general, perpetuate a more Roman Catholic interpretation of the Articles such as that advocated by Newman, despite such an interpretation being in contrast to what the primary architects of the Articles (Cranmer and Latimer) had in mind, as well as what the history of interpretation of the Articles until the time of Newman had been. In most cases, Anglo-Catholic groups have found it more convenient simply to neglect the Articles. This negative view of the Articles is common among Anglo-Catholics, including not only those within the ACNA but also among the Continuing Churches that came out of TEC in the 1970s. While they often regard the Prayer Book as a formulary, they rarely accept the Articles as a binding Anglican norm.

Anglo-Catholic resistance to the Articles is a well-known phenomenon. Some Anglo-Catholics have a negative view of the ACNA, not just because of the issue of women's ordination but also because of the place and use of the Articles in the ACNA. Bishop William Ilgenfritz, the bishop of the Missionary Diocese of All Saints (an Anglo-Catholic diocese in the ACNA) has said: "While the 39 Articles are an important historical document within Anglicanism, they were written to address specific issues at a certain time. Their meaning is contextual. As Anglicans, we affirm our faith when we recite the Nicene Creed. We are not Confessional Christians."[28] It is likely, therefore, that Anglo-Catholics will continue to reject, revise, or hold the Articles with mental reservation in such a way that their normative nature is effectively reduced.

Some Evangelicals, the largest orthodox Anglican "party," are also likely to undermine a clear appeal to the authority of the Articles as well, although not for the same reasons as Anglo-Catholics. Some are prone to use the Articles as a sufficient confession, apart from the entire context in which they were created and designed to be used, and in this way are also allowing for greater innovation and diversity. This context includes not only Scripture but also the Prayer Book (and not alternative prayer books), the Ordinal, the Homilies, the creeds, the councils, and the witness of the church of the first several centuries. Some Evangelical Anglicans seem to forget or ignore the fact that both the Articles and Prayer Book were largely the work of the same man in the same historical context: Archbishop Thomas Cranmer. Removed from the original milieu in which they were

28. Virtue, "Dual-Integrity Over Women's Ordination."

designed to function, the Articles do not adequately address many issues or deal with them insufficiently. Attempts to interpret Scripture in light of the Articles alone are likely to produce interpretations in conflict with traditional Anglican interpretations and the patristic witness the Articles were meant to protect. This view is reflected in a belief held by some Evangelical Anglicans that the Articles are a doctrinal standard above the Prayer Book, a view that became much more common after the Tractarians appealed to the Prayer Book for their distinctive emphases. Such a valuing of the Articles over the Prayer Book is reflected by D. B. Knox's view that "the other formularies of the Church of England, for example the *Book of Common Prayer*, ought to be interpreted in the light of the Articles and not the Articles in the light of the Prayer Book . . ."[29] This view, however, pits the Articles against the Prayer Book and also seems to assume that the two are inconsistent in some ways. Furthermore, such a move undermines the possibility of appealing to a catholic tradition of biblical interpretation that lies behind both the Articles and the Prayer Book.

One example of how the Articles interpreted apart from the Prayer Book or other contexts of tradition might be used in such a way as to weaken an orthodox Anglican identity is the doctrine of the church some Anglicans derive from the Articles and Scripture, apart from other parts of the tradition. John Woodhouse, principal of Moore Theological College from 2002–2013, an Evangelical seminary in Sydney, Australia, argues that the definition of a "church" contained in Article XIX is one that is difficult to improve on. However, Woodhouse proceeds to interpret this Article apart from its larger traditional context and further argues that the language of Article XIX may suggest a structure that is not essential and that the church is complete wherever God gathers two or three to himself by his Word. In so arguing, Woodhouse is aware that his ecclesiastical position is one of congregationalism but seems unconcerned that such congregationalism is in contrast to the traditional ecclesiology that Anglicanism has inherited from the early church. Woodhouse derives his minimalist ecclesiology from his interpretation of Scripture, supported by a minimalist reading of Article XIX.[30]

29. Knox, *Thirty-Nine Articles*, 57.

30. Woodhouse, "Unity of the Church." A similar claim is made by Peter Baron against the English Evangelical group, Reform, which Baron believes elevates the local parish at the expense of the catholic nature of the church (Baron, "The Case against Reform.")

N. T. Wright, a leading Evangelical Anglican, sees a similar willingness to re-interpret the ecclesiology of the Articles in order to promote congregationalism in "A Covenant for the Church of England" that was released in December of 2006 by a group of Evangelicals who are in sympathy with the goals of Federal Conservatives. To Wright, this document bases unity on the idea of an invisible church and exhibits a "breathtaking congregationalism" when it states that the local congregation is the seed-bed for recognizing, authorizing, and raising up and releasing new leaders. Wright contends that such an ecclesiology is based on a faulty reading of Article XXIII, which cannot mean "the local church, doing its own thing."[31]

A final group of orthodox Anglicans who undermine such a turn to the Articles are Communion Conservatives such as Radner and Turner, authors of *The Fate of Communion* and representative members of the Anglican Communion Institute (ACI). Throughout *The Fate of Communion*, Radner and Turner are critical of turns to formularies, including the Articles, as a means of preserving communion, and Communion Conservatives, in general, are concerned about what they consider attempts to establish a confessional form of Anglican identity. Any turn to the Articles within TEC (where Communion Conservatives are still members) is effectively blocked by how TEC has relegated the Articles to a "Historical Documents of the Church" section in the back of the 1979 Prayer Book, where they have been safely ignored for the past four decades. The few remaining orthodox leaders in TEC are unlikely to use the Articles in any meaningful way.

The resistance of some Communion Conservatives to using the Articles as a formulary raises the related problem of the ecclesial identity of orthodox Anglicanism, which is a third way in which a turn to the Articles will be problematic. How strictly will the Articles be enforced? The present Anglican Communion has no mechanism for enforcing any Communion-wide decisions, and provincial autonomy prevails. In addition, it is largely the Global South provinces that claim the Articles as a norm. When the Anglican Communion was restricted to the Church of England, the subscription that the state required was a potent force in maintaining Anglican unity. Without the aid of the state, orthodox Anglicans in the Anglican Communion are less likely to require adherence to the Articles or 1662 Prayer Book in order for communion to be preserved, especially if the Articles have not historically been an important part of provincial life, as may be the case with many newer, global, provinces.

31. Wright, "A Confused 'Covenant.'"

In order for this appeal to the Articles to act as a solid bond of communion and effective orthodox Anglican norm, the Articles would have to be enforced to some degree at every level. Dioceses would have to hold parishes accountable, and provinces would have to hold dioceses accountable. Seminaries would have to find ways effectively to enforce subscription to the teaching of the Articles, and as orthodox provinces and groups continue to realign, they would need to determine what part the Articles should play in intercommunion. While GAFCON and the ACNA have forcefully claimed the Articles one of their theological norms, it remains to be seen how forcefully they will actually enforce them, especially among the clergy.

A fourth and final limitation on the effectiveness of the Articles to limit diversity and establish a clear orthodox Anglican identity is the fact that the Articles are of increasingly limited relevance. The Articles only deal with a limited number of issues, related to the historical exigencies present at the time of their writing. If the Articles are insufficient to prevent some orthodox Anglicans from reading them out of context and continuing to innovate on issues which they do address, then they will be an even weaker brake on innovations related to issues that they do not directly address, such as lay confirmation. The Articles are silent on women's ordination (although the traditional Prayer Books assume a male clergy). The Articles are also silent on moral issues, such as the issue of homosexuality that is at the forefront of the orthodox Anglican realignment. Because such moral issues were part of a shared consensus at the time of the writing of the Articles, the Articles cannot serve as a guide for orthodox Anglicans in judging them.

In the Anglican Communion as a whole, the Articles increasingly have been marginalized as an Anglican norm and considered irrelevant. Resolution 19 of the 1888 Lambeth Conference recommended that newly-constituted churches of the Anglican Communion should provide evidence "that they hold substantially the same doctrine as our own, and that their Clergy subscribe Articles in accordance with the express statements of our own standards of doctrine and worship; but that they should not necessarily be bound to accept in their entirety the Thirty-nine Articles of Religion."[32] As early as 1930, the Lambeth Conference appears to have chosen to demote the normative status of the Articles even further. The Conference declared that the Anglican Communion includes those "whose

32. "Resolution 19," 1888 Lambeth Conference, in *The Six Lambeth Conferences*, 124. See also the "Encyclical Letter," 1888 Lambeth Conference, in *The Six Lambeth Conferences*, 116; and "Committee Report No. XII," 1888 Lambeth Conference, in *The Six Lambeth Conferences*, 174.

faith has been grounded in the doctrines and ideals for which the Church of England has always stood,"[33] defining this doctrine in terms of Scripture, the creeds, the sacraments, the Prayer Book, and the three-fold ministry, but not the Articles. The 1968 Lambeth Conference made this deletion of the Articles more explicit when it suggested "that each Church of our Communion consider whether the Articles need be bound up with its Prayer Book" and "that assent to the Thirty-nine Articles be no longer required of ordinands."[34] Archbishop of Canterbury, Michael Ramsey, commented to the 1968 Lambeth Conference that Articles had differing degrees of importance to different churches. The attitude of the Lambeth Conferences reaffirms, then, that the Articles are generally normative for the Church of England but that a diversity of attitudes towards the Articles among the Anglican provinces properly exists.

The attitudes of specific Anglican provinces are especially important to a discussion of the place of the Articles because, unlike the Lambeth Conferences, individual provinces have the authority to define and defend particular Anglican norms. Because of the normative place the Articles have had in the Church of England, those churches claiming to retain the doctrine of the Church of England, therefore, are at least implicitly acknowledging the Articles as an Anglican norm. As of 1988, Peter Toon found that the Churches of Ireland, Scotland, Wales, Australia, Canada, New Zealand, Uganda, Ruanda-Burundi-Zaire, Nigeria, and West Africa had retained the Articles as a norm, while Kenya and Tanzania gave individual dioceses the option to adopt them. Furthermore, it is possible that the Articles are implicitly included in the constitutions of provinces that claim the same faith as the Church of England.[35] However, six of those who had retained them, the provinces of Ireland, Scotland, Wales, Australia, Canada, and New Zealand, are heavily influenced by liberal Anglicanism and are not likely to hold them with a very great degree of strictness. It's very likely that the Articles are even less authoritative today in Anglican provinces, even in those that still officially claim them.

---

33. "Committee Report No. IV," 1930 Lambeth Conference, in *The Lambeth Conferences, 1867–1948*, 246.

34. "Resolution 43," 1968 Lambeth Conference, in Coleman, *Resolutions*, 165. The thirty-seven bishops who dissented from this resolution were mainly English Evangelicals (Simpson and Story, *Long Shadows of Lambeth X*, 147). This point is important in considering specifically orthodox attitudes towards the Articles.

35. Toon, "The Articles and Homilies," 141.

While GAFCON has adopted the Articles as one of their theological norms, it's not clear how widely used they are in the practical life of GAFCON or Global South provinces. They may never have been the norm in such provinces and are likely not to have played a prominent part in their provincial life. As John Pobee concludes, in an article on authority in African Anglicanism: "So, then, authoritative as the Thirty-nine Articles may be, they are not authoritative for all the communion and *certainly not for the churches in Africa*"[36] (emphasis added).

The appeal to the Articles made by GAFCON, the ACNA, and others is a promising development in orthodox Anglicanism, in terms of establishing a clear and coherent identity. However, many practical questions about the strictness with which the Articles will be held present important difficulties, and orthodox Anglicans will have to set the Articles more clearly in their larger context, including that of the Prayer Book, if they hope for them to be an effective norm. If orthodox Anglicans are finding it difficult to discipline what they consider to be clear departures from biblical orthodoxy, what mechanism or resolve will they find to enforce the Articles as a clear Anglican norm? Given the diversity of interpretation of the Articles present among orthodox Anglicans, such as some Evangelicals and some Anglo-Catholics, and their relative unimportance globally, the ability of a turn to the Articles to act as a strong norm to shape a clear orthodox Anglican identity is not likely to be as strong as many orthodox Anglicans hope for. This diversity in interpretation and use will render the Articles relatively impotent unless orthodox Anglicans develop some mechanism to effectively enforce the Articles as a meaningful norm.

As with the appeal to Scripture, orthodox Anglicans are likely to find themselves caught between a desire to require assent to the Articles while also desiring to continue to allow divergences from them.

THE BOOK OF COMMON PRAYER

The third important Anglican norm that orthodox Anglicans are likely to continue to appeal to is the *Book of Common Prayer*, especially the 1662 Prayer Book.[37] Archbishop Thomas Cranmer's first Prayer Book was pub-

36. Pobee, "Take Thou Authority," 193.

37. The 1928 American Prayer Book is so close to the 1662 that, despite a general consensus that it is more Catholic than the 1662 Prayer Book, it is practically equivalent to the 1662. Other Prayer Books that represent minor revisions to the 1662 Prayer Book

lished in 1549 and took its most normative shape in the 1662 Prayer Book. While the Articles have had a long and broad history of acting as an Anglican norm, the influence of the Prayer Book as a specifically Anglican norm has been even greater.

The Importance of the Prayer Book

The propositional and confession-like character of the Articles may make them a natural candidate to be an Anglican norm, but the normative character of the Prayer Book is both less obvious and also more powerful. The Prayer Book has helped create and maintain a distinctly Anglican identity in four related ways.

First, the Prayer Book acts as a specifically Anglican formulary, an aspect represented by its official normative status in various provinces, especially the Church of England. The Anglican formularies were devised to preserve the doctrine, discipline, and worship that the Church of England had received from the undivided church. The Prayer Book, as a distinctly Anglican formulary, therefore gives shape and unity to Anglicanism by serving not only as a standard for doctrine, discipline, and worship but also by serving to tie Anglicanism back to the standards or formularies of the early church. The Prayer Book, as an Anglican formulary, has been acknowledged widely by Anglicans to be a faithful transmission of the normative apostolic and catholic tradition as reflected in Scripture, the creeds, the ecumenical councils, and the patristic mind. A 1948 Lambeth Conference report stated that the Prayer Book is the embodiment of the Reformed Catholic character of Anglicanism and is not only an important source of teaching but also the means by which the Anglican tradition has been maintained.

A second way in which the Prayer Book has created and preserved Anglican identity is in its role as a repository of Anglican doctrine. Anglicans sometimes assert that there is no distinctively Anglican doctrine, and yet this statement is undermined by the historic use of the Prayer Book to define the limits and use of Anglican doctrine. The Church of England declares in its canon law that its doctrine may be found in particular in its Articles, Prayer Book and Ordinal, and these Anglican formularies have, until recently, been seen as *theological* norms among Anglicans. The Prayer

---

can be assumed to be included when I use the term "Prayer Book." However, it is still the 1662 Prayer Book that is the most important norm.

Book manifests a Reformed Catholicism in its doctrines, which negatively proscribes certain doctrinal beliefs and positively prescribes others, and these doctrines are still officially the doctrinal standard for much of the Anglican Communion. The Prayer Book historically has been the context within which Anglicans have read the Bible, and so even the most authoritative standard for orthodox Anglicanism, the Bible, is colored by the doctrinal standards and expressions contained in the Prayer Book. Because Anglicans generally believe the adage *lex orandi, lex credenda* ("the law of praying is the law of believing"), what is continually experienced in worship shapes the way that the worshiper believes; in this way, the Prayer Book is a uniting force in Anglican theology.

The Prayer Book is, thirdly, also the source for a distinctively Anglican spirituality or way of life. The Christian life is always incarnated into particular forms, each of which represents its own way of understanding the priorities and emphases of a particular Christian community. Regardless of what might be said of English spirituality before Cranmer's Prayer Books, since that time, the Prayer Book has been at the heart of Anglican spirituality. This conclusion is supported by a consensus of scholars studying Anglican spirituality.[38]

The fourth and perhaps greatest reason why the Prayer Book has been the essence of Anglican spirituality is that it is the Prayer Book that especially creates a common life and a living tradition in continuity with the apostolic tradition. Until recently, it was possible for Anglicans to go to most parts of the world and experience the same liturgy in the same words, even when local flavors were present. Even after a few decades of prayer book revision, there is something of a common core to both the structure and the words of Anglican worship that unites Anglicans, although this commonality is rapidly perishing.

Historically, therefore, the Prayer Book has been essential to Anglican identity. The 1920 Lambeth Conference stated that "at the date of the first Lambeth Conference, 1867, this Communion had taken the form of a federation of self-governing Churches, held together for the most part without legal sanctions by a common reverence for the same traditions and *a common use of a Prayer Book*"[39] (emphasis added). Archbishop of Canterbury

38. See, for example: Thornton, *English Spirituality*, 257, and Wakefield, "Anglican Spirituality," 259–63.

39. "Report No. 8," 1920 Lambeth Conference, in *The Lambeth Conferences, 1867–1948*, 122.

Fisher offered his opinion in 1948 that the Prayer Book was the authoritative expression of the unity of faith and order among Anglicans and that it provided "our accepted pattern of liturgical order, worship, and doctrine which is to be everywhere maintained."[40] In summary, so strongly has the Prayer Book been connected with Anglican identity that Edward Norman believes that "in the absence of a coherent ecclesiology, the Prayer Book *was* the authority of the Church of England. Its forms of words and its teaching office is really all there is that joins present Anglicans with their predecessors."[41] Some believe that as the place of the Articles went down in authority, the place of the Prayer Book went up. But what would happen if the Prayer Book were no longer a strong norm and force for Anglican unity?

The future of the Prayer Book is therefore closely related to the future of any Anglican identity, including a specifically orthodox Anglican identity.

The Turn to the 1662 Prayer Book

Mainly in response to the growing theological liberalism of the West, and not necessarily as a response to liturgical revision, some orthodox Anglicans desire to establish more forcefully the Prayer Book as an Anglican norm. Among Prayer Books, the 1662 Prayer Book is the most important, for it is the one that has been the most widely accepted Anglican norm. The 1662 Prayer Book, despite the introduction of the *Alternative Service Book* and then *Common Worship*, as well as their widespread use, is still the official standard of worship and doctrine in the Church of England. Canon A5 of the Church of England asserts the authority of the Prayer Book when it states that the doctrine of the Church of England is to be found in the Thirty-nine Articles of Religion, *The Book of Common Prayer*, and the Ordinal. In the Church of Nigeria, the second largest province in the Anglican Communion with twenty million members, the 1662 *Book of Common Prayer* is explicitly claimed to be the standard for the church. The Constitution of the Anglican Church of Australia, as just one more example of one of the larger provinces (with four million members), contains a similar statement concerning the Prayer Book as its authorized standard of worship and doctrine.

40. "Encyclical Letter," 1948 Lambeth Conference, Part I, in *The Lambeth Conferences, 1867–1948*, 23.

41. Norman, *Anglican Difficulties*, 17.

Most significantly, both GAFCON and the ACNA also clearly state the 1662 Book of Common Prayer as one of their theological norms. Bishop Robert Duncan, the first primate of the newly formed ACNA, issued perhaps the strongest and most remarkable statement of the need for a return to the Prayer Book:

> I want to be so bold as to suggest the following: that Anglicanism's practical magisterium—its reliable teaching authority—has been its Book of Common Prayer, and that without a restored Book of Common Prayer, reasserting the theological propositions of medieval Catholicism as reshaped by the English Reformation, best represented in the prayer book of 1662, Anglicanism will continue its theological disintegration apace. For that Western Church whose popular and practical believing was more nearly lex orandi, lex credendi than any other tradition—for that Western Church whose practical magisterium was its prayerbook—a fixed prayer book is essential.[42]

Even more than a turn to the Articles, a turn to the 1662 Prayer Book has the potential to help to create a clear and coherent orthodox Anglican identity.

Difficulties with the Turn to the 1662 Prayer Book

As with the Articles, however, the turn to the 1662 Prayer Book involves many difficulties. Because of the very practical and regular nature of the liturgy, a turn to the Prayer Book has the critical challenge of having to confront a mismatch between the stated norm, the 1662 Prayer Book, and the actual lived-out standard, which is usually not the 1662 Prayer Book. In addition, while the actual use of the Articles in a given province may remain obscured and only become visible occasionally, the actual use of the Prayer Book or its alternatives is recognizable by all within a particular jurisdiction because of the practical nature of the Prayer Book.

The difficulties posed by a turn to the 1662 Prayer Book all relate to one primary problem: the disuse of the 1662 Prayer Book in practice and the corresponding large amount of diversity in actual liturgical and prayer book practice. An evaluation of the actual state of use of the 1662 Prayer Book, particularly among orthodox Anglicans, is, therefore, critical in assessing the possible effectiveness of a turn to the Prayer Book as an effective agent in

42. Duncan, "Future of Anglicanism."

creating a coherent orthodox Anglican identity. In spite of the acceptance of the 1662 Prayer Book as an official standard by many orthodox Anglicans, the 1662 Prayer Book is not likely to be as effective as orthodox Anglicans hope in establishing a clear orthodox Anglican identity because it will continue to be undermined by orthodox Anglicans in two ways. First, some provinces and Anglican groups have entirely replaced the traditional Prayer Book as their norm, and, second, even in provinces or churches where the 1662 Prayer Book is the official standard, its use is undermined by the widespread use of alternative prayer books and liturgies.

The first source of difficulty for an orthodox Anglican turn to the Prayer Book is the fact that many provinces, including primarily orthodox ones, have replaced it with other prayer books that often represent significant changes to the traditional Prayer Books. As of 2006, most of the Anglican provinces had an official prayer book that was not the 1662 Prayer Book (or one of its equivalents). Provinces that have replaced the 1662 Prayer Book or authorized additional ones include: TEC, Canada, the West Indies, the Philippines, Japan, Myanmar, Tanzania, Sudan, Kenya, Central Africa, South Africa, Burundi, Congo, Korea, Ireland, Scotland, Wales, Papua New Guinea, Australia, New Zealand, Melanesia, and Nigeria.[43] Even the churches that have retained the 1662 Prayer Book as an official standard have another official Prayer Book in use in addition to 1662 (Nigeria); have replaced the 1662 with a contemporary Prayer Book even though the 1662 is the constitutional standard (Australia); or have effectively replaced the 1662 with a modern book of services, even while 1662 is the official standard (Church of England). To the list above should be added the united churches of Asia (South India, North India, Pakistan, and Bangladesh), which are not specifically Anglican and do not use Anglican prayer books. As time goes on, this list will only grow.

The replacement of the traditional Prayer Book (1928 in this case) is most dramatically the case in TEC, even among orthodox Anglicans in TEC. While in 1980 alternative services began to displace Prayer Book services in the Church of England, in 1979 TEC did more than displace the Prayer Book: it *replaced* it in an unprecedented move in Anglicanism

43. Hefling and Shattuck, *The Oxford Guide to The Book of Common Prayer*. See individual chapters for detailed information about each province discussed. It may be that the provinces not listed here have also replaced the 1662 Prayer Book, but information on such provinces as Brazil, the Indian Ocean, and others is difficult to come by. In fact, it is possible that only a very few provinces such as England, Australia, Nigeria, and Uganda have actually retained the 1662 Prayer Book as their official standards.

at the time. TEC does not consider the 1979 Prayer Book as an alternative prayer book but as *the* Prayer Book in the United States, as evidenced by the official title: *The Book of Common Prayer*. The 1928 American Prayer Book was no longer to be considered the Prayer Book of TEC, a point confirmed by a resolution of the 1979 General Convention.

Because the Prayer Book acts in Anglicanism as a formulary, a standard of doctrine, a primary source of spirituality, and the most powerful bond of a common life, the replacement of the traditional Prayer Book with an entirely new one is a radical step that changes the identity of Anglicanism. The 1979 American Prayer Book contains a different theology than the traditional Prayer Books. Urban Holmes, a TEC insider, revealed that the Standing Liturgical Commission knew that the 1979 Prayer Book represented a clear theological change.[44] This shift in theology is reflected, for example, in "An Outline of the Faith" that replaced the traditional catechism. The new catechism begins not with God but with humanity, replaces the old theology of righteousness and salvation with the concept of harmony, and omits the doctrine of original sin that has been crucial to traditional Anglican theology. This reduction of the doctrine of sin and the need for confession and repentance is also reflected throughout the 1979 Prayer Book, for example, in the revised baptismal service.

If it were only liberal Episcopalians who were dedicated to the use of the 1979 Prayer Book, the turn to the 1662 Prayer Book by orthodox Anglicans in the US might represent a meaningful and effective means of preserving a clear orthodox Anglican identity. Liberal Episcopalians might continue to use the 1979 Prayer Book or revisions of it, while orthodox Anglicans might return to the 1662 or 1928 Prayer Books. However, the majority of the orthodox Episcopalians who are either in TEC or who came out of TEC used the 1979 Prayer Book, and not the 1928 Prayer Book.

This situation has changed in recent years with the completion of the new ACNA Prayer Book in 2019. This Prayer Book is a new Prayer Book and not just a revision of a previous Prayer Book, such as the 1979 TEC Prayer Book or the 1928 American Prayer Book. The ACNA Prayer Book contains elements of both the 1979 Prayer Book, as well as the traditional Prayer Books, and has been revised in a more clearly orthodox direction from the 1979 Prayer Book. However, it seems to have used the 1979 Prayer Book as its foundation and, therefore, has a less direct connection to the traditional Prayer Book. It also severs the historical connection with the

44. Holmes, "Education for Liturgy," 134.

theology and practice of the traditional Prayer Books, a point that will not be immediately apparent but will reveal itself visibly over time. The gravitational pull of its very existence is likely to rein in some of the substantial liturgical diversity that has existed within the ACNA, a process that will facilitate greater unity in theological norms and liturgical and ecclesiastical practices. In this way, the new ACNA Prayer Book is a favorable force to a renewed ecclesial orthodox Anglican identity.

On the other hand, its very presence makes it less likely that all members of the ACNA will all actually be using a *common* Prayer Book. The new ACNA Prayer Book is now one more option for orthodox Anglicans in the ACNA, although many will choose to use it. Its advent highlights the way that trends in religious identities may manifest forces both conducive to and destructive of a clear and coherent identity. Since the Prayer Book is a practical norm, it gains its authority by actual use, and not by using it as a propositional theology, such as the Articles, which are easily referenced on any point of doctrine it treats. Not only must the Prayer Book actually be used, it is not merely a collection of random liturgical rites but is instead a Rule of Life that binds its members into a common life. Members of a church can only very imperfectly be united if those members are living by different Rules of Life. The 1662 Prayer Book (or its traditional equivalents such as the 1928 American Prayer Book or the Reformed Episcopal Church's 2003 Prayer Book), which both GAFCON and the ACNA portray as a crucial theological norm, is not being used by most within GAFCON or the ACNA. This renders the 1662 Prayer Book in ACNA as a less potent force for normative orthodox Anglican identity than it might otherwise be.

The problem for a turn to the 1662 Prayer Book as an orthodox norm because of its replacement with other prayer books is also raised by the desire for liturgical inculturation in places such as Africa. Orthodox Anglicans, especially Federal Conservatives, are turning to the Global South primates as a uniting authority that will help create and enforce a new Anglican covenant, which will contain the 1662 Prayer Book as a norm: the status of the Prayer Book in the Global South is therefore crucial.

Earlier in this chapter, the number of provinces that still have the 1662 Prayer Book as the official Prayer Book was discussed. How widely is the 1662 Prayer Book (or its equivalents) used, more specifically, in the mostly orthodox Global South provinces that are so important to the future of orthodox Anglicanism? Information is available for fifteen of the twenty-five Anglican communion provinces that are a part of the Global

South, primarily from *The Oxford Guide*. Nine of these fifteen provinces discussed have produced their own prayer book or use a prayer book that is not the 1662 Prayer Book. These provinces include: Burundi, Central Africa, the Church of South India, Congo, Kenya, Myanmar, the Philippines, Tanzania, and the West Indies. Three of the provinces allow for the 1662 Prayer Book but also have at least one other official prayer book and include: Jerusalem and the Middle East, Nigeria, and Southern Africa. Only three of these Global South provinces that *The Oxford Guide* discusses have the 1662 Prayer Book as their sole official Prayer Book: Rwanda, Sudan, and Uganda.[45] Although it is difficult to find information on the Church of Bangladesh, this church is also very unlikely to have the 1662 Prayer Book as its standard or to use it in its worship services.

This cross section of Global South provinces, which are predominantly orthodox, indicates that the 1662 Prayer Book is no longer the dominant prayer book it once was, either officially or in actual use. Officially, less than half of these fifteen provinces have the 1662 Prayer Book as their official prayer book (and only three have it as their only official Prayer Book). The evidence suggests that even in the ones that do, the 1662 Prayer Book is falling into disuse, as will be discussed below with reference to the Church of England and in chapter 5 with reference to the Church of Uganda. Many of the new prayer books being used have been introduced in the past two decades, and in some provinces the process of prayer book revision is a relatively new one that has only recently been undertaken in earnest. Prayer book and liturgical revision are likely to continue to increase, with which will come an increase in diversity that will make the effective use of the 1662 Prayer Book as an orthodox Anglican norm improbable.

The 1988 Lambeth Conference resolved that "each province should be free, subject to essential universal Anglican norms of worship, and to a valuing of traditional liturgical materials, to seek that expression of worship which is appropriate to its Christian people in their cultural context."[46] However, as discussed in chapter 3, there are no reliable means by which the Anglican Communion can guard these norms of worship or traditional

---

45. See Hefling and Shattuck, *The Oxford Guide*, which discusses the Prayer Book, region by region. In 2013, the Church of Uganda published a new *Book of Common Worship* to be used alongside the 1662 Prayer Book. This *Book of Common Worship* represents another innovation among orthodox Anglicans: it does not contain a service for confirmation.

46. "Resolution 47," in *Truth Shall Make You Free*, 232.

liturgical materials. Also, these "essential universal Anglican norms" rarely have been specified.

The second way in which the turn to the 1662 Prayer Book is likely to be undermined by orthodox Anglicans is in the effective replacement of the traditional Prayer Book in churches that still officially hold the 1662 Prayer Book as the standard. This kind of undermining is taking place in two ways. First, officially sanctioned alternative service books and liturgies are being used more commonly than the 1662 Prayer Book, and, secondly, liturgical innovation even outside of officially sanctioned books is taking place. In both cases, the amount of diversity represented by the worship of orthodox Anglicans effectively undermines any turn back to the 1662 Prayer Book as a forceful and effective norm. As long as alternative service books are used as supplements to a normative Prayer Book in actual use and remembrance they might serve as valuable sources of enrichment; if, however, they supplant the Prayer Book, then the Prayer Book, which can only be a norm if people are actually familiar with it, ceases to be an effective norm. This is, in fact, what has happened in some provinces and seems likely to continue.

Most dramatically, Anglicans in the Church of England, including orthodox Anglicans, have effectively replaced the 1662 Prayer Book with alternative service books to a large degree. By 1987 Gareth Bennett could already state that "no change in Anglicanism during the last thirty years has been more remarkable than the virtual disuse of the prayer books based on the English Book of Common Prayer."[47] As early as 1980, David Martin was concerned that the Prayer Book was being marginalized by being used only at eight o'clock services and believed that some who might prefer Prayer Book services were going to non-Prayer Book services that were held later in the day and were emphasized as the main service.[48] David Bebbington writes, "Even before the publication of *The Alternative Service Book* in 1980, most Evangelicals had ceased to use the 1662 order except for an early morning communion service."[49] Thus, disuse of the 1662 Prayer Book in the Church of England is an *orthodox* Anglican problem, and not just a general Anglican one. Furthermore, there were many indications that clergy at all levels were making deliberate efforts to marginalize the use of the 1662 Prayer Book. In 1995, an extensive survey of recently trained ordinands in the Church of England revealed that

47. Bennett, "Preface to Crockford's Clerical Directory," 197.

48. Martin, "A Plea for Our Common Prayer," 20–21.

49. Bebbington, *Evangelicalism in Modern Britain*, 257.

many had not been exposed to the theology and practice of traditional services and were ill-equipped to conduct them.[50]

In spite of the status of the 1662 Prayer Book as the official norm and formulary of the Church of England, it has been marginalized: this same marginalization is likely to be occurring in other provinces that also use alternative service books, for example, the *Book of Alternative Services* in Canada.

One problem presented by the displacement of the Prayer Book by alternative service books is the sheer amount of diversity they represent. For example, in the Church of England, the alternative service books have been based on the idea of a directory of resources, from which local parishes pick and choose, designing their own liturgies for local use. A directory approach to liturgical services is built on a minimal basic foundation, with local churches choosing from a variety of materials to produce their own liturgies. *Common Worship* (2000) continues the trend toward a directory of resources with a great diversity of choices and consists not only of a single book but also of a series of books, CDs, a website, and other electronic resources to help to cope with the overwhelming number of options. Such worship, while it may succeed in its aim of allowing for a wide variety of choices for local use, is not "common" in the way that the *Book of Common Prayer* is, with a common liturgical use for a province. Because of the number of choices available, there is often little continuity between parishes that use *Common Worship*, even though they are technically using the same alternative service book.[51] The unifying effect of a common Prayer Book is thus lost when the diversity of prayer books or services is too great.

To put it bluntly: in the Church of England, the "Mother" church of Anglicanism, there is no longer "common" prayer.

The theology of alternative service books is likewise a problem for maintaining a common identity. As long as the Prayer Book and its accepted teachings and norms are well known, the diversity of theology contained in alternative service books may be limited because there is a recognized standard. However, as the Prayer Book falls into disuse, the theologies of

---

50. Homan, "The Liturgy," 46.

51. My experience in the Church of England when I lived there for a year to begin my PhD studies was that the liturgy varied widely from parish to parish and that often there was little in common between the liturgies. One Evangelical parish kept experimenting with various elements and was so unsure of the inner logic of the liturgy they had created (or they had changed the liturgy so frequently) that the worship leader felt it necessary to frequently explain why the service was moving from one element to the next.

alternative prayer books, cut loose from a definite norm, are more likely to be interpreted in diverse and even heterodoxical ways. *Common Worship* does not contain the Thirty-nine Articles, the Athanasian Creed, or the Catechism, and a confession of sin appears to be optional. There does not seem to be much evidence that liturgical practices are monitored for undesirable diversity or are disciplined when violations do occur. In fact, with as many choices as *Common Worship* offers, it would be impossible for any church authority to assess the theology and practice of each local parish. This fact means that churches in the Church of England can be producing heretical or otherwise deficient liturgies, by which the laity will be habitually instructed and formed. Even if it were certain that the theologies of alternative service books are sound, they would still represent an increasing diversity of theologies that could not be easily evaluated or confined within any common orthodox Anglican norms.

To these problems inherent in alternative service books must be added the destruction of a common and comprehensive spirituality. Traditional Anglican spirituality has been founded upon *The Book of Common Prayer* as a common and comprehensive Rule of Life, something no collection of myriad, local rites can produce. The rationale for alternative service books appears to be that such books are merely a collection of services or a collection of resources for services. There is no notion, as was true with the Prayer Book, that a single book would be used in every room and for every occasion, and there is no notion that a single book serves as the basis for a complete spiritual life. Even if such a spirituality were desired, it would be impossible because the repetition and memorization that make such an intense and internalized familiarity possible cannot be accomplished when the diversity of services is too large and the service one encounters week by week and year by year keeps changing.

In addition to the displacement of the traditional Prayer Book by alternative service books, many orthodox Anglicans are using even more radically diverse liturgies that often exceed even the generous limits of alternative service books such as *Common Worship*. Some Anglo-Catholics in England do not use the 1662 Prayer Book or *Common Worship* but liturgies that are more Roman Catholic in nature. Some Anglo-Catholics in the US also replace the Prayer Book with the Anglican Missal or mix worship between the two. An assortment of other Anglo-Catholic communities uses the *Anglican Breviary*, which is an English translation of the pre-Vatican II

Roman Catholic Breviary. Some Anglo-Catholics in England even use the Roman Catholic Mass.

Evangelicals in England, who are primarily orthodox, manifest an even greater diversity in the liturgies they use. Paul Roberts chronicles some of the radical departures from Prayer Book worship and even outside of the *Alternative Service Book* (replaced in 2000 by *Common Worship*). That a mainstream Evangelical publisher publishes Roberts's book and that Roberts himself, an Evangelical, is an advocate of more expansive worship options emphasize the acceptability of and widespread nature of such views among orthodox Anglicans within the Church of England, a province that has retained the 1662 Prayer Book as a norm. According to Roberts, the words and liturgies of alternative worship are normally home-grown. Roberts himself favors a church that defines itself through worship and not creedal subscription, as well as a "postmodern" church that advocates the reduction of the value placed on logical, word-based reasoning; the move toward open-ended and open-minded approaches; suspicion of centralized structures of authority in favor of more local and *ad hoc* structures; and a continued openness to individual experience.[52]

Roberts's approach is represented by the radical worship of the *Nine O'Clock Service*, a non-canonical and often bizarre form of worship in the 1990s that was nevertheless supported by many in the Church of England. Although the *Nine O'Clock Service* was short-lived, the fact that it was supported by high-level Church of England officials reveals the pervasiveness of departures for Prayer Book worship. As Roberts writes, "When alternative worship happens in the Church of England, most diocesan bishops welcome it, but normally adopt the stance of 'please don't tell me what you're doing'—since to do so would implicate the bishop in non-canonical liturgy."[53] Supporters of the *Nine O'Clock Service* included the Archdeacon of Sheffield (the diocese which hosted the *Nine O'Clock Service*), Professor John Rogerson, Head of Sheffield University's Biblical Studies Department, scores of senior clergy and theologians who were enthusiastic visitors, and future Archbishop of Canterbury George Carey, an orthodox Evangelical. Such attitudes towards clear canonical violations and the great diversity of liturgies in use indicate the difficulty of using the 1662 Prayer Book as a standard if it cannot or will not be enforced in any meaningful way. If such diversity in prayer book and liturgical usage

52. Roberts, *Alternative Worship*.

53. Roberts, *Alternative Worship*, 23–24.

exists within the Church of England itself, it is likely that the diversity in global Anglicanism is at least as great.

Perhaps the greatest challenge to the Prayer Book is its state in global Anglicanism, not only because of liturgical inculturation and Prayer Book revision but also because of competition from new church groups and Pentecostals. This competition is inciting some global Anglicans to reject the Prayer Book and to worship in ways that have more in common with non-denominational or Pentecostal worship than they do with historic Anglican worship. The inculturation of the Prayer Book into the local cultures of the newer Anglican provinces has produced an increasing array of diverse prayer books. Some are still based on the 1662 Prayer Book, while other provinces have produced prayer books more fully revised with local theologies and cultures in mind. These revisions have often only taken place in recent decades, and the divergence of global Anglican liturgies and prayer books from the 1662 Prayer Book will continue in the future. Given the increasingly global nature of Anglicanism, including orthodox Anglicanism, such diversity undermines any clear return to the 1662 Prayer Book.

When Vinay Samuel visited the Province of Nigeria in 1988, he discovered that priests led the 1662 Prayer Book service for forty-five minutes and that "after that, lay leaders take over for a time of exuberant and lively worship, sometimes lasting over two hours. There seems to be no real link with the preceding 1662 worship or with their own cultural tradition."[54] The Anglican Church of Kenya has historically had a very strong connection to the 1662 Prayer Book, a relationship that is weakening, and some younger Anglicans have been told that they cannot pray using a Prayer Book, since prayer must come from the heart. The "formalism" of the Prayer Book has become a source of frustration to some Kenyan Anglicans who are concerned about the new Pentecostal churches drawing many young people to them. Sometimes, due to a lack of available Prayer Books, the worship of the churches in some of the global provinces develops without it.

The turn to the 1662 Prayer Book is, in theory, a move that makes sense, based on the critical importance the Prayer Book has had in creating and maintaining a specifically Anglican identity. The fact that various orthodox Anglican provinces and churches have officially adopted the 1662 Prayer Book as a norm is a good indicator of an understanding of its continuing importance to orthodox Anglican identity. However, the turn to

---

54. Samuel and Sugden, *Lambeth: A View from the Two Thirds World*, 26. I've been told similar things by several Nigerian priests.

the 1662 Prayer Book is not likely to prove as effective as many orthodox Anglicans hope it will be for these four reasons: its replacement in various provinces; the challenge presented to it by alternative service books; its virtual replacement in actual use by alternative service books and other liturgies; and a continuing desire by many orthodox Anglicans to worship outside any official limits.

If Bishop Duncan's words about the importance of a restored Prayer Book were indicative of a united desire among orthodox Anglican leaders to return to the Prayer Book, then a turn to the 1662 Prayer Book might become a remarkable instrument of unity for orthodox Anglicans. Given the actual usage of prayer books, however, this is an unlikely possibility, although the force of an official 1662 Prayer Book might potentially become one means by which diversity could be made somewhat more manageable and identity maintained.

As the Prayer Book increasingly continues to be unused, disused, and revised by orthodox Anglicans (and Anglicans in general), the continuity of orthodox Anglicanism with the ancient church and the Church of England through the common theology and liturgy of the Prayer Book is weakened, and with it, orthodox Anglican identity. One of the characteristics of a developing fourth stage of Anglican identity, of which orthodox Anglicanism is a vital part, will, therefore, be an increase in liturgical and prayer book diversity.

CONCLUSION

While a turn to the Articles and Prayer Book as clear norms is likely to provide a point of focus for orthodox Anglicans and may retard the process of innovation and diversification to some degree, it is unlikely to stop the process of increasing diversity that threatens a clear orthodox Anglican identity. Without either a strong authority or clear norms, or more effectively *both together*, a clear orthodox Anglican identity will prove difficult to establish or maintain. Without a clear and robust ecclesial definition of orthodox Anglicanism, a move to a more clear, normative orthodox Anglican identity is less likely.

As with an ecclesial analysis of orthodox Anglicanism, a normative one suggests that the orthodox Anglicanism that is being asserted and is undergoing a realignment may be in the process of entering a fourth stage of Anglican identity. In this fourth stage, which may be likened to a "post-Anglican" Anglicanism, there will be less continuity with the Church of England and its historical norms, the Thirty-nine Articles, and the Prayer Book. As a result, there will be less continuity with the doctrine, discipline, and worship of the Church of England and through it continuity with the early church.

As with the ecclesial aspects of Anglican identity, orthodox Anglicans officially seek a more definite identity based on the norms of Scripture, the Articles, and the Prayer Book, an identity that is related to an *integrated* concept of culture. At the same time, orthodox Anglicans are continuing to adhere to these norms in individual and increasingly diverse ways and will manifest aspects of a *globalized* concept of culture.

Orthodox ecclesial and normative identities are likely to be a mix of both *integrated* and *globalized* identities and will not be as clear and coherent as orthodox Anglicans assume or desire them to be. One final possibility exists for serving as the foundation of a more clear and coherent identity: practical definitions of Anglicanism based on the principle of comprehension, which is the subject of chapter 5.

Chapter 5 —————————————

Orthodox Anglican Spiritualities

INTRODUCTION

IF APPEALS TO ECCLESIAL and normative identities are likely to produce mixed results for orthodox Anglicans asserting a clear and coherent identity, are there any other options? By embracing a diversity of orthodox Anglicanism spiritualities, all of which are identified as both orthodox and Anglican, an orthodox Anglican comprehension may be one definition that could account for the increasing diversity within orthodox Anglicanism and yet allow for a common core identity that is Anglican. In other words, Anglicanism may be defined not so much as churches in communion with Canterbury or as churches that interpret the Scriptures in light of a Reformed Catholicism and adhere theologically to the 1662 Prayer Book and the Thirty-nine Articles but defined on the basis of an orthodox Anglican comprehension.

COMPREHENSION AND ORTHODOX ANGLICAN SPIRITUALITIES

Historically, Anglicans have dealt with the problem of diversity through the ideal of comprehension, an ideal that developed mainly as a consequence of the English Reformation and the Elizabethan Settlement, after which the Church of England identified itself as a church that was both Catholic and Protestant. Elizabeth achieved political and religious stability by comprehending in one national church as many religious positions and identities as possible while still setting limits on comprehension so that the extremes of Roman Catholicism and Anabaptism or Puritanism were proscribed. The ideal of a limited comprehension was put into effect to a large degree by the ecclesial authority of the state, including the use of legal power in such instruments as the Act of Uniformity as well as the use of state-mediated norms of Anglican identity such as the Prayer Book and Articles.

Along with the Catholic and Protestant elements that Anglican identity in the Church of England comprehended, it was later also assumed that Anglicanism contained a Liberal element in it, one that affirmed the role of reason in the church. In response to the Oxford Movement and the Ritualism that succeeded it, a new Anglo-Catholic identity was asserted in the nineteenth century that, to some degree, expanded the previous definition of Anglicanism. The ideal of comprehension was also expanded in the nineteenth century by Anglican thinkers such as F. D. Maurice at a time when the division between Anglican parties was so intense that a view of comprehension as the union of opposites or as things held in tension emerged. Historically, comprehension was not a celebration of toleration or diversity for its own sake but was a principled agreement on where fundamentals lie and where non-essential *adiaphora* (not in conflict with the fundamentals) lie.

Practical definitions are those based on the practices, behaviors, and ethos of a church. One important practical definition of Anglicanism, then, has been in terms of the ideal of comprehension. To include as much as possible, Elizabeth and others attempted to include both Protestant and Catholic ideals; to include as many orthodox Anglicans as possible, orthodox Anglican leaders are also assuming and accepting a kind of comprehension. Such an orthodox comprehension is mostly implicit and has not been expressed very often in terms of comprehension; however, it is related to the more openly expressed idea of convergence, which is the third aspect of the orthodox Anglican realignment. As the institutional realignment in orthodox Anglicanism may be evaluated in terms of ecclesial identity and the theological realignment in terms of a normative identity, the convergence aspect of the orthodox Anglican realignment may be evaluated in terms of the ideal of comprehension (a kind of practical definition).

Convergence is the attempt to have orthodox Anglican churches and groups work together toward a common, united orthodox Anglicanism. This convergence is evident in the emergence of the ACNA. In their letter to the Archbishop of Canterbury announcing the creation of the Common

Cause Partners (a precursor to the ACNA), representatives of the partners wrote of their "commitment to make common cause for the gospel of Jesus Christ and common cause for a united, missionary and orthodox Anglicanism in North America."[1] Behind the creation of the ACNA, which emerged from the Common Cause Partners, lies the desire of the orthodox Global South primates to have a united orthodox Anglican province in the United States that they may officially recognize. This convergence of the Global South and orthodox Anglicans in the US (discussed in greater detail later in this chapter) represents another important part of the growing orthodox Anglican convergence.

The ideas of realignment and convergence are predicated upon the existence of a common identity strong and clear enough to establish an Anglican orthodoxy distinct from liberalism and also to serve as the basis for greater unity among orthodox Anglicans. Orthodox Anglican leaders and groups have developed a strong network of connections with each other and generally recognize who other orthodox Anglicans are, even if they also acknowledge their differences. This is especially true in terms of their common *orthodox* identity. Orthodox Anglicans generally recognize the orthodoxy of other Anglicans if they accept the literal truth of the statements of the historic Christian creeds; consider the Bible to be the inspired Word of God; adhere to the traditional biblical interpretation that homosexuality is a sin; and identify themselves as orthodox. There also appears to be little desire by orthodox Anglicans to deny the Anglican identity of any of the orthodox Anglican churches and groups. Diverse orthodox Anglicans such as Evangelicals in Sydney, Australia, Charismatics in the Church of England, Anglo-Catholics in the US, and Global South Anglicans in Africa, for example, generally see both themselves and each other as orthodox Anglicans.

If, however, orthodox Anglicans are working toward a realignment into which all orthodox Anglicans are invited, especially as such a realignment takes the shape of an orthodox Anglican communion of some sort, they must clearly articulate the terms of such a comprehension. Convergence, so far, has taken place primarily in terms of *orthodoxy* as orthodox Anglicans unite to distinguish themselves from liberal Anglicans. In terms of a specifically *Anglican* identity, however, will such a convergence take place? Will this attempt to establish a clear and coherent Anglican

---

1. "Anglican Groups to Make Common Cause," https://virtueonline.org/anglican-groups-make-common-cause.

identity on an orthodox comprehension of all orthodox Anglican spiritualities fare any better than orthodox Anglican ecclesial or normative identities are likely to?

To gauge orthodox Anglican identity in terms of such a comprehension, the degree of diversity that is present among orthodox Anglicans should be assessed, a work that few have undertaken. The typical approach to defining an Anglican identity has been deductive, attempting to sketch a historical development based from a fundamental point of historic origin. An inductive approach, on the other hand, would examine the diversity that is present among Anglicans today to determine what shared identity can encompass such diversity. In the remainder of this chapter, I will explore the degree of diversity already present in orthodox Anglicanism and, from that point, begin to understand what definition of orthodox Anglicanism would be necessary to comprehend this diversity.

The diversity among Anglicans that must be comprehended may be understood mostly in terms of the distinctive spiritualities[2] that are to be included within orthodox Anglicanism. The traditional understanding of the spiritualities comprehended within Anglicanism is being modified by orthodox Anglicans from a comprehension of three spiritualities (Catholic, Protestant, and Liberal) to a comprehension of four *orthodox* spiritualities (Anglo-Catholic, Evangelical, Charismatic, and Global). Paul Avis, among others, discusses a classical understanding of Anglicanism as being a synthesis or comprehension of Catholic, Evangelical, and Liberal elements. It's possible to see the origins of three Anglican "spiritualities" as being inherent in the English Reformation. The English Reformers asserted the catholic nature of the Church of England in their controversies with the Roman Catholic Church, while insisting to the Puritans that they were also fully Protestant. In both of these polemics, English Reformers made use of the new humanist learning of the Renaissance and made constant appeals to sound learning that are earmarks of a kind of liberalism (although in a very different form from what would emerge later).[3]

The orthodox Anglican spiritualities that currently exist represent several modifications to this traditional ideal of a comprehension of Catholic, Protestant, and Liberal spiritualities. One of the most notable changes from the traditional Catholic-Protestant-Liberal trichotomy has been the

2. I am using "spirituality" to mean the distinctive style, ethos, or characteristic piety that marks certain groupings of Anglicans, especially orthodox Anglicans.

3. Avis, "What is 'Anglicanism'?," 408.

reluctance of contemporary orthodox Anglicans to affirm a specifically liberal aspect. Although some orthodox Anglican theologians continue to make appeals to the freedom of inquiry that liberalism classically represented, for most orthodox Anglican leaders today, "liberalism" is often equated with a radical form of liberalism that undermines the supreme authority of Scripture. While orthodox Anglican leaders do not now commonly appeal to a Liberal spirituality, this is not to say that orthodox Anglicans have jettisoned a desire to use reason as an interpretive tool. Instead, the appeal to reason appears to have been absorbed within the identity of the four orthodox spiritualities.

The Catholic spirituality has been modified slightly so that the most common Catholic spirituality now referenced is the Anglo-Catholic spirituality. Following the Oxford Movement of the 1830s and 1840s, the Catholic spirituality in the Church of England expanded to include not only the High Church party, the traditional Catholic constituency in the Church of England, but also those who eventually became identified as Anglo-Catholics. As a result of the great influence of the Oxford Movement and the consequent Ritualist Movement, the Catholic spirituality within Anglicanism has been, to a large degree, an Anglo-Catholic one. While many who would consider themselves Catholic Anglicans would not consider themselves to be Anglo-Catholics, this more general Catholic identity, traditionally associated with the High Church position, has not had a particularly diversifying or innovating influence on Anglican identity. For this reason, as well as because of the influence of Anglo-Catholics, the Anglo-Catholic spirituality will be considered, instead of a more diffuse and generalized Catholic spirituality.

The Protestant spirituality is usually no longer referenced as a separate orthodox spirituality: the Evangelical spirituality in some ways has taken its place. In response to both the Evangelical Revival and the Oxford Movement, the Protestant face of Anglicanism has become, essentially, the Evangelical party. Paul Avis claims that "the Protestant elements in Anglicanism, detached however from high ecclesiology of the High Church tradition and from liberal humanism of Latitudinarian or Broad Church tradition, became the special preserve of the Evangelicals."[4]

Additionally, two new spiritualities have now become a part of a new orthodox Anglican comprehension: the Charismatic spirituality and what I will be calling the Global spirituality, both of which are primarily

4. Avis, "What is 'Anglicanism'?," 410.

twentieth-century developments and both of which are related especially to a pre-existing Evangelical spirituality.

To understand the challenge of maintaining an identity based on a comprehension of orthodox Anglican diversity, we must evaluate each of these four orthodox Anglican spiritualities in terms of the kind and degree of diversity each contributes to any contemporary notion of comprehension, as well as the ways in which they may tend to produce a more *globalized* and less coherent orthodox Anglican identity.

DIVERSITY IN THE ANGLO-CATHOLIC SPIRITUALITY

The first orthodox Anglican spirituality is the Anglo-Catholic one, a form of Catholic spirituality. In some ways, the Catholic spirituality is most characterized by its impulse to adhere to the Vincentian Canon ("that which has been believed everywhere, always and by all"). At its heart, the Catholic aspect of Anglicanism has been concerned with what is universal or "catholic," and therefore, continuity with the historical traditions of the church—its doctrine, worship, and order, especially in relation to the patristic era—is especially important to Catholics. Catholic emphases that the Church of England recognized and made part of the church's Reformed identity in the sixteenth century include: the priority and authority of Scripture, the doctrinal guidance of the creeds, the use of liturgy that is faithful to Scripture and embodies the experience of the church over the centuries, the historic episcopate, the threefold ordained ministry, the unity of Word and sacrament in the Holy Communion service, and a desire for the visible unity of the church on earth. Such a catholicity is rooted not only in Scripture but also in the first five centuries of church tradition.

A precise definition of Anglo-Catholicism within this broader Catholic spirituality may not be possible, but Anglo-Catholics appear to range from those who would look little different from traditional High Church Anglicans to those who are sometimes called "Anglo-Papalists" and who seek to approximate Roman Catholicism in various ways. Anglo-Catholicism is, essentially, the attempt to inject a Catholic (often Roman Catholic) ethos of worship and religious life on the Church of England and other Anglican churches, and therefore Anglo-Catholics are in general associated with beliefs and practices related to the Roman Catholic Church. Although the diversity of Anglo-Catholic beliefs and practices is not expanding as

rapidly or as diversely as those of the other orthodox Anglican spiritualities, it is still important to gauge the expanded comprehension necessary
to encompass current Anglo-Catholic beliefs and practices, as well as the
diversity represented by the other spiritualities.

The proclivity of some Anglo-Catholics to reject the Prayer Book and
to reject the Articles to an even greater degree, and, therefore, to contribute to an expansive definition of Anglicanism, was discussed in chapter 4.
Another representative of Anglo-Catholic spirituality that necessitates an
expansion of the definition of Anglicanism is the various Anglo-Catholic
churches and communities that not only reject the traditional Prayer Book
but also, in fact, appeal to a large degree to the spirituality, beliefs, and practices of the Roman Catholic Church.

Anglo-Papalists are Anglo-Catholics who are especially desirous to
approximate a Roman Catholic spirituality and may be seen as those who
believe the true nature of the Church of England can only be recognized
when it is once again united with the Roman Catholic Church. Michael Yelton understands the mission of the Anglo-Papalists as desiring to make the
Church of England as much like the Roman Catholic Church on the Continent as possible. To demonstrate their belief that the Church of England
was part of the catholic Church, they produced the religious communities,
shrines, pilgrimages, and popular piety of the Roman Catholic Church.[5]
One of the most visible reminders of this goal was the re-establishment of
the shrine of Our Lady of Walsingham and the pilgrimages to this shrine.
This re-establishment of the shrine and pilgrimage brought together two
Anglo-Papalist goals: the desire to look back to medieval precedents and
the need to show that the Church of England was a true part of the catholic
church by its outward demonstrations of faith.[6] At the parish church of
Our Lady of Walsingham, the interior was filled with statues, candles, and
other objects to bring the look into keeping with Continental Roman Catholicism. Initially, the Prayer Book was used, with silent insertion of the
canon from the Roman Mass. Later the Prayer Book was adapted to make
it appear like the Roman Mass, and, finally, the Roman canon was used. At
present, the Sacrament is reserved, and the rite of Benediction, in which
the Sacrament in a monstrance is presented before the people, has become
a regular devotion (in seeming violation of the Thirty-nine Articles). Each

5. Yelton, *Anglican Papalism*, 13.

6. Yelton, *Anglican Papalism*, 130–31.

day, the rosary is said. A Procession of Our Lady is made, and Mary is seen as a point of entry for the Gospel life.

A list of some of the innovations characteristic of Anglo-Catholics includes: perpetual reservation of the Sacrament on the high altar; Benediction; the Rosary; shrines of the Sacred Heart, Our Lady, and of St. Joseph; Corpus Christi processions; the complete disuse of the English language; the regular use of the Latin Missal; and others. The rite of Benediction is only one example in which the Anglo-Catholic spirituality has brought innovations into Anglican identity and has contributed to the increasing diversity within orthodox Anglicanism. Benediction is common among Anglo-Catholics and is repugnant to the majority of Evangelicals who often see it as a form of idolatry and are quick to point out its violation of Article XXVIII of the Thirty-nine Articles. In turn, this is one of the reasons Anglo-Catholics often reject the Thirty-nine Articles as an authentic Anglican norm.

The Roman Catholic tendency of some Anglo-Catholics is also represented not only by the defections to the Roman Church by John Henry Newman and others in the nineteenth century but also by the establishment of three Anglican Ordinariates in 2011–2012, including ones that include England[7] and the United States. The Ordinariate is a structure within the Roman Catholic Church that allows Anglicans to join the Roman Church while preserving elements of their liturgical and spiritual heritage. While reports that the Anglican Church in America (ACA), a continuing Anglo-Catholic body, had voted to join the Roman Church may have been greatly exaggerated, the fact that it was even considered and that one of the bishops of the ACA had gone to Rome still substantiates the fact that many Anglo-Catholics continue to look to Rome.

The original Anglican comprehension excluded both Roman Catholics and radical Reformers. If the new orthodox Anglican comprehension includes Anglo-Catholics who are virtually Roman Catholic, with the exception of the acceptance of papal infallibility or acknowledgment of the Pope's universal jurisdiction, then the identity of orthodox Anglicanism and the terms of comprehension will need to be expanded in a Roman Catholic direction. The rejection of both the Articles and the Prayer Book by some Anglo-Catholics also expands the degree of comprehension

---

7. Interestingly enough, the Ordinariate that includes England is called the Personal Ordinariate of Our Lady of Walsingham, a point which confirms the Rome-ward looking gaze of many Anglo-Catholics.

necessary to incorporate them. Some Anglo-Catholics assert an exclusively Catholic identity, and even an almost Roman Catholic one, in a church that has often clearly identified itself as Protestant. Such a process has, of course, already begun, but has to a large degree already been incorporated into the orthodox Anglican identity, at least partially because the Anglo-Catholic spirituality has been around for well more than a century now. It is also relatively limited[8] and static and, therefore, represents the least significant of the four orthodox spiritualities that challenge an orthodox Anglican identity. Anglo-Catholics are not very numerous or influential in the key Global South provinces, to which many orthodox Anglicans are looking for leadership, or in Anglicanism as a whole, and they are a clear minority in the ACNA as well.

DIVERSITY IN THE EVANGELICAL SPIRITUALITY

The diversity present in the Evangelical Anglican spirituality is greater than that present in the Anglo-Catholic spirituality and is still growing. Since the Evangelical spirituality has become the dominant form of orthodox Anglican spirituality, the diversity present among Evangelicals is especially important to consider. This Evangelical diversity is also crucial because the Charismatic and Global spiritualities are often closely related to a pre-existing Evangelical spirituality that has become a part of them.

Principles of Evangelicalism that Evangelical leaders state include: Scripture as the supreme authority and a personal message to individuals; the necessity of conversion; prioritizing preaching, evangelism, and church extension; the centrality of the Cross and the penal substitutionary theory of the Atonement; assurance of salvation; the priesthood of all believers; and often a Reformed emphasis on the sovereignty of God and the five solas of the Reformation. These distinctives form a reasonably consistent constellation of primary Evangelical concerns, although Evangelicals are not monolithic in their beliefs and emphases, and diversity exists within each of the four orthodox Anglican spiritualities.

The Evangelical spirituality that exists today is different in significant ways from the traditional Evangelical spirituality that was mostly, until about the 1960s, content with Anglican Prayer Book spirituality. The contemporary

8. Barrett and Johnson, for example, count less than two million Anglo-Catholics out of a total Anglican population of more than seventy-four million (Barrett and Johnson, *World Christian Trends*, 390).

Evangelicalism in both the UK and the US traces its roots not only through the English Reformers and the Evangelical Revival of the eighteenth century but also to an Evangelical resurgence that did not begin until the late 1960s. Evangelical Anglicanism in the Church of England was at a low point from 1900 to 1960, and no classical Evangelical party in TEC existed from about 1900 until the 1960s. The re-emergence of classic Evangelicals in TEC began with isolated individuals in the 1950s through the 1970s, most of whom were influenced by English Evangelicals.

The Evangelical resurgence is often attributed in part to the Keele Conference in 1967 when Evangelical Anglicans began the process of becoming more "open" in a variety of ways, especially to engaging the larger church and world. J. I. Packer, one of the most important representatives of the older Evangelicalism, speaks of a division among Evangelicals between "conservationists" and "innovationists." He believes that the Charismatic influence among Evangelicals is at least partially responsible for the increased Evangelical emphasis on emotional freedom, spontaneity, charismatic phenomenon, and ad hoc liturgies.[9] The openness of the new Evangelicals may be seen as well in the movement towards "post-evangelicalism" led by Evangelicals such as David Tomlinson.[10] It is more likely these "innovationists," rather than "conservationists," who are expanding the boundaries of an orthodox Anglican identity.

The significant changes in the Evangelical Anglican spirituality in the past four decades have facilitated an Evangelical diversity that is challenging the limits of a clear orthodox Anglican identity. One of the most critical changes that some Evangelical Anglicans have made is a reversal of the traditional Anglican biblical hermeneutic that the traditions of the church are to be received unless contrary to Scripture. Such a view is reflected in Article XXXIV of the Thirty-nine Articles, which states that those who openly break the traditions of the church that are not repugnant to the Word of God ought to be rebuked. However, certain Evangelicals argue and act on the basis of a reversal of this traditional Anglican hermeneutic and employ a more "Puritan" hermeneutic in which only what is positively proved by Scripture is binding. This new hermeneutic is one of the reasons a naked appeal to Scripture as a norm without reference to the Prayer Book or broader catholic tradition is weaker than imagined. It is resulting in a rejection of a number of essential traditions that historically have defined

9. Packer, *Evangelical Identity Problem*, 26–31.

10. Tomlinson, *The Post-Evangelical*.

Anglicanism, including issues related to ecclesiology, ministry, liturgy, and identity. This new hermeneutic is significant because in removing traditions that have acted as markers of Anglican identity, Evangelical Anglicans are helping to expand the definition of orthodox Anglicanism beyond previous, more recognizable boundaries.

This new hermeneutic is described by Gerald Bray (himself an Evangelical Anglican) as *sola exegesis*, in contrast to *sola Scriptura*, and is related to the method of interpretation of some Evangelical Anglicans that Bray describes where proof texts are selected to confirm an inspiration or experience. Bray argues that a hermeneutic which relies on *sola exegesis* will soon discover many areas of human experience of which no single verse speaks clearly and argues as well that the support of Evangelical Anglicans for women's ordination is an example of how *sola exegesis* may lead to innovations.[11]

The first important issue where this new hermeneutic is removing traditions and therefore expanding the boundaries of an orthodox Anglican comprehension is the issue of ecclesiology. Traditionally, Anglicans have placed a great emphasis on the visible church and on the bishop as the locus of unity. While Evangelicals have historically also equally desired to affirm the invisible nature of the church, they often still retained a sense of the importance of the visible church. This was reflected in the Evangelical acceptance of the three-fold ministry advocated by the Prayer Book and in the standard Evangelical view that while bishops are not of the *esse* ("essence") of the church (a more Anglo-Catholic position), they were necessary for either the *bene esse* ("for the well-being") or *plene esse* ("of the fullness") of the church.

Some Evangelical Anglicans from a variety of provinces are now arguing, however, that the church is essentially the local congregation; a congregational, rather than an episcopal, ecclesiology is, therefore, now common among certain Evangelicals. Michael Wilcock, writing as a Church of England Evangelical, asks what the word "church" would mean if all the traditional structures had been blown away. His answer is that "it would mean *the people of God*: nothing more, nothing less. Wherever a group of men and women and boys and girls met in the name of Christ, there would be the Church."[12] John Woodhouse, principal of the leading Evangelical

---

11. Bray, "Authority of Scripture?," 61–67.
12. Wilcock, "Ministry of Parish Clergy," 133.

seminary in Sydney, Australia, Moore Theological College, argues the point even more forcefully:

> My point is that the church is complete wherever two or three have been gathered by God to himself by his word. The trappings that we have added, and now associate with 'church', do not add *anything* essential—or even important—to the reality of church. We must stop thinking that the home Bible study group is *less church* than the gathering at 11 am on Sunday. The home Bible Study group or any other gathering of believers in the name of Christ lacks *nothing of any consequence* as the church of God.[13]

Woodhouse accepts the term "congregational" as an adequate description of his ecclesiology but does not see this as a problem.

Such a view of the church is at odds with Anglicanism as it has been defined historically and is also inconsistent with the Thirty-nine Articles, to which Evangelicals often appeal. Article XXIII states that anyone preaching or ministering the sacraments in the congregation must be lawfully called and sent, implying a very different and more visible view of the church than some Evangelicals hold. Likewise, Article XX accepts the idea of a *national church* that has the right to create or change ceremonies and rites. The view of the 1662 Prayer Book concerning the nature of the church and her ministers is even clearer. It is, therefore, difficult to comprehend how a "church" of two or three laypersons can be faithful to the view of the church expressed in the Articles and Prayer Book, and such an ecclesiology moves Evangelicals away from a clearly defined Anglicanism.

This congregationalist polity effectively undermines the importance of bishops, a part of Anglicanism that has been enshrined in the Lambeth Quadrilateral as one of the four components necessary for ecumenical union with other churches. On the basis of the Articles, David Holloway of Reform argues not only that the local congregation is the visible church of the Articles but also that parishes have an independent identity from dioceses and that, therefore, the diocese is not the ultimate spiritual reality. Instead, the Church of England is a federation of parishes that are grouped into dioceses for the sake of convenience.[14] Such a view appears to be a rejection of the significant role of bishops that the Prayer Book assumes, for example. Many Evangelical Anglicans seem to approve of episcopacy only on pragmatic, and not theological, grounds.

13. Woodhouse, "Unity of the Church."
14. Holloway, "Semper Reformanda," 23–24.

The natural outcome of such a pragmatic Evangelical view of episcopacy would seem to be the rejection of episcopacy as unimportant to the life of the true church, which is seen as local and parochial. For example, Melvin Tinker's view of episcopacy is that episcopacy is neither of the *esse* nor the *bene esse*. Employing the "Puritan" hermeneutic, Tinker argues (citing Article XIX) that Anglicans are only required to believe what may be demonstrated from Scripture and that episcopacy, although not contrary to Scripture, is not demanded by it. Tinker not only argues as an Evangelical but also believes that "as far as *traditional historic Anglicanism* is concerned, episcopacy is a matter of indifference"[15] (emphasis added). The ultimate conclusion of such a view would seem to be that bishops are entirely optional. Such a position extends the boundaries of orthodox Anglican diversity even beyond the minimal requirements of the Lambeth Quadrilateral. For orthodox Anglicans who desire to assert the 1662 Prayer Book as a norm, a congregationalist ecclesiology in which bishops are optional would also be contrary to the theology of that norm.

A second area where Evangelical Anglicans are expanding the boundaries of orthodox Anglicanism is in the field of ministry. Some Evangelicals are not only arguing for the priority of the local church, and acting accordingly, but are also arguing that there is nothing distinctive about the ordained clergy. If the local church is complete whenever two or three Christians are gathered together, as some Evangelicals argue, then it is not only bishops that are optional but, ultimately, also all ordained clergy. While the view of many Evangelical Anglicans regarding bishops is a pragmatic one, Gillian Sumner states that the opinion of many Evangelicals regarding the ordained ministry is also a "functional" one in which "any ministerial role within the body of Christ can, theologically speaking, be carried out by any lay member."[16] John Woodhouse argues on this basis, employing the hermeneutic that Bray calls *sola exegesis*, that there is no word in the New Testament about who should take the leading role at the Lord's Supper. More than merely allowing for laypersons to celebrate, Woodhouse argues that the practice of absolutely prohibiting a non-priest from administering the Lord's Supper contradicts, or obscures the gospel, and he is unconcerned that his belief is a violation of what the Prayer Book prescribes.[17]

15. Tinker, "Evangelical View of the Church," 106.

16. Sumner, "Evangelicalism and Patterns of Ministry," 161.

17. Woodhouse, "Lay Administration," 145–54. In acknowledging this, Woodhouse demonstrates the practical resistance to using the 1662 Prayer Book as a norm that

The Evangelical position in the ACNA Task Force on Holy Orders Report (discussed earlier) similarly demotes the traditional Anglican understanding of ordination and the role of clergy in the church. Some Evangelicals are willing to extend this lay involvement to lay confirmation as well.

This new Evangelical "Puritan" hermeneutic is leading some Evangelical thinkers to continue to argue for innovations beyond lay presidency and lay confirmation. Arguing that the Bible is mostly or entirely silent regarding issues related to baptism, Mark Thompson believes that a good case can be made for both infant and adult baptism and that ultimately the issue is a matter of Christian freedom.[18] This "Puritan" hermeneutic is contrary to the theology of the Prayer Book and the Articles, and by using the same hermeneutic, some Evangelical Anglicans could potentially reject a large number of historic Anglican beliefs and practices.

A third way in which Evangelical Anglicans are facilitating an expanded view of comprehension to include their beliefs and practices is in the common Evangelical attitude that they are "Evangelicals first and Anglicans second." This belief is evident in the preference many Evangelicals have to think of themselves as Anglican Evangelicals (with the emphasis on Evangelical) rather than Evangelical Anglicans (with the emphasis on Anglican). This attitude is held by Archbishop Peter Jensen of Sydney, Australia, as well as Melvin Tinker, the editor of *The Anglican Evangelical Crisis*, whose title itself represents the Evangelical first position. In his Preface, Tinker criticizes fellow Evangelical Anglicans France and McGrath, editors of a volume titled *Evangelical Anglicans*, precisely because they see the term "Evangelical" functioning as an adjective, describing the type of Anglicans they are, rather than the primacy being given to Evangelicalism. Tinker and his fellow authors assert that they are first Evangelical before they are Anglican, believing that Evangelicalism is not simply one tradition amongst many, but is instead the authentic Christianity which is one with, and arises out, of the New Testament.[19]

The relationship between Tinker's Evangelicalism and Anglicanism is a crucial one because the identity of such Evangelical Anglicans is a broadly Evangelical one that frequently sees more in common with Evangelicals outside of Anglicanism than it does with fellow Anglicans. Such an identity that emphasizes the Evangelical character over the Anglican is more

---

Evangelicals like Woodhouse are offering.

18. Thompson, "Saving the Heart of Evangelicalism," 40.

19. Tinker, "Preface," 9–12.

likely to have a relatively weak affinity with a specific, clear, and coherent *Anglican* identity. Such Evangelicals have a pragmatic view of Anglicanism, similar to their pragmatic view of bishops and the ordained ministry, which is represented by the Evangelical sentiment that the Church of England is "the best boat to fish from," suggesting a merely pragmatic reason for Evangelicals to remain Anglicans.

Such Evangelicals are likely to retain an Anglican identity only weakly. Although historically Anglican and willing to maintain the label "Anglican," they are first and foremost Evangelicals who are likely to be willing to live within multiple identities. Among the identities affirmed by these Evangelicals, such as the "local congregation as church" identity, a broad Evangelical identity, and an Anglican identity, the specifically Anglican identity is not likely to be the strongest one.

Given the composite picture of what some Evangelical Anglicans are already advocating or practicing (and not including innovations that may eventuate using their expansive liturgies, theologies, ecclesiologies, and hermeneutics), it is difficult to identify many characteristics of a particularly *Anglican* identity that remain. While many Evangelical Anglicans are not concerned about this, it does, however, present serious difficulties for maintaining any specifically orthodox Anglican identity in the future.

The diversity present among the Anglo-Catholic and Evangelical spiritualities is, therefore, already breaking down the definition of Anglican comprehension as excluding Roman Catholic and Puritan extremes: some Anglo-Catholics are almost Roman Catholic in their theology and practice, while some Evangelicals are practically Puritans. The diversity present in the Evangelical spirituality is especially important when considering the next two spiritualities, the Charismatic and the Global, because of the convergence taking place among all three.

DIVERSITY IN THE CHARISMATIC SPIRITUALITY

The first of the two new spiritualities that have become a part of orthodox Anglicanism is the Charismatic spirituality, a new Anglican spirituality that emerged only in the 1960s. Being related to revivalism and Pentecostalism on the one hand, and Evangelicalism on the other, the Charismatic spirituality is sometimes difficult to define, as are the other spiritualities.

The modern Pentecostal movement is often dated from the Azusa Street Revival of 1906, although others acknowledge antecedents in other movements such as the Welsh Revival, the Irvingite movement, Wesleyism, and others. When the Pentecostal movement moved into the historic denominational churches, the term "charismatic renewal" began to be used, and as the Charismatic movement migrated into the mainline churches, its excesses were to some degree mitigated. Dennis Bennett, an American Episcopalian who came under the influence of international Pentecostal leader David Du Plessis, is usually seen as the first (in 1960) to bring the Charismatic renewal experience, or the Charismatic spirituality, into Anglicanism. Within Anglicanism, the Charismatic spirituality has been commonly understood as a renewal movement from within, although not exclusively so. Since the 1960s, the Charismatic spirituality has grown to the point where it is widely acknowledged to be one of the "three streams" of orthodoxy that many orthodox Anglicans want to see converge, the other two being the Catholic and Evangelical spiritualities.

In common with Pentecostalism, the Charismatic spirituality within Anglicanism emphasizes baptism in the Spirit, attended by miraculous outpourings of the Spirit such as speaking in tongues and prophesying, as well as a "restorationist" view that the church is experiencing what the church in the book of Acts was experiencing. In addition to these two characteristics, Charismatic Anglicans also emphasize the charismatic spiritual gifts, a "renewed" style of worship, healing, every member ministry, spiritual warfare, the end times, and evangelism.

This Charismatic Anglican spirituality is a rapidly growing one, and through its sheer size and momentum, it is a vital force. Worldwide, there were 810,000 Charismatic Anglicans in 1978, while by 2000 there were 17,000,000.[20]

The Charismatic spirituality, like the Anglo-Catholic and Evangelical spiritualities, continues to exert a diversifying influence that necessitates a more expansive orthodox Anglican identity that is moving beyond previously recognizable Anglican boundaries. The two most important influences of the Charismatic spirituality in changing orthodox Anglican identity involve, first, the Charismatic impulse to base unity on experience instead of theology and, second, the Charismatic challenge to Anglican ecclesiology and ministry.

20. Barrett and Johnson, *World Christian Trends*, 271.

Unity through Experience and Not Theology

One of the essential ways in which Charismatic Anglicans are challenging orthodox Anglican identity is in their belief that "experience unites but theology divides." This attitude, expressed in a variety of beliefs and practices, is especially important because it diminishes a specifically theological underpinning for a united orthodox Anglicanism and allows for an increasing diversity of practices, since theological resistance to innovative practices is sometimes removed. Whereas doctrine usually has relatively well-defined boundaries, experience is often a vague category that allows for a significant degree of diversity within a common identity. This downgrading of theology is also crucial to understand because it represents a turn from the traditional Anglican and Evangelical emphasis on theology, which was one of the primary motives for the English Reformation and the subsequent Anglican identity that emerged.

Avoidance of theological rigidity appears at times to be essential to the movement. Restorationists, or Charismatics who believe they are restoring the church to its primitive origins, expect doctrine to be in perpetual flux as God reveals fresh themes, and the Charismatic emphasis on "God doing a new thing" is frequently employed. Restoration Charismatics, desiring to pattern their belief and practice on the New Testament, and the book of Acts in particular, are sometimes dissatisfied with the traditional Anglican beliefs and practices, for example, infant baptism. Some Charismatics call into question practices that are part of the Anglican tradition but not found explicitly in the New Testament, such as infant baptism. Some Charismatic Anglicans thus repeat the new Puritan biblical hermeneutic of some Evangelicals.

The Charismatic devaluation of theology is accompanied by a corresponding emphasis on experience as primary in the life of Christians and as the primary means of achieving unity. Charismatics' characteristic use of music, for example, sometimes represents an elevation of experience over theology. The use of worship songs and praise choruses, unlike the didactic nature of hymns such as those of the Wesleys, appears existential. In the tradition of revivalism, one goal of such music is that the feelings are to be changed first by music before the mind is changed by teaching. This use of music creates a community of feeling based on individual believers whose emotional states have been changed, and in Charismatic worship the songs are often repeated many times and are sung for approximately thirty minutes to lead the worshiper into a spirit of worship. In fact, for many

Charismatics (and not only Anglicans) who worship this way, "worship" has become a term almost equivalent to "music." This theologically unsophisticated "renewal" tradition was initially met with a hostile reaction by some older Evangelicals. "Conversationist" Evangelicals sometimes believe that the majority of such praise choruses are not only poorly written and set to banal music but have been used by Charismatics as the spearhead to push liturgical worship into the background or out altogether. The potential for "renewal," or Charismatic, style worship to replace Prayer Book worship is important as well because it has become a part of the experience of the Global Anglican spirituality in many places and is also quite frequent in the orthodox Anglicanism of the ACNA.

The Charismatic Anglican tendency to elevate experience over theology is visible in the hugely influential Alpha course, an evangelistic program based on a series of videotaped talks by Nicky Gumbel. Holy Trinity, Brompton, in London (HTB), the church at which the Alpha course was developed, had close contact with John Wimber's Association of Vineyard Churches beginning in the 1980s.[21] HTB and a majority of large Charismatic churches in the UK were involved in the Toronto Blessing that developed from Wimber's churches, in which Charismatics manifested various supernatural experiences, most notably barking like dogs.[22] Martyn Percy's investigation into the Charismatic spirituality of Wimber is relevant to this discussion because Wimber's influence has been so great on Charismatic Anglicans and on Alpha. Percy believes that for Wimber the heart of Christian faith resides in an experience of the power and love of God, not in a creed, and that any articles of faith are expressed precisely because they have the power to induce this experience. There seems to be little place in Wimber's theology for the Trinity because it does not feature prominently in either the Bible or experience.[23]

The connections between Alpha and the theology and practices of Wimber's churches are meaningful, therefore, in considering the impact of the Charismatic spirituality on orthodox Anglicanism. This is especially true because of the large numbers of Anglicans who have attended the Alpha course as an introduction to or renewal of their Christian faith and

21. Hunt, *Alpha Enterprise*, 14.

22. Hunt, *Alpha Enterprise*, 52.

23. Wimber's influence on Alpha is felt throughout the course. There are at least four places where Wimber is referenced in Gumbel, *Questions of Life* (the Alpha course in book form), sometimes at length: 53–54, 158, 199–200, and 226.

because of the attention and popularity Alpha has gained for itself within orthodox Anglican circles. As of 2001, over seven thousand churches in the UK were sponsoring the program, and twenty thousand courses were being run worldwide,[24] a point that has great significance for the Global Anglican spirituality. On a global scale, Alpha had attracted more than twenty-three million people by 2007.[25] The fact that Alpha has become a part of mainstream Anglicanism, and must be considered carefully, is further indicated by the fact that seven Anglican archbishops endorsed it.

Alpha distorts orthodox theology, as is evident in its skewed presentation of the doctrine of the Trinity. An analysis of the topics of the Alpha talks[26] reveals that there are two talks about Jesus Christ, three about the Holy Spirit, and none about the Father. Furthermore, the doctrine of the Trinity does not have a talk devoted to it and is rarely mentioned throughout the series, while the Father is mentioned only incidentally. This lack of discussion of the Trinity is related to Wimber's teachings and is representative of both Wimber and Alpha's tendency to exalt experience over theology. The feedback from participants appears to confirm the doctrinal emphases of the course itself, which include the Holy Spirit and experience and not the Father and theology. One study found that the answers to the question, "Which session was the most helpful?" were:

> Holy Spirit sessions—21 percent
> All—11 percent
> "Why and how do I pray?"—8 percent
> "Who is Jesus?"—4 percent
> "Does God heal today?"—4 percent[27]

Of the topics of the fifteen talks, four are more clearly theological, but the overall emphasis tends to be on experience, with titles such as "How Can I be Sure of My Faith?," "How Does God Guide Us?," "How Can I Be Filled with the Spirit?," "How Can I Resist Evil?," and "Does God Heal Today?"

---

24. Hunt, *Alpha Enterprise*, 11.

25. Bell, "Alpha."

26. The text of the talks is largely contained in Nicky Gumbel, *Questions of Life*. I will be referring to *Questions of Life*, rather than the videotaped talks, since it is easier to document.

27. Other sessions had 3 percent or less. "What about the Church?" was considered the most helpful by only 1 percent of the participants (Hunt, *Alpha Enterprise*, 194).

Another notable distortion of orthodox Anglican theology and practice is the devaluation in Alpha of the role of the sacraments. *Questions of Life*, the Alpha course in book form, devotes one paragraph to baptism in a chapter titled "What About the Church?" The importance of Holy Communion in the life of the convert is never discussed, again representing an important omission of a traditional Anglican emphasis and one of the four points of the Lambeth Quadrilateral.

Alpha devotes an entire talk to healing and assumes a Restorationist view that the healings which Christ and the apostles performed in the first century are also normative for today, claiming that "Jesus expected *all* of his disciples to do the same."[28] In the talk "How Can I be Filled with the Spirit?" Gumbel spends most of his time arguing for the fact that speaking in tongues is to be expected when one converts to Christ and discussing hindrances to people speaking in tongues as a sign of the power of the Holy Spirit.

The Charismatic distortion of theology represented by Alpha is matched by its elevation of the role of experience. In discussing healing, it is a person's feelings that govern the experience and are, therefore, in some ways, normative. Gumbel writes, "After we have prayed we usually ask the person what he or she is *experiencing*. Sometimes the person *feels* nothing, in which case we continue to pray. . . . We continue praying until we *feel* it is right to stop"[29] (emphasis added).

The experiential nature of Alpha is most evident in the "weekend away" or "Holy Spirit weekend," which seems to be carefully orchestrated to produce the intended effect of a supernatural outpouring of the Holy Spirit. Hunt reports that in his experience at the "Holy Spirit weekend," the psychological environment was carefully controlled to produce increasing pressure to respond to the events of the day and a supernatural outpouring of the Holy Spirit. Hunt felt that the suggestibility of this time was enhanced by the mantra-type lyrics of the songs and choruses, the group conformity, and the influence of charismatic leaders.[30]

Charismatic Ecclesiology

The ecclesiology of some Charismatic Anglicans is another crucial challenge to orthodox Anglican identity, since it undermines traditional Anglican

28. Gumbel, *Questions of Life*, 205.

29. Gumbel, *Questions of Life*, 213.

30. Hunt, *Alpha Enterprise*, 236–44.

ecclesiology. The house church movement, associated with Charismatics in the Church of England, demonstrates this radical restructuring of ministry that not only replaces the three-fold ministry with five different offices but also, in some cases, seeks to do away with the ordained ministry altogether. One house church leader stated, "The house church movement doesn't have any ordained 'ministers' as such in the accepted sense of the word, we believe that we are all priests. There is not a special breed and class of priests. We certainly don't believe in setting people aside with peculiar clothes and titles."[31] The Charismatic re-ordering of ministry is closely related to the Charismatic revision of Anglican ecclesiology. As with some Evangelicals, the local church is viewed by some Charismatics as being the true church, and there is often more of an allegiance to Charismatic groups outside of Anglicanism than there is to any Anglican identity.

It is not surprising, therefore, in light of the devaluation of the ordained clergy and suspicion of received authority by some Charismatics that they may also denigrate the institutional church. Michael Harper, a prominent Charismatic Anglican leader, claims that Charismatics "reject altogether the concept of the Church as an institution."[32] For some, denominations are contrary to the divine will, and denominationalism is a sin. This breaking down of boundaries extends to the traditional parochial model within Anglicanism. Charismatics often see parish boundaries as transient structures, and Sandy Millar, associated with HTB, Alpha, and then the Church of Uganda, states that "every recent church report has recognized that the parish is no longer the appropriate geographical area with which to work."[33] Some Charismatic leaders believe that Anglicans are faced with the choice of maintaining boundaries and continuing to decline or declaring mission areas where any congregation can plant a mission. This same willingness to break down traditional boundaries is demonstrated in the founding of the AMiA in the US, in spite of much opposition from other orthodox Anglican leaders, as well as in the 2006 "Covenant for the Church of England" that was sponsored by a number of different Evangelical and Charismatic groups. That document boldly asserts that "existing ecclesiastical legal boundaries should be seen as permeable;" that "there cannot be any no-go areas for gospel growth and church planting;" and that "we will support mission-shaped expressions of church through prayer, finance and personnel, even

31. Scotland, *Charismatics and the Next Millennium*, 73.

32. Bebbington, *Evangelicalism in Modern Britain*, 244.

33. Scotland, *Charismatics and the Next Millennium*, 240.

when official permission is unreasonably withheld."[34] Evangelical bishop N. T. Wright views these statements as meaning that "we intend to plant churches wherever we like and claim that they are Anglican;" "the spread of our particular type of church;" and "churches which do their own thing and cock a snook at any bishop who questions them."[35]

Another significant sign that the Charismatic view of ecclesiology will prove challenging to an orthodox Anglican identity is the presentation of the Charismatic position in the ACNA's Holy Orders Task Force Final Report. This Charismatic presentation outlines a recurrent pattern of restoration and cites the heretical group, the Montanists, as a positive example of a Restorationist impulse to correct the church when it was becoming too hierarchical in the early centuries. The Report goes on to quote John Wesley as a Restorationist hero who cited Montanus favorably: "one of the best men then upon earth . . . under the character of a Prophet, as an order established in the Church, appeared (without bringing any new doctrine) for reviving what was decayed, and reforming what might be amiss."[36] The Report repeats, favorably a few times, the Charismatic idea that relationships are first and practices are second. This is further explained as meaning that while relationships are essential to the church, practices are for the good of the church, vary, and are mutable, thus paving the way theologically for the ordination of women.

This Charismatic ecclesiology drives a wedge between gospel and church, and relegates the church and her ecclesial institutions to a secondary and mutable (even optional) status, a point reinforced when The Report states: "The more the Church concentrated on structure and authority, the further from its original model it became."[37] Perhaps most dramatically, The Report summarizes John Wesley's willingness to break with church tradition and reject the church's authority by saying "that the New Testament prescribed 'no determinate plan for church-government,' but that pastoral necessity and the authority of the Holy Spirit gave him the right to violate extant canon law in the interests of spreading the Gospel."[38] For this reason, Wesley was justified in consecrating bishops when he was not a bishop, crossing parochial and other boundaries against the will of church

---

34. Church Society, "Covenant for the Church of England."

35. Wright, "A Confused 'Covenant.'"

36. Fairfield, "Anglican Charismatics," 203.

37. Fairfield, "Anglican Charismatics," 229.

38. Fairfield, "Anglican Charismatics," 205.

authorities, and on this basis, according to the report, Anglicans are justified in ordaining women.

Charismatic Hybridity and Postmodernism

The Charismatic spirituality is pushing orthodox Anglicanism in a more *globalized* and less *integrated* direction, not only because of its natural affinities with a more *globalized* and diffuse Anglican identity but also because of its power to hybridize or produce an Anglicanism with a new identity based on the mixing of spiritualities. Schreiter believes that hybridity results from an erasure of a boundary between two entities and a redrawing of a new boundary. Hybrid religious cultures serve as strategies for negotiating life in a globalized world and often experience life as a *tiempos mixtos*, or mixture of times, in which they develop strategies for moving between different times—premodern, modern, or postmodern. In addition, hybrid cultures take differences less seriously.[39]

In many ways, this description of hybridity applies to the Charismatic spirituality that mixes its spirituality with others, especially the Evangelical and Global spiritualities. This Charismatic spirituality draws new boundaries based more on shared experiences than on common theological boundaries and the theological differences that have marked orthodox Anglicanism traditionally become less important.

The blending of Evangelical and Charismatic spiritualities in TEC, the ACNA, and the Church of England is one good example of this crucial process of hybridization to which the Charismatic spirituality lends itself. In some ways, Charismatics and Evangelicals are natural allies. Both emphasize a biblical orthodoxy (and one that does not depend much on church tradition as a primary interpretive guide), both are keenly interested in propagating the gospel message through evangelism, and both stress the importance of inner conversion, experience, and testimony of conversion, sometimes diminishing or undermining the institutional church.

The Evangelical Anglicanism re-emergent in TEC was from its inception connected with the new Charismatic spirituality of the 1960s and 1970s, a fact that has consequences for the nature of American Evangelical Anglicanism. This premise is supported by the establishment of Trinity Episcopal School for Ministry (now Trinity School for Ministry, TSM) in 1976, which had connections with English Evangelicals such as John Stott,

39. Schreiter, *The New Catholicity*, 76–77.

J. I. Packer, and Michael Green, as well as important American Evangelicals such as Peter Moore and John Rodgers. Half of the first class of students at Trinity were Charismatic, and TSM has tended to speak of itself more as serving the renewal movement than serving the Evangelical movement. Given that TSM is the only self-consciously Evangelical Episcopal seminary in the US, its clear connections with the Charismatic spirituality and its training of priests with a Charismatic spirituality are crucial. It is important to note, therefore, that the resurgent Evangelical spirituality in the US (and the UK) is closely related to the Charismatic renewal that occurred during approximately the same period.

The Charismatic devaluing of theology discussed earlier is, therefore, not a self-contained phenomenon so that only Charismatic Anglicans stress experience over theology. In some ways the Charismatic spirituality has become the center of much of the Evangelical spirituality, and its stress on experience over theology is likely to have effected Evangelical theology. Tomlinson, writing of Charismatics in the Church of England, believes that "it is now clear that the whole centre ground of evangelicalism has become gradually charismaticized, adopting the style and ethos of the charismatic movement."[40] Packer agrees and believes that by bringing Charismatic emphases into the center of Evangelicalism, the Charismatic spirituality has demoted a concern for sound doctrine and continuity with the Evangelical past. By treating God's exceptional modes as the norm, the Charismatic spirituality has altered the temper of evangelical piety.[41]

The Charismatic spirituality is, therefore, one of the most potent forces in orthodox Anglicanism today that is moving orthodox Anglicans in a direction that represents a more *globalized* concept of culture. The Charismatic de-emphasis on theology and emphasis on experience is compatible with a *globalized* identity that is willing to live with multiple identities, question the structures and authority that have been received, and blur boundaries and definitions. Charismatics, as a whole, including Anglicans, are willing to live with vague or even contradictory boundaries and norms shorn of a theological clarity: this lack of boundaries is not only theological but also ecclesial.

It is likely, therefore, that Charismatic Anglicans, with their willingness to have permeable boundaries and no hard theological edges, will continue to claim and often adhere to a specifically Anglican identity while sometimes

---

40. Tomlinson, *The Post-Evangelical*, 15.

41. Packer, *Evangelical Identity Problem*, 27.

speaking, acting, and believing in ways much closer to Pentecostals or Charismatics outside Anglicanism than to other Anglicans. The inclusion of the Charismatic Anglican spirituality in a larger orthodox Anglican identity, and its convergence with both the Evangelical and Global spiritualities, is, therefore, creating an enlarged definition of orthodox Anglicanism and one that is more diffuse and less clearly Anglican.

The Prosperity Gospel

One final way that the Charismatic spirituality is challenging an orthodox Anglican identity is a Charismatic theology known as the Prosperity Gospel theology, which is also known as the Word of Faith movement or the Health and Wealth Gospel. The Prosperity Gospel theology teaches that Jesus Christ came to make men healthy and prosperous. These blessings are achieved in this life in a kind of speech-act theology by which one can invoke the blessings of God by speaking them into existence. It is related, in general, to the Charismatic theology with its emphasis on the miraculous and instantaneous, as well as a de-emphasis on the boundaries of traditional Christian theology and a privileging of individual experience.

The Word of Faith theology is prevalent in certain parts of Global orthodox Anglicanism, particularly in the African churches, and presents a genuine challenge to orthodox Anglicanism. So significant is the challenge of the Prosperity Gospel, and so widespread among the African churches, that GAFCON 2018 felt it necessary to condemn it in the same terms with which it condemned homosexuality. When the regional GAFCON churches met in separate sessions, the African meeting had a lively discussion of the place of the Prosperity Gospel, with a few delegates in favor of it. GAFCON 2018's final statement, "Letter to the Churches," condemned the practice with these strong words: "Internally, the 'prosperity gospel' and theological revisionism both seek in different ways to recast God's gospel to accommodate the surrounding culture, resulting in a seductive syncretism that denies the uniqueness of Christ, the seriousness of sin, the need for repentance and the final authority of the Bible."[42]

42. GAFCON, "Letter to the Churches." Several African Anglican Facebook groups are filled weekly, if not daily, with posts declaring or decreeing that you will be healed, you will not bury your children, every spiritual bondage is broken, and that anyone planning your death will attend their own funeral service (a curious but common declaration on such sites). One such post has a picture of Jesus, captioned by the words: "I will bless anyone that type [sic] 'Amen.'"

DIVERSITY IN THE GLOBAL
ANGLICAN SPIRITUALITIES

The fourth orthodox Anglican spirituality is what may be called the Global Anglican spirituality or the Global spiritualities (plural). Many discussions of the nature of Anglicanism and Anglican spiritualities have continued to center on an Anglicanism that still is based on a relatively homogenized (compared to contemporary global Anglicanism) identity that centers on the Church of England and TEC. However, with the expansion of Anglicanism into the parts of the former British Empire and with the post-colonial situation that now exists, the traditional categories of Anglican spiritualities in terms of Catholic, Evangelical, and Liberal are insufficient, even if the Charismatic spirituality is added.

The Global Anglican spirituality is represented by the ways in which Anglicanism, especially orthodox Anglicanism, has been inculturated into the former English colonies. The Global South provinces are representatives of this Global spirituality, and not just the more visible leaders and official statements but also the actual Anglican life in these provinces. The Global Anglican spirituality is a key to understanding the future of orthodox Anglican identity, since Anglicans in post-colonial provinces, such as Nigeria, Uganda, and Kenya, now constitute the majority of Anglicans worldwide and since a large percentage of new Anglicans each year come from these provinces. Such Global Anglicans are also mostly orthodox. The Global spirituality is a complex one for at least two reasons, and these complexities hold key clues to the probable future of orthodox Anglican identity. First, although the term "Global Anglican spirituality" suggests a single entity, in reality, each Anglican province has a unique context. It is more accurate and appropriate, therefore, to think in terms of Global Anglican *spiritualities*, even when it is referred to in the singular. What the provinces have in common is the fact that the Anglican form of Christianity, which represents the catholic and universal aspect, is in the process of being inculturated into a local environment. The diversity in the global provinces is the result of the different cultures and histories into which Anglican Christianity is being inculturated, and various provinces are inculturating at different speeds, from different starting points, and in different ways.

The second complexity is that the Global spirituality of each particular province is itself a complex phenomenon that is both similar to the Anglicanism from which it originated (often, as embodied in particular mission groups) but that also incorporates other elements. It would be a mistake to conceive of a single spirituality even within a sole province. The identity of any particular Global spirituality is, therefore, not a single process or picture that represents the logical and organic outgrowth of what was originally planted but a succession of identities in which the earlier identities remain to interact with newer identities. This complex identity is captured by the word *hybridity*, a concept explored earlier with reference to the Charismatic spirituality.

Spiritualities in the Church of Uganda

To limit adequately the discussion of what I am calling the Global Anglican spirituality, I will focus on the situation in Africa, using the Church of Uganda (COU) as an example. The COU is an important Anglican province because it is one of the largest in terms of numbers: its nine million members make it the second most populous Anglican province. Because of the relative abundance of literature on the COU, compared to other Global South provinces, as well as its size, the COU is a useful exemplar of the Global spirituality. The COU is a good representative of the Global Anglican spiritualities because its most visible leaders, such as Archbishop Stanley Ntagali, are orthodox, and it is one of the most important provinces in the predominantly orthodox Global South and in GAFCON. The orthodox COU is also an important representative of the Global spirituality because of the networked relationships between the COU and orthodox Anglicans in the United States. The present identity of the COU is the result of at least five different Anglican movements or spiritualities that interact: the origins in the mission work of the Church Mission Society (CMS), the East African Revival, the traditional Prayer-Book and clerical Anglican identity, the indigenization of Anglicanism into the local culture, and the global Charismatic/Evangelical spirituality that has been imported from the West in recent decades.

An understanding of the Global Anglican spirituality represented by the COU begins with an understanding of the Anglican mission work done in Uganda by Western Anglicans, who brought with them their own forms of Anglican spirituality. While Anglo-Catholic missionaries predominated in a few areas of Africa, the Evangelical spirituality, and particularly the revivalistic Evangelical spirituality, prevailed in the Anglican missionaries to Uganda, Kenya, and other future Anglican provinces and was, therefore, transmitted to these Anglican colonies. In response to Henry Stanley's 1875 letter to the *Daily Telegraph* romanticizing the kingdom of Buganda, the Church Mission Society (CMS), an Evangelical Anglican mission group, rushed to send a group of missionaries, the first of whom arrived in 1877. This Evangelical spirituality had its roots not so much in the Prayer Book Evangelicals of England but in the revivalistic Evangelicalism that had swept England in 1875 under the influence of Moody and Sankey. This form of Evangelical spirituality stressed an instantaneous conversion that would create an immediate revolution in life in which the old habits would die away. This original revivalistic Evangelical spirituality was reinforced in the COU by the Pilkington Revival of the 1890s.

The revivalistic Evangelical spirituality was later further reinforced by the East African Revival that had come to Uganda through the Ruanda Mission of the CMS. Kevin Ward believes that not only in spite of but also at least partially because of the Pilkington Revival of the 1890s, Anglican Christianity had grown in terms of numbers and prestige at the expense of deeper faith and genuine commitment. The East African Revival was a response to the spiritual malaise that had apparently set in and was particularly associated with the collaborative work of Simeoni Nsibambi (a Ugandan Anglican) and Joe Church (a CMS missionary doctor) that began in 1929. Ward notes in particular that the East African Revival was influenced by the Keswick Movement in England, a movement related to the holiness or second blessing movement, which is a species of Charismatic spirituality.[43]

Joe Church's presentation of the gospel, out of which the East African Revival in Uganda grew, stressed not only a turn to a stricter morality and emphasis on repentance and testimony, but also the second-blessing type of theology, in which dreams, visions, trembling, noise, and confusion were associated. Such phenomena, importantly, are also often associated with the Charismatic spirituality that came to Uganda from England and the US at a later date. This revivalistic spirituality, associated with those who are called the *balokole* ("the saved ones"), has, in many ways, become the dominant spirituality in the COU. By 1949 the Revival had been accepted into the mainstream of the life of the church, and in Western Uganda the Revival has become so much a part of Anglican Christianity that it is difficult to distinguish the Revival from the church. The first Anglican Archbishop of the COU, Erica Sabiti, was a pioneer of the Revival, and at least two other Archbishops in the COU were leaders coming out of the Revival.

---

43. Ward, "Balokole Revival," 113–14.

This strongly revivalistic spirituality has been in some degree of competition with a more traditional, more church-oriented, Anglican spirituality, a third spirituality present in the COU. From the beginning, Anglican Christianity in Uganda has been closely associated with the centers of political power, beginning from the period when the chiefs of Buganda overwhelmingly became Anglican, and Buganda was more resistant to the *balokole*, who became dominant in other regions of Uganda. While never officially established as the state church of Uganda, the COU approximated an established church, which was accompanied by a hierarchical structure of dioceses and, eventually, an Archbishop for Uganda as a separate province. Bishops are still integral to the COU but are sometimes seen as part of a colonial legacy that is no longer tenable or desirable. In contrast to the anti-clericalism of many Revivalists, Bishop Tucker was instrumental in ordaining native clergy, beginning in 1893. The more traditional Anglican emphasis in the COU was represented by the fact that relatively early on, in the nineteenth century, the Morning Prayer, Evening Prayer, and Baptismal services were printed. Tucker wrote that as of 1893 those in the Anglican Church knew their Bibles and "knew something of their Prayer Book—something of Church order and history."[44] The fact that some older Anglicans in Uganda still prefer traditional Anglicanism, including Prayer Book worship, demonstrates that a traditional Anglican spirituality, and not just a revivalistic Evangelical spirituality, has been a part of the COU, even if that historic Anglicanism is waning in strength.

A fourth kind of spirituality that is part of the COU involves the process of indigenization. Although a common complaint against the *balokole* of the Revival is that they show little interest in indigenization and, in many cases, are deeply critical of African values, this very critique of African values proceeds from an African cultural perspective and thus represents a form of indigenization. Areas of African thought and social organization have penetrated the *balokole*. The pattern of the local Christian community centers around the head of a household, who gathers a community of "revived" Christians around him. This group then functions in the same way the large family did in Uganda when the clan system was stronger. The Pentecostal movement has been more readily accepted in African churches because of its flexibility and freedom, which some see as being related to indigenization or Africanness. Pentecostals also recognize charismatic leadership and

---

44. Taylor, *Growth in an African Church*, 11.

indigenous church patterns, and so in this way the Charismatic spirituality may symbiotically facilitate an indigenization of African Anglicanism.

A final kind of spirituality that is now a part of the COU is the Charismatic/Evangelical spirituality that has been imported from England and the US since the 1970s. This spirituality shares many characteristics of the earlier, revivalistic Evangelical spirituality that has existed in the COU since its origins, as well as a common orientation toward the supernatural that existed before any form of Anglicanism or Christianity was present. With its emphasis on healing and deliverance, demons, dreams, ecstatic and prophetic utterances, and other supernatural phenomena, the Charismatic spirituality is, in some ways, a natural ally of the worldview that many Global Anglicans already share. The convergence of the Charismatic and Global spiritualities is, therefore, a powerful force that any future studies on Anglican identity should consider more carefully.

Anglican missionaries from England and the US are generally Charismatics or Evangelicals who favor a "renewal" style of freer worship and praise choruses. Groups such as SOMA (Sharing of Ministries Abroad), committed to Charismatic renewal, are active in Uganda, and Trinity School for Ministry (TSM) has trained Ugandan ministers who bring back the Charismatic influence from the US. A former TSM professor, Stephen Noll, was Vice-Chancellor of Uganda Christian University from 2000–2010. Thus, the complex network of churches and ministries that exists in ecclesial orthodox Anglicanism acts, especially in terms of the Charismatic/ Evangelical spiritualities in England and the US since the 1970s, to forge a *global* Charismatic/Evangelical spirituality that interacts with previous Anglican identities. In the COU this means that the revivalistic spirituality already present is reinforced and is a significant factor in understanding its contemporary orthodox Anglican identity.

Anglican Identity in the COU

The Anglican identity in the COU that is a mixture of the five spiritualities just discussed is often a weakly held and loose identity for two essential reasons. Traditional Anglican views of the church, ministry, the sacraments, and the Prayer Book are relatively weak, and orthodox Anglicans in the COU often have more in common with other Christian traditions and identities than they do with Anglicanism. As Anglicanism interacts with local cultures and other church traditions in global contexts, a specific and clear orthodox Anglican identity is likely to be weak in other Global Anglican spiritualities as well.

The first reason the Anglican identity of the COU is somewhat weak is because traditional Anglican views of the church, ordained ministry, sacraments and Prayer Book are somewhat weak, at least partially because the revivalistic Evangelical spirituality remains very influential. Many believe that the key to understanding the COU, its vitality, and what it has to offer the rest of the world, is the East African Revival. In this spirituality, the church, the sacraments, the ordained ministry, and liturgy are sometimes relatively unimportant. This is true not only because of the theology and practice of this revivalistic Evangelical spirituality but also because of the mission mindset that accompanied the establishment of Anglicanism in Uganda. This mission mindset, enhanced by the practical exigencies of mission work, included a desire to plant Christianity with urgency and speed and often apart from any ecclesiastical structures or church practices that might be perceived to slow down the work of the gospel. Throughout the history of the COU, in spite of the eventual development of the episcopacy and the persistence of a strand of Anglicanism that affirms more traditional Anglicanism, a strong element of anti-clericalism has existed. This anti-clericalism and anti-ecclesiastical attitude were present in Joe Church and the Ruanda Mission, and some aspects of the East African Revival have affirmed a radical egalitarianism. The Revival brought in a new form of Christianity whose power and authority did not come from missionaries, bishops, or clergy, and the Revival has been heavily lay-led. An anti-clerical strand persisted through the 1950s when those called Strivers or Trumpeters sometimes attacked church members during services or disrupted services by using megaphones. Although, in some ways, the division between the church and the Revival has been healed, and while there is a diversity of relationships between the church and the Revival, a tension and difference in understandings of religion and Anglicanism persist.

The relatively low place given to the church and the clergy has led to less of an emphasis on the sacraments. The revivalistic Evangelical spirituality centers primarily on Scripture and personal piety, and thus the liturgy and the sacraments are often given a lower place in theology and practice. This propensity toward a low view of the sacraments is reinforced by the practical consideration that there have not been sufficient clergy, catechists, or other means of propagating a more complete Anglican identity. Since the pastor is often a deacon, and, therefore, unable to celebrate the Holy

Communion, a high proportion of church members are denied Holy Communion. Partaking of communion has also been less frequent because of how, for example, the English planters of the COU restricted participation in the Holy Communion to those married in the COU. While the *balokole* may sometimes decry the overbearing presence of the clergy, in many circumstances it is the very lack of the presence of clergy that has reinforced an Anglican identity without clergy or a high place for the sacraments. Taylor's extensive look at one parish in 1958 found that the parish covered thirty-four square miles, contained a dozen sprawling hamlets, and had a total population of around five thousand. All of the church work in this particular parish was the work of a single parish catechist, a common position in the church, especially since the growth of Anglicanism in Uganda was closely related to the education and literacy that was offered by the missionaries. The nearest ordained minister lived seven miles away and had charge over five such parishes. In the Buganda region of Uganda, Taylor found that four to seven parishes shared one pastor. Catechists, and not just priests, have often been in short supply, and they were rarely given an adequate living wage. Taylor summarized the situation by stating that it was very difficult to see the church in such a parish.[45] In some cases, it has still been difficult to have sufficient clergy because the clergy transfer to parachurch ministries or similar organizations that offer better remuneration.

Until 2013, the 1662 Prayer Book was the only authorized prayer book in the COU; however, the COU is an example of how an Anglican norm, the 1662 Prayer Book, can be strictly held at the official level, even while it is becoming less and less of a meaningful standard or norm. Where the Prayer Book has been in short supply, the absence of this essential foundation for traditional Anglicanism has led to an Anglican identity that has assimilated only part of this larger, traditional Anglican identity. The lack of access to the Prayer Book has also contributed to an already existing tendency to diminish the importance of the sacraments and the life of the church as centered on the liturgical year. Some churches don't have enough Prayer Books to go around, and the liturgical calendar may not be respected. Even where the Prayer Book has been in regular use, some see its use as being spiritually dead. This same kind of negative attitude toward the Prayer Book and liturgical worship, along with a desire for a more Pentecostal style of worship, has also been noted in the Anglican Church in Kenya.

---

45. Taylor, *Growth in an African Church*, 18–19.

Ugandan Anglicans feel competition from Pentecostal churches; as a result, they often borrow from the Pentecostal churches and use a less Prayer Book-bound service. Ugandans who still want to worship more traditionally often feel alienated by the new styles of worship and belittled by the advocates of the freer worship. Whether because of competition from Pentecostal churches and a desire for a "renewal" style of worship or because of a lack of Prayer Books, the Ugandan Church, like other African Anglican churches, appears to be moving away from use of the Prayer Book, regardless of the official status of the Prayer Book.

This picture of worship in one of the few provinces with the 1662 Prayer Book as its official norm is confirmed by a 2006 article by James Short, who writes that worship in the province of Uganda may sometimes be characterized as "high Baptist." A typical worship service in a village or field worship service is part worship, part notices, part fellowship and socializing, and part eating. Catechists lead most services and not by priests, and were it not for the catechists, the whole province would grind to a halt, since, for example, in the diocese of Masindi-Kitara there are three hundred local churches but only twenty-six pastors. Short observes that the services are not followed slavishly and that he has attended Holy Communion services where the priest did not use the whole prayer of consecration. In summary, Short states, the Church in Uganda does not concern itself too much with the correct form of worship or correct liturgical vocabulary.[46]

In 2013 the COU authorized the *Book of Common Worship* to be used alongside the 1662 Prayer Book. It's uncertain how much this has led to the disuse of the 1662 Prayer Book, but over time another authorized prayer book, written because of some perceived need, will only lead to a lessening of the 1662 Prayer Book as a book in actual use. As one more example of how even orthodox Anglicans are presenting challenges to Anglican identity by their innovations, the *Book of Common Worship* has no service for Confirmation but only a reaffirmation of baptismal vows, without the laying on of the hands of a bishop. This is a significant departure from traditional Anglicanism, all the more significant because it has happened in a solidly orthodox province.[47]

A second way in which Anglican identity is weak in the COU is because in the COU orthodox Anglicans often have more in common with other Christian traditions and identities than they do with Anglicanism. In

46. Short, "Ugandan Field Worship," 14–15.
47. Tovey, "End of Anglican Confirmation."

the COU, Anglican identity often is not easily distinguished from a more generic Protestant identity. Gifford states that the fundamental division between Protestant (Anglican) and Catholic is also a political division and that for this reason it is important to identify oneself as either Protestant or Catholic, perhaps even if a specifically Anglican identity is not particularly defined. Amos Kasibante confirms that the term "Protestant" essentially means "Anglican" in the COU.[48] Anglican identity in Uganda may appear weak in two ways. First, there may be some Protestants who are counted as Anglicans because the only other alternative is to be counted as a Roman Catholic. Second, some may consider themselves Anglican as a means for achieving political or cultural power, and not for any reasons related to a specific religious identity. To be Anglican, then, may almost be to consider oneself (in American terms) a Democrat or Republican.

A specific Anglican identity in the COU is weakened as well by a strong affinity orthodox Anglicans in the COU have for other Christian traditions, especially Pentecostal churches. One diocese has formal links with a Swiss Reformed body, but, more importantly, many non-Anglican groups, including Pentecostals, Baptists, and Presbyterians are involved in teaching and otherwise supporting the COU. Since 1984, conservative American Presbyterians have been involved in an extensive education mission to the COU, and it seems possible that financial considerations override theological ones. But what happens to a specifically Anglican identity in the COU when that church is catechized by Presbyterians?

The most important challenge from other Christian traditions to an Anglican identity in the COU comes from the Charismatic and Pentecostal churches. The revivalistic spirituality planted in the nineteenth century and subsequently reinforced, coupled with the Charismatic/Evangelical spirituality more recently imported, appears to be leading to an identity for many in the COU that is more clearly Charismatic and Pentecostal than it is Anglican. The emphasis on revival in the COU is a marked one and one that has much in common with the "experience over theology" identity of the Charismatic spirituality. The revivalistic spirituality, from its origins through the various forms of revival the COU has experienced, has continually stressed the significance of certain experiences as markers of the true Christian or "saved one:" as with some Charismatic Anglicans, what counts is often the *experience* of "being saved." This emphasis on experience has often led to conflict, sometimes to schism, and has created an attitude that

48. Kasibante, "Beyond Revival," 366.

if one does not manifest these experiences, then one is not truly a Christian. Many joined the Revival because it alone had a positive moral message, and not because of particular theological beliefs. Thus, the specifically Anglican identity in the COU may often be more perceived than real, and more of a label than a clear and coherent identity.

This previously existing revivalistic spirituality is often not enough to keep people in the COU, and some are making a conscious turn in a Charismatic or Pentecostal direction. Those who are part of the revived communities with a relatively weak Anglican identity are sometimes tempted to change to become more like the Pentecostal churches outside Anglicanism that appear to be more flourishing. Many in the COU are concerned about losing the youth to Pentecostal churches that have grown up since the 1980s. The free style of worship and lively music, along with the dramatic healings seen on Pentecostal TV programs, has enticed many young Anglicans to leave to join Pentecostal churches. One Ugandan priest explained that the only way out the Church of Uganda was for it also to take the direction of the Charismatic movement. Many Anglican churches, and not just ones affected more by the Revival, have been encouraged by archbishops and other leaders to add or alter services to lure back those who have left the church.[49] As some church leaders told a delegation of COU bishops, "The massive desertion was so alarming that checking measures should be taken."[50] This recognition that different spiritualities and churches are in competition for members is indicative of the *globalized* and hybridized identity of the Global Anglican spirituality in the COU. A large proportion of those becoming Pentecostals in Uganda is from the COU: even after they have left the COU for the Pentecostal churches, many still regard themselves in some way as members of the COU.

The vital connection between the Global Anglican spirituality and the Charismatic spirituality (and one that is not always specifically Anglican) is seen in the emerging networks and connections between Ugandan Anglicans and orthodox Anglicans in the US that Miranda Hassett, in particular, has studied. One of the markers of such a Global/Charismatic Anglican spirituality is the shared renewal style of worship, expressed in the COU. Hassett found that there was a great desire on the part of Ugandan Anglicans to have the "renewed" style of worship they have seen in Pentecostal churches. This renewed style includes: worship services less based on the

49. Hassett, "Episcopal Dissidents, African Allies," 54.
50. Gifford, *African Christianity*, 146.

Prayer Book; an extended time of music at the beginning of the service, often composed of Western praise choruses; rock style instrumentation and audiovisual aids; a lay-led "worship team" to lead music; healing and deliverance ministry; times in the worship service designated for the expression of the supernatural gifts and for the giving of testimonies; more time for extemporaneous prayer; and other practices associated with the Charismatic spirituality. Some Ugandan clergy and lay leaders claim they have a desperate need for new musical equipment, including electronic keyboards, electric guitars, drum kits, amplifiers, and speakers to perform the "revival" style of soft rock. This "renewal" style of worship is coming to the COU not only from Pentecostal churches in Uganda and from Pentecostal TV programs but also from the Western Charismatic/Evangelical missionaries and groups such as SOMA and TSM.[51] The emergence of a particularly Charismatic style of worship in churches in the Global South has been noted by others and is what Geoff Morgan calls the "international New Pentecostalist liturgical style."[52]

Another powerful Charismatic influence that is well known to many Ugandans is the Alpha course, discussed earlier. In an especially noteworthy occasion, Sandy Millar, a priest associated with Holy Trinity, Brompton (HTB), the church from which the Alpha course emerged, was consecrated a bishop by Archbishop Orombi of Uganda in 2005. Millar himself appointed Nicky Gumbel to work on HTB's Alpha course in 1990, and, therefore, he represents a direct link between the Charismatic spirituality of Alpha and the Global spirituality of Uganda. Furthermore, Orombi himself studied in England and during that time was supported by HTB. Although consecrated in Uganda by a Ugandan archbishop and canonically bound to Archbishop Orombi, Millar will serve as Assistant Bishop for Mission in the Diocese of London. Orombi was enthusiastic that the consecration would put the COU on the global Christian map, and Millar's consecration emphasizes the new orthodox Anglican conception of the nature of a diocese and the work of a bishop, emphasizing a network of personal relationships over traditional geographical lines.[53]

---

51. Hassett, "Episcopal Dissidents, African Allies," 54–55.

52. Morgan, "Study of Anglican Mission," 143.

53. Sugden, "7000 Sing and Dance."

The Place of Anglican Identity
in the Global Spiritualities

Through these means, and others, the Global Anglican spirituality is becoming a Global *Charismatic* Anglican spirituality. It may be that a broader Charismatic spirituality that is not particularly Anglican is transforming Global Anglicanism into a Charismatic identity more than traditional orthodox Anglicanism is coherently incorporating the Charismatic spirituality into itself. In this case, it would be more accurate to speak in terms of an Anglican *Charismatic* spirituality rather than a Charismatic *Anglican* spirituality. The same *globalized* Anglican identity that the Charismatic spirituality was found to manifest is, therefore, also present in the Global Anglican spirituality, but with perhaps even more indefinable boundaries, a more complex and chaotic mixture of time, cultures, and spiritualities, and an even higher degree of hybridity. Anglicans in Africa, and not just in the COU, are becoming Pentecostals. Some are leaving the Anglican Communion, but many others are remaining Anglican while also practicing a Pentecostal form of Christianity. In such cases, an Anglican identity may be asserted while at the same time the spirituality that is lived out has more in common with Pentecostalism than with any traditional or identifiable Anglican identity. The influence of the Charismatic spirituality on the Anglicanism of other global provinces is also significant: the COU is, therefore, only one representative of a significant and widespread movement in Anglicanism.

The relatively low place given to the church and the relatively weak Anglican identity so characteristic of parts of the COU is also characteristic of some other parts of the Global South provinces where Anglicanism was first planted by Evangelical mission societies such as the CMS. As early as 1838 Samuel Wilberforce recognized the problem of Anglican missions being planted without a full view of the church, writing that "the great object . . . we now ought to aim at in our missionary exertions is to give them a much more Church character than we have done—to send out the Church, and not merely instruction about religion. This is the way in which in primitive times the world was converted."[54]

The Global Anglican spirituality may often have as its primary foundation a particular traditional Anglican spirituality, such as the revivalistic Evangelical spirituality found in Uganda, and not a more complete spectrum of Catholic, Evangelical, and Liberal spiritualities. So dominant

54. Jacob, *Making of the Anglican Church*, 106.

has the Low Church emphasis been in the COU that a COU minister ordained in Uganda writes that the churchmanship of the COU is mono-lithic in its Low Church character.[55] Often, it is the Catholic spirituality with its emphasis on apostolic tradition and continuity with the past that is missing, and the Evangelical and Charismatic spiritualities, without the Catholic spirituality, are often sometimes only weakly identifiable as Anglican. An example of an Anglican identity shaped with less reference to the Catholic spirituality may be found in the new Evangelical, Kenyan liturgy, which, according to Morgan, did not need to accommodate to Catholic theology because, unlike neighboring Tanzania, there was no Catholic-Protestant ecumenical incentive and a broader range of church-manship to provoke it into doing so.[56] The Anglican identity present in Global Anglican spirituality may often be weak due to political connec-tions or a connection to Anglican Christianity that was only partial to begin with. The ideal of comprehension that existed in the Church of England, in which the different spiritualities were all represented and had to be incorporated, did not often exist in the colonies. Converts to Anglicanism in the colonies, growing up under a particular missionary society (typically Evangelical), were often unaware of a different type of churchmanship than that which was planted in their land.

In fact, in some Global Anglican provinces, a specifically Anglican identity may have been very weak or even non-existent from the begin-ning. Earlier Anglican missionaries focused their energy in establishing local churches in the mission field (or even missions works which were not clearly a part of a church) and did not consciously seek to form lo-cal "Anglican churches," often because of the Evangelical and Charismatic ecclesiologies in which church structures are secondary matters. Often, a shift occurred only later, when a deliberate attempt was made to impose Anglican polity on local churches in the mission fields. The Anglican churches planted in China, Hong Kong, Japan, and Korea did not necessar-ily have a specifically Anglican identity and were called "Sheng Kung Hui," or the "Holy Catholic Church," and not *Anglican* churches. Anglicans in China have now become part of the Christian China Council, which does not have an Anglican polity, and, in fact, such churches are effectively post-denominational. What does it mean for Anglicans in the Three-Self Church

---

55. Gakuru, "Anglican's View of the Bible," 58.

56. Morgan, "Study of Anglican Mission," 183.

in China to be Anglican, and is there any reason for people in countries like China to cultivate a specifically Anglican identity and heritage?

The challenge of maintaining a clearly Anglican identity is present in many different global Anglican provinces, each with a relatively unique situation, and inculturation in other provinces may play an even greater role in their Global Anglican spiritualities than in the COU. A process of inculturation uninhibited by colonial control is relatively new in many provinces and is still resisted by some in those provinces who want to remain faithful to the ways of the missionaries. As inculturation begins in earnest and develops over time, the inculturation of Anglicanism into many different cultures with no clear controls or limits on the diversity it produces is, therefore, an enormous, yet still little recognized, potential source of increasing diversity. The Global spiritualities have been vastly underrepresented in most discussions of Anglican identity and the future of Anglicanism, a situation that must change to understand properly orthodox Anglican identity.

Recognition of the great diversity among orthodox Anglicans worldwide is a very recent phenomenon and one that even now is rarely taken into account as much as it should be. The 1998 Lambeth Conference highlighted the significance of the Global South in terms of articulating an orthodox Anglicanism against an Anglicanism that is liberal in terms of human sexuality, but the diversity of that Global South has so far been only a footnote in understanding the impact of the mostly orthodox and increasingly influential Global South. Now, however, the new technologies and modes of communication have begun to make an awareness of this diversity much more readily available, while at the same time facilitating the networking of orthodox Anglicans globally.

It is especially crucial that orthodox Anglicans come relatively soon to a better understanding of the Global Anglican spiritualities present in the mostly orthodox Global South. Some orthodox Anglicans, Federal Conservatives, in particular, are poised to allow the Global South primates to determine the future of orthodox Anglicanism. Do they adequately understand the diversity present in these provinces and the dynamics of continued inculturation and diversification? A Global South bishop, quoted favorably by John Pobee, a leading Anglican scholar from the Anglican Church in Ghana, suggests the degree of diversity that the Global spirituality may represent when he says that "there is no one tradition to which all Anglicans must conform."[57] Often, Anglicans do not know the ways in which many other Anglicans understand the meaning of Anglican touchstones. We might wonder what ordinary Anglicans around the world mean by identifying themselves as Anglican.

CONCLUSION

Given the increasing diversity within orthodox Anglicanism and its four spiritualities, the Anglican ideal of comprehension seems unlikely to be able to act as an instrument to establish and maintain a clear and coherent orthodox Anglican identity, in spite of a continuing orthodox Anglican desire to do so. Due to a weak ecclesial authority, weak norms, and diversifying spiritualities that include a strong element of post-colonial inculturation, diversity is likely to continue increasing among orthodox Anglicans.

What happens to the ideal of comprehension when a strong authority such as the English Crown or state does not exist on the global level, and the specifically Anglican norms of the Articles and Prayer Book have become weakened? In such situations, religious diversity would be the norm, and identity would be relatively weak. A study of the four orthodox Anglican spiritualities suggests that such diversity is, in fact, large and increasing and is making it more difficult to articulate a clear and coherent orthodox Anglican identity.

Orthodox Anglican comprehension now includes the following extremities and more. Each of the four orthodox spiritualities, to some degree, manifests a practical and sometimes official denial of the Prayer Book and Articles as Anglican norms. Some Anglo-Catholics use the Roman Catholic liturgies and breviaries and the celebration of Roman Catholic services such as Benediction and the Assumption of Mary. Some Evangelicals employ non-liturgical worship services, a Puritan biblical hermeneutic, a congregationalist polity, a desire for lay presidency and lay confirmation, and an Anglican identity that is merely pragmatic. Some Charismatics assert a five-fold order of ministry in place of the catholic three-fold one, a substitution of experience for theology and the accompanying tendency to innovate, and a denial of the importance of infant baptism. Global Anglicans sometimes have little Catholic spirituality, are weakly Anglican, and are changing to compete with Pentecostals and more fully inculturate.

---

57. Pobee, "Newer Dioceses," 399.

We might ask the question, then: "What does an Evangelical who allows for women priests, has a congregational ecclesiology, and subscribes to the Articles but uses no Prayer Book have in common with an Anglo-Catholic who does not recognize women priests, maintains a historic ecclesiology, uses the Missal, and does not adhere to the Articles?" Aside from being Christian and having some degree of historical connection to the Church of England, the answer seems to be "Not very much."

What, therefore, would constitute a clear and coherent identity for orthodox Anglicans who want to encompass this kind of diversity? At a minimum, it would involve being able to say with some certainty who is an orthodox Anglican and who is not. This is precisely what orthodox Anglicans are likely to have more and more difficulty determining, as diversity continues to increase.

Comprehension is a useful term for defining religious identities, but only if both what is comprehended and what is excluded are clear. However, orthodox Anglicans are likely to find themselves unable to qualify precisely the terms of comprehension as they attempt to articulate a specifically *Anglican* identity.

While orthodox Anglicans have the desire to exclude liberal positions and are seeking the ecclesial authority to do so, they are not likely to exclude other kinds of diversity, such as deviations from the Articles or Prayer Book. Historic norms such as the Prayer Book and the Articles will not be consistently used as Anglican identity norms, even though there may be some attempt officially to do so. The power of establishment that held together Anglican comprehension in the Church of England does not exist within contemporary, global Anglicanism, and the strength of the replacement authority of GAFCON and the ACNA is uncertain.

While no clear answer to the question of what makes an orthodox Anglican an *Anglican* is likely to be articulated, it appears that if a group identifies itself as Anglican, then it is. While being in communion with Canterbury has been a marker of being Anglican for the last fifty years or so, this is no longer the case in the eyes of many orthodox Anglicans. Orthodox Anglicans, therefore, are seemingly asserting (even if only implicitly) a subjective definition of Anglicanism similar to one given by others: you are an Anglican if you self-identify as one. While orthodox Anglicans would not wish to follow this subjective definition with its inability to exclude or discipline, they sometimes seem implicitly to affirm that all that is necessary to be an orthodox Anglican is to be orthodox in terms of the view of the creeds, Scripture, and biblical morality and to claim some sort of Anglican identity. Whether one uses the 1662 Prayer Book or any prayer book or not; whether one subscribes to the Articles or not; whether one holds to particular theological views or certain ancient, catholic practices or not; one is an orthodox Anglican if one is biblically and creedally orthodox and claims an Anglican identity. This means, primarily, the national and regional churches that came out of colonial Anglicanism but would also include any other groups that have emerged as well.

The ideal of comprehension itself may still be desired and employed, and yet given the degree of diversity present in orthodox Anglicanism, it will not be able to function as a clear and coherent preserver of identity. Thus, the orthodox Anglican acceptance of competing and even contradictory spiritualities, all clearly orthodox and yet not so clearly Anglican, will ensure that practically speaking a strongly *globalized* concept of culture will exist in orthodox Anglicanism, even as a more *integrated* one is desired and asserted. This actual *globalized* identity will continue to frustrate orthodox Anglican attempts to establish and maintain a clear, specific, and ideal orthodox Anglican identity that is more *integrated* in conception. In this way, orthodox Anglican identity is likely to be a hybrid of both *globalized* and *integrated* identities.

While orthodox Anglicans may be *converging* or working more closely together to assert a particularly Christian *orthodox* identity as part of the realignment they are seeking, they are also *diverging* from each other as each of the orthodox Anglican spiritualities is acting to move from a common, identifiable *Anglican* identity. Desiring, therefore, to affirm both a common Anglican identity and the large degree of diversity that undermines any clearly Anglican identity, orthodox Anglicans may be heading into a fourth stage of identity which we may call a "post-Anglican" Anglicanism.

Conclusion

How clear and coherent is the Anglican nature of this orthodox Anglican identity on which the orthodox Anglican realignment has been predicated? Orthodox Anglicans will continue to desire a relatively clear and coherent identity, even while their actual lived-out identities will often be more ambiguous and messier. While they will seek a more *integrated* identity, they will actually achieve a more *globalized* identity: their identity is thus likely to be a hybrid of both *integrated* and *globalized* identities.

Ecclesially, the Anglican Communion has relatively weak ecclesial structures and is unwilling to enforce any norms at the Communion level. GAFCON and the ACNA have been created as orthodox Anglican alternatives to the Anglican Communion, while at the same time desiring to maintain connections to the Communion. Both are also experiencing difficulty in creating an ecclesial structure with an authority any greater than that of the Anglican Communion.

Normatively, orthodox Anglicans desire to assert a more clear and coherent identity by rallying around the Bible and by reclaiming the Prayer Book and Articles as specifically Anglican norms. However, orthodox Anglican interpretations of the Bible appear to be increasingly diverging on several issues, especially as many orthodox Anglicans are willing to read the Bible with less reference to tradition and more outside of the context of the Prayer Book and Articles. In fact, despite their reassertion of the Prayer Book and Articles, both of these norms are already becoming less important to orthodox Anglicans.

Practically, orthodox Anglican identity is being challenged by the diversity presented by four orthodox Anglican spiritualities that would have to be comprehended in a single orthodox Anglican identity. Each of the four orthodox Anglican spiritualities, Anglo-Catholic, Evangelical, Charismatic, and Global, manifests a degree of diversity and innovation that necessitates an ever-expanding definition of Anglicanism.

Here, then, is the central dilemma for orthodox Anglicans: if they adhere to a strict, *integrated* definition of Anglicanism with strict boundaries, then a strong authority would likely be necessary to act forcefully in conjunction with clear norms to limit diversity and establish and maintain such an identity. Doing this, however, would mean restricting the current practices of some orthodox Anglicans or identifying some as outside the realm of orthodox Anglicanism, neither of which is particularly likely. However, if a looser, *globalized* definition of orthodox Anglicanism prevails, then increasing diversity is likely to make any specifically orthodox *Anglican* identity challenging to identify and maintain. In terms of a common *orthodox* Anglican identity, as distinguished by an orthodox view of homosexuality and the authority of Scripture, orthodox Anglicans will likely achieve a relatively clear and coherent ecclesial and theological identity as they converge or work together to distinguish themselves from liberal Anglicans. However, in terms of a common orthodox *Anglican* identity, their ecclesial, theological, and practical identities will not be as clear and coherent as assumed or desired, and orthodox Anglicans will, in fact, increasingly *diverge* from one another and a clearly Anglican identity.

The reality that orthodox Anglicans will live in will, therefore, be a hybrid of both *globalized* and *integrated* identities. This hybrid of both *globalized* and *integrated* identities is characteristic of a fourth stage in Anglican identity. This fourth stage might be called "post-Anglican" Anglicanism, a term that helps to reflect the irony of orthodox Anglicans (but not solely orthodox Anglicans) in the retention of the notion of a single, identifiable Anglican identity, even while identifiably Anglican commitments and markers of identity become increasingly less important and difficult to discern. This identity is "post-Anglican" in the sense that the continuity with the early church through continuity with the doctrine, discipline, and worship of the Church of England has weakened to the point that the specifically "Anglican" nature of Anglicanism is not only different from what has come before but is also increasingly difficult to define and locate.

If both ecclesial authority and norms are weak in the present Anglican Communion, then a generally weak identity should be expected, according to the model of religious identity I have presented. In this "post-Anglican" Anglicanism, the diversity that has been increasing within Anglicanism will also be present within orthodox Anglicanism, and the mechanisms by which diversity within Anglicanism has been allowed and not limited (weak authority and weak norms), leading to a weakened identity, will also be present within orthodox Anglicanism and are likely to remain so. Provincial autonomy, inculturation, a desire for relevance, and reception are principles and processes that are all reshaping Anglican identity, including orthodox Anglican identity. "Post-Anglican" Anglicanism will, therefore, continue to have a problem managing diversity, and one of the present difficulties which orthodox Anglicans are attempting to remedy is likely to continue to exist for them in a different guise.

Anglicans are used to diversity within Christianity but may still assume that a greater uniformity within their own tradition is both desirable and inherent. Such uniformity may not be a realistic expectation for eighty-five million Anglicans in 167 countries, and although this does not mean there will not be or should not be recognizably Anglican qualities, it does mean that we should expect that there will be as much diversity within Anglicanism as is found within world religions in general.

The "post-Anglican" Anglican identity of this fourth stage is also represented by the orthodox Anglican ecclesial realignment that is reshaping Anglicanism, not only by potentially excising liberal Anglican churches but also by reshaping the ecclesial foundations of Anglicanism. The result of this process is likely to be a continued fragmentation in which networks are becoming more important than geography, a point that has implications for the place of the Church of England in this "post-Anglican" Anglicanism. The reality of this fourth-stage identity of "post-Anglican" Anglicanism is something that has only recently begun to be seen "through a glass darkly," and it is, in part, the emergence of technologies enabling Anglicans to know more about each other that has created this recognition. Hassett, discerning this emerging Anglican identity, writes,

> The controversies, tensions, and discoveries of affinities, differences, and antagonisms with which the Anglican Communion is currently struggling have much to do, then, with its member provinces simply learning more about one another—and finding that they don't, after all, have as much in common as they perhaps assumed, in days when all they knew about one another was that they shared allegiance to Canterbury.[1]

She adds, "The Anglican Communion's current struggles are not a matter of global communion being torn apart, but rather being examined for its implications, possibility, and desirability, for the first time . . ."[2] In other

1. Hassett, "Episcopal Dissidents, African Allies," 624.
2. Hassett, "Episcopal Dissidents, African Allies," 625.

words, the more *globalized*, diverse, and complex nature of Anglicanism may have existed for some time before it was recognized and more visibly created problems for Anglican identity, including orthodox Anglican identity. This recognition, however, once made, precipitates a desire for understanding and generates a dialogue concerning what Anglicanism is and should be. Arguing that the current crisis in Anglicanism between orthodox and liberal Anglicans is about decision-making in the church and the interpretation and authority of Scripture, former Archbishop of Canterbury Rowan Williams writes, "But my real point is that we have never really had this discussion properly. It surfaced a bit in our debates over women's ordination, but for a variety of reasons tended to slip out of focus. But we were bound to have to think it through sooner or later."[3] Issues that have been inherent in Anglicanism but which have only recently been fully illuminated appear to be at the center of the Anglican identity crisis, both in terms of the debate over homosexuality and in its more general form.

In grappling with the place of the Bible and the process of decision-making in a global family of churches, orthodox Anglicans are struggling once again with the issues of authority, norms, and a practical ethos, and therefore with issues of identity. As Anglicanism has progressed through its first three stages of identity and has now entered a more diverse and messier fourth stage, it may be that orthodox Anglicans will reinvent Anglican identity in meaningful and unexpected ways, and the future of orthodox Anglicanism may be seen in either a negative or positive light. With the possible fracture of the Anglican Communion, the imminent dissolution of a clear and coherent identity, and the present trauma in the lives of Anglicans at stake, it is possible to assess the future of orthodox Anglicanism and Anglicanism with pessimism.

ESCHATOLOGICAL AND ECUMENICAL HOPE

I began this book by quoting Dickens's *A Tale of Two Cities*. So far, it may seem as if I've forcefully presented only "the worst of times" face of Dickens's introduction. Where, in my analysis of orthodox Anglicanism, are the elusive best of times? If I've been quick to portray difficulties, I want to be just as quick to express hope. I'm sure many will be troubled by the complex, fragmented, and contentious nature of orthodox Anglicanism: I know I was. When I began my work on orthodox Anglicanism, I

3. Williams, "Archbishop's Presidential Address."

experienced a year of grieving for the Anglicanism I hoped would be, the one I had read about and which could easily be defined. But then a bold spirit of encouragement seized me, and I had the epiphany that there was no Golden Age of the church and that what orthodox Anglicanism looked like in the twenty-first century was what the church had always looked like in all places and in all times! Furthermore, the fact that orthodox Anglican identity is messier, more ambiguous, and less definable than desired does not mean that an authentic Anglican identity is an impossible or fatuous thing. Religious identities are inherently complex and ambiguous while also being livable and essential realities.

Jesus Christ prayed: "I do not pray for these alone, but also for those who will believe in Me through their word; that they all may be one, as You, Father, are in Me, and I in You; that they also may be one in Us, that the world may believe that You sent Me," (John 17:20–21). That is the orthodox Anglican hope because it is the Christian hope.

Christian and Anglican unity implies, like marriage, a unity that emerges through diversity and which can only be accomplished by the love of God, which *loves the other* as himself. The disputes and diversities of orthodox Anglicans may be seen, then, as marriage spats, even if the actions of TEC and others may, ultimately, lead to divorce. While the diversity within orthodox Anglicanism is great, so is the commitment to walk together in love and unity. GAFCON and the ACNA are hopeful signs of Christian and Anglican unity. Despite the difficulties and differences, GAFCON and the ACNA are committed to walking together as orthodox Christians. Although the convergence of different spiritualities and even norms is fragile, one cannot attend either GAFCON or ACNA events and not experience a palpable unity and good will.

Whether these are enough to bind orthodox Anglicans together in the future remains to be seen. At some point in time, for example, the issue of women's ordination in the ACNA will have to be decided, and this will test whether the ACNA, or any church so conceived and so dedicated, can long endure. But hopefully, this book is a starting point for the ecclesial spouses to know who it is they have married. Hopefully, the members of GAFCON, the ACNA, and others will not experience the embarrassing shock of Jacob, who, although he had agreed to marry Rachel, in the morning discovered that "Behold: It was Leah!" It may be that the new orthodox Anglicanism, most exemplified by GAFCON and the ACNA but certainly not limited to them, is the new wineskin into which God is pouring the new wine of Anglican identity in the postmodern world.

Anglicanism is a microcosm of the entire Christian church and has often been the most ecumenical of churches. Its inherent identity, derived from both Catholic and Protestant principles, and from the kind of ecclesial comprehension manifested most formatively by the Elizabethan Settlement, allows it to look to the one, catholic church as a whole, and to extend Christian communion to Roman Catholics, Orthodox Christians, and Protestants alike. The kind of diversity manifested in orthodox Anglicanism is a microcosm of the kind of diversity that is true for the one, catholic church. Both the brokenness and the hopefulness of the orthodox Anglican identity, therefore, has the ability to illuminate the struggles with identity caused by the interplay between unity and diversity that is replicated on a grander scale by the church as a whole, as well as by other Christian ecclesial bodies. It is not only Anglicanism that is diverse, messy, and divided but the entire catholic church. But perhaps out of this hybrid Anglican identity may come a new way of imagining Christian unity, one that compels us to look both beyond and before the Constantinianism in which ecclesial unity is compelled by the state and is imagined in terms of national identities.

One future for orthodox Anglicans, then, may be that they succeed in their quest for ecclesial and normative realignment, as well as practical convergence. Alternatively (though not necessarily contrarily), orthodox Anglicans may proceed, in its "post-Anglican" Anglican identity, to fulfill some twentieth-century prophecies that it is destined to work towards the extinction of its own separate identity through its unique service to the whole church in the work of Christian unity. The Anglican identity crisis is compelling Anglicans to re-examine their common life and assess not only its identity but also its place within the one catholic church. Other churches are also struggling with identity, in large part due to the issue of homosexuality. They are watching the orthodox Anglican realignment—watching, learning, and hoping. The ecumenical moment inaugurated by Vatican II has manifested itself not only in the orthodox Anglican realignment but also in renewed ecumenical dialogue between the ACNA and a host of ecumenical partners, including the Roman Catholic Church, Old Catholic churches, Orthodox churches, Lutherans, and others. This is the kind of ecumenical dialogue that TEC has short-circuited by its innovations.

Finally, the struggle of the emerging orthodox Anglicanism and the issues of religious identities that it lays bare speak prophetically about the nature of all religious identities in the postmodern world we now inhabit. All religions are experiencing similar changes and challenges, from hybridity, competing spiritualities, weakening of ecclesial structures and norms, and the general fluidity and fragmentation of the postmodern world.

Just as heresies throughout church history provoked a vigorous orthodox response and re-definition that has encouraged and shaped the church, so the challenges to the new orthodox Anglican identity may, hopefully, prompt orthodox Anglicans to work out their own identity with fear and trembling for the sake of the greater church.

Bibliography

ACNA. "ACNA Fact Sheet." http://www.anglicanchurch.net/media/ACNA_Fact_Sheet_2-21-17.pdf.

———. "Appendix II: Chart on Women's Ordination in the Anglican Provinces." In *The Holy Orders Task Force Final Report*. ACNA, 2017. http://anglicanchurch.net/?/main/page/1448.

———. "Theological Statement." http://www.anglicanchurch.net/index.php/main/Theology/.

Ammerman, Nancy T. "Religious Identities and Religious Institutions." In *Handbook of the Sociology of Religion*, edited by Michele Dillon, 207–24. Cambridge: Cambridge University Press, 2003.

Anderson, Allan. "African Anglicans and/or Pentecostals: Why So Many African Anglicans Become Pentecostals or Combine Their Anglicanism with Pentecostalism." In *Anglicanism: A Global Communion*, edited by Andrew Wingate et al., 34–40. New York: Church, 1998.

———. *African Reformation: African Initiated Christianity in the 20th Century*. Trenton: Africa World, 2001.

Anderson, William B. *The Church in East Africa: 1840–1974*. Dodoma: Central Tanganyika, 1977.

"Anglican Communion Primates' Meeting Communique, February 2005." https://www.anglicannews.org/news/2005/02/the-anglican-communion-primates-meeting-communique,-february-2005.aspx.

"Anglican Groups to Make Common Cause." https://virtueonline.org/anglican-groups-make-common-cause.

Avis, Paul. *Anglicanism and the Christian Church*. Minneapolis: Fortress, 1989.

———. "Keeping Faith with Anglicanism." In *The Future of Anglicanism*, edited by Robert Hannaford. Leominster: Gracewing, 1996.

———. "What is 'Anglicanism'?" In *The Study of Anglicanism*, edited by Stephen Sykes and John Booty, 405–24. London: SPCK, 1988.

Baron, Peter. "The Case against Reform." In *Has Keele Failed? Reform in the Church of England*, edited by Charles Yeats, 64–80. London: Hodder and Stoughton, 1995.

Barrett, David B., and Todd M. Johnson. *World Christian Trends: AD 30–AD 2200*. Pasadena, CA: William Carey Library, 2001.

Bebbington, David. *Evangelicalism in Modern Britain: A History from the 1730s to the 1980s*. Grand Rapids: Baker, 1992.

Bell, Matthew. "Alpha: The Slickest, Richest, Fastest-Growing Division of the Church of England." https://www.spectator.co.uk/2013/11/alpha-rising/.

Bennett, Gareth. "Preface to Crockford's Clerical Directory 1987/88." In *To the Church of England*, 189–228. Worthing: Churchman, 1988.

Booty, John. *The Episcopal Church in Crisis*. Cambridge, MA: Crowley, 1988.

Bray, Gerald. "Whatever Happened to the Authority of Scripture?" In *The Anglican Evangelical Crisis*, edited by Melvin Tinker, 57–71. Fearn: Christian Focus, 1995.

Bridge, G. Richmond. *Women and the Apostolic Ministry?* Halifax: Convent, 1997.

Butler, Sarah. "The Ordination of Women: A New Obstacle to the Recognition of Anglican Orders." *Anglican Theological Review* 78 (1996) 96–113.

Called to Be a Faithful Church in a Plural World: Section III Report. 1998 Lambeth Conference. Harrisburg: Morehouse, 1999.

Castells, Manuel. *The Rise of the Network Society*. Malden, MA: Blackwell, 1996.

Chadwick, Henry. "Tradition, Fathers and Councils." In *The Study of Anglicanism*, edited by Stephen Sykes and John Booty, 91–105. London: SPCK, 1988.

Chadwick, Owen. "Introduction." In *Resolutions of the Twelve Lambeth Conferences: 1867–1988*, edited by Roger Coleman, i–xxvii. Toronto: Anglican Book Centre, 1992.

Chiwanga, Simon E. "Beyond the Monarch/Chief: Reconsidering Episcopacy in Africa." In *Beyond Colonial Anglicanism: The Anglican Communion in the Twenty-First Century*, edited by Ian T. Douglas and Kwok Pui-Lan, 297–317. New York: Church, 2001.

Church of England. "Canon A2." https://www.churchofengland.org/more/policy-and-thinking/canons-church-england/section-a#b2.

———. "Canon A5." https://www.churchofengland.org/more/policy-and-thinking/canons-church-england/section-a#b2.

"Church of Nigeria Redefines Anglican Communion." https://virtueonline.org/church-nigeria-redefines-anglican-communion.

Church Society. "A Covenant for the Church of England." https://churchsociety.org/issues_new/communion/division/iss_communion_division_cofecovenant.asp.

Coleman, Roger, ed. *Resolutions of the Twelve Lambeth Conferences: 1867–1988*. Toronto: Anglican Book Centre, 1992.

"Communion and Discipline." https://www.wycliffecollege.ca/archive/document/communion-and-discipline-submission-lambeth-commission-anglican-communion-institute.

Day, David. "The Ministry of the Laity." In *Has Keele Failed? Reform in the Church of England*, edited by Charles Yeats, 104–16. London: Hodder and Stoughton, 1995.

Duncan, Robert. "The Future of Anglicanism." https://virtueonline.org/future-anglicanism-robert-duncan.

Episcopal News Service. "What is the Anglican Consultative Council?" https://www.episcopalnewsservice.org/2019/04/27/what-is-the-anglican-consultative-council/.

Fairfield, Leslie. "Anglican Charismatics in the Modern West." In *The Holy Orders Task Force Final Report*. ACNA, 2017. http://anglicanchurch.net/?/main/page/1448.

———. "The Ecclesiology of the Anglican Evangelical Tradition." In *The Holy Orders Task Force Final Report*. ACNA, 2017. http://anglicanchurch.net/?/main/page/1448.

Finke, Roger. "Innovative Returns to Tradition: Using Core Teachings as the Foundation for Innovative Accommodation." *Journal for the Scientific Study of Religion* 43 (2004) 19–34.

GAFCON. "The Complete Jerusalem Statement." https://www.gafcon.org/resources/the-complete-jerusalem-statement.

———. "GAFCON Final Statement." https://www.gafcon.org/news/gafcon-final-statement.

———. "Jerusalem 2018—Introduction." https://www.gafcon.org/jerusalem-2018/introduction.

———. "Letter to the Churches—GAFCON Assembly 2018." https://www.gafcon.org/news/letter-to-the-churches-gafcon-assembly-2018.

Gakuru, Griphus. "An Anglican's View of the Bible in an East African Context." In *Anglicanism: A Global Communion*, edited by Andrew Wingate et al., 58–62. New York: Church, 1998.

Gibson, Paul. "What Is the Future Role of Liturgy in Anglican Unity?" In *Liturgical Inculturation in the Anglican Communion*, edited by David R. Holeton, 17–22. Bramcote: Grove, 1990.

Gifford, Paul. *African Christianity: Its Public Role.* Bloomington: Indiana University Press, 1998.

Gumbel, Nicky. *Questions of Life: A Practical Introduction to the Christian Faith.* Colorado Springs: Cook, 1996.

Harris, David. "Lay Presidency Issue Heats Up." *Anglican Journal*, Oct 1, 1998. http://www.anglicanjournal.com/opinion/029/article/lay-presidency-issue-heats-up/.

Hassett, Miranda. "Episcopal Dissidents, African Allies: The Anglican Communion and the Globalization of Dissent." PhD diss., University of North Carolina, 2004.

Hefling, Charles, and Cynthia Shattuck, eds. *The Oxford Guide to The Book of Common Prayer.* Oxford: Oxford University Press, 2006.

Holloway, David. "Semper Reformanda." In *The Anglican Evangelical Crisis*, edited by Melvin Tinker, 13–27. Fearn: Christian Focus, 1995.

Holmes, Urban T. "Education for Liturgy: An Unfinished Symphony in Four Movements." In *Worship Points the Way: A Celebration of the Life and Work of Massey Hamilton Shepherd, Jr.*, edited by Malcolm C. Burson, 116–41. New York: Seabury, 1981.

———. *What is Anglicanism?* Harrisburg: Morehouse, 1982.

Homan, Roger. "The Liturgy: Experiments and Results." In *The Real Common Worship*, edited by Peter Mullen, 31–47. Norfolk, UK: Edgeways, 2000.

Hunt, Stephen. *The Alpha Enterprise: Evangelism in a Post-Christian Era.* Aldershot: Ashgate, 2004.

Jacob, W. M. *The Making of the Anglican Church Worldwide.* London: SPCK, 1997.

Jensen, Peter. "The Windsor Report is Bound to Fail." https://virtueonline.org/windsor-report-bound-fail-peter-jensen.

Kasibante, Amos. "Beyond Revival: A Proposal for Mission in the Church of Uganda into the Third Millennium." In *Anglicanism: A Global Communion*, edited by Andrew Wingate et al., 363–68. New York: Church, 1998.

Kaye, Bruce. *Reinventing Anglicanism: A Vision of Confidence, Community, and Engagement in Anglican Christianity.* New York: Church, 2003.

"Kigali Communiqué, September 2006." http://www.globalsouthanglican.org/comments/kigali_communique/.

Kings, Graham. "Shechem, Corinth, and Columbus: ECUSA's Choices." https://www.fulcrum-anglican.org.uk/articles/shechem-corinth-and-columbus-ecusas-choices-fulcrum-newsletter-8-june-2006/.

Knox, David Broughton. *Thirty-Nine Articles: The Historic Basis of Anglican Faith.* London: Hodder and Stoughton, 1967.

The Lambeth Conference Resolutions Archive from 1998. Anglican Communion Office, 2005. https://www.anglicancommunion.org/media/76650/1998.pdf.

The Lambeth Conferences, 1867–1948. By the Conference of Bishops of the Anglican Communion. London: SPCK, 1948.

Martin, David. "A Plea for Our Common Prayer." In *Ritual Murder*, edited by Brian Morris, 18–30. Manchester, UK: Carcanet, 1980.

McGrath, Alister E. *The Renewal of Anglicanism*. Harrisburg: Morehouse, 1993.

Moore, Peter C. "Why Some Godly Women Should Be Ordained." Trinity Episcopal School for Ministry. http://www.tesm.edu/articles/moore-why-godly-women-can-have-true-calling.html.

Morgan, James Geoffrey Selwyn. "An Analytical, Critical and Comparative Study of Anglican Mission in the Dioceses of Nakuru and Mount Kenya East, Kenya, from 1975." MPhil thesis, Oxford Centre for Mission Studies, 1997.

Newman, John Henry. "Tract XC: Remarks on Certain Passages of the Thirty-Nine Articles." Tracts for the Times 90. London: Rivington's, 1841. http://anglicanhistory.org/tracts/tract90/.

Norman, Edward. *Anglican Difficulties: A New Syllabus of Errors*. London: Morehouse, 2004.

Packer, J. I. *The Evangelical Anglican Identity Problem: An Analysis*. Oxford: Latimer, 1978.

———. *A Kind of Noah's Ark? The Anglican Commitment to Comprehensiveness*. Oxford: Latimer, 1981.

Packer, J. I., and R. T. Beckwith. *The Thirty-Nine Articles: Their Place and Use Today*. Oxford: Latimer, 1984.

"Pastoral Letter from Gregory Venables," http://www.theroadtoemmaus.org/RdLb/32Ang/Ang/DarEsSalaam-Venbles.htm.

Paul, Robert S. *The Church in Search of Its Self*. Grand Rapids: Eerdmans, 1972.

Percy, Martyn. *Words, Wonders and Power: Understanding Contemporary Christian Fundamentalism and Revivalism*. London: SPCK, 1996.

Pobee, John S. "Newer Dioceses of the Anglican Communion." In *The Study of Anglicanism*, edited by Stephen Sykes and John Booty, 393–405. London: SPCK, 1988.

———. "Take Thou Authority: An African Perspective." In *Authority in the Anglican Communion*, edited by Stephen W. Sykes, 189–201. Toronto: Anglican Book Centre, 1987.

Poon, Michael Nai Chiu. "Deliver us from 'Corporate Perversion': A Conversation with Drs Ephraim Radner and Graham Kings on the State of our Communion." https://virtueonline.org/deliver-us-corporate-perversion.

"Preface." *The Book of Common Prayer: According to the Use of the Protestant Episcopal Church in the United States of America*. 1789. http://justus.anglican.org/resources/bcp/1789/FrontMatter_1789.htm#Preface.

Presler, Titus. "Old and New in Worship and Community: Culture's Pressures in Global Anglicanism." *Anglican Theological Review* 82 (2000) 709–23.

Quantin, Jean-Louis. *The Church of England and Christian Antiquity: The Construction of a Confessional Identity in the 17th Century*. Oxford: Oxford University Press, 2009.

Radner, Ephraim, and George R. Sumner, eds. *Reclaiming Faith*. Grand Rapids: Eerdmans, 1993.

Radner, Ephraim, and Philip Turner. *The Fate of Communion: The Agony of Anglicanism and the Future of a Global Church*. Grand Rapids: Eerdmans, 2006.

Roberts, Paul. *Alternative Worship in the Church of England*. Cambridge: Grove, 1999.

Roozen, David A. "National Denominational Structures' Engagement with Postmodernity: An Integrative Summary from an Organizational Perspective." In *Church, Identity, and Change: Theology and Denominational Structures in Unsettled Times*, edited by David A. Roozen and James R. Nieman, 588–624. Grand Rapids: Eerdmans, 2005.

Roozen, David A., and James R. Nieman. "Introduction." In *Church, Identity, and Change: Theology and Denominational Structures in Unsettled Times*, 1–34. Grand Rapids: Eerdmans, 2005.

Sachs, William. *The Transformation of Anglicanism: From State Church to Global Communion*. Cambridge: Cambridge University Press, 1993.

Samuel, Vinay, and Christopher Sugden. *Lambeth: A View from the Two Thirds World*. Harrisburg: Morehouse, 1989.

Schaff, Philip. *Creeds of Christendom, with a History and Critical Notes*. Vol. 1, The History of Creeds, 6th ed. New York: Harper, 1919.

Schreiter, Robert J. *The New Catholicity: Theology between the Global and the Local*. Maryknoll, NY: Orbis, 1997.

Scotland, Nigel. *Charismatics and the Next Millennium: Do They Have a Future?* London: Hodder and Stoughton, 1995.

Short, James. "Ugandan Field Worship." *Mandate* 19 (2006) 14–15.

Simpson, James B., and Edward M. Story. *The Long Shadows of Lambeth X*. New York: McGraw-Hill, 1969.

The Six Lambeth Conferences: 1867–1920. Edited by Randall Davidson. London: SPCK, 1920.

Stark, Rodney, and Roger Finke. *Acts of Faith: Explaining the Human Side of Religion*. Los Angeles: California University Press, 2000.

Stark, Rodney, and William S. Bainbridge. *The Future of Religion: Secularization, Revival, and Cult Formation*. Los Angeles: California University Press, 1985.

"Statement from the Bishops of the Anglican Church of Nigeria," https://www.anglicannews.org/news/2003/11/statement-from-the-bishops-of-the-anglican-church-of-nigeria.aspx.

"Statement from the House of Bishops, Tanzania," https://www.anglicannews.org/news/2006/12/statement-from-the-house-of-bishops,-tanzania.aspx.

Stuart, Mary. *Land of Promise: A Story of the Church in Uganda*. London: Highway, 1957.

Sugden, Chris. "7000 Sing and Dance as Sandy Millar Consecrated Bishop." https://virtueonline.org/uganda-7000-sing-and-dance-sandy-millar-consecrated-bishop.

Sumner, Gillian. "Evangelicalism and Patterns of Ministry." In *Evangelical Anglicans: Their Role and Influence in the Church Today*, edited by R. T. France and Alister E. McGrath, 160–71. London: SPCK, 1993.

Sykes, Stephen W. *The Integrity of Anglicanism*. Oxford: Mowbray, 1978.

———. *Unashamed Anglicanism*. London: Darton, Longman and Todd, 1995.

Taylor, John V. *Processes of Growth in an African Church*. London: SCM, 1958.

Thompson, Mark. "Saving the Heart of Evangelicalism." In *The Anglican Evangelical Crisis*, edited by Melvin Tinker, 28–41. Fearn: Christian Focus, 1995.

Thornton, Martin. *English Spirituality: An Outline of Ascetical Theology according to the English Pastoral Tradition*. London: SPCK, 1963.

Tinker, Melvin. "Preface." In *The Anglican Evangelical Crisis*, edited by Melvin Tinker, 9–12. Fearn: Christian Focus, 1995.

———. "Towards an Evangelical View of the Church." In *The Anglican Evangelical Crisis*, edited by Melvin Tinker, 94–110. Fearn: Christian Focus, 1995.

Tomlinson, Dave. *The Post-Evangelical*. London: SPCK, 1995.

Toon, Peter. "The Articles and Homilies." In *The Study of Anglicanism*, edited by Stephen Sykes and John Booty, 133–43. London: SPCK, 1988.

———. *Reforming Forwards? The Process of Reception and the Consecration of Women as Bishops*. London: Latimer Trust, 2004.

Tovey, Phillip. "End of Anglican Confirmation." https://www.academia.edu/26334987/End_of_Anglican_Confirmation.

The Truth Shall Make You Free: The Lambeth Conference 1988. London: Church House, 1988.

"The Virginia Report." London: Anglican Communion Office, 2004. https://www.anglicancommunion.org/media/150889/report-1.pdf.

Virtue, David. "Dual-Integrity over Women's Ordination Heightens Tension in ACNA." https://virtueonline.org/dual-integrity-over-womens-ordination-heightens-tension-acna.

Wakefield, Gordon. "Anglican Spirituality." In *Christian Spirituality III: Post-Reformation and Modern*, edited by Louis Dupré and Don E. Saliers, 257–93. New York: Crossroad, 1989.

Ward, Kevin. *A History of Global Anglicanism*. Cambridge: Cambridge University Press, 2006.

———. "Tukutendereza Yesu: The Balokole Revival in Uganda." In *From Mission to Church: A Handbook of Christianity in East Africa*, edited by Zablon Nthamburi, 113–44. Nairobi: Uzima, 1991.

Whitacre, Rodney. "Women, Ordination, and the Bible." Trinity Episcopal School for Ministry. http://www.tsm.edu/2014/09/03/women_ordination_and_the_bible/.

White, Gavin. "Collegiality and Conciliarity in the Anglican Communion." In *Authority in the Anglican Communion*, edited by Stephen W. Sykes, 202–20. Toronto: Anglican Book Centre, 1987.

White, Stephen Ross. *Authority and Anglicanism*. London: SCM, 1996.

Wilcock, Michael. "The Ministry of Parish Clergy." In *Has Keele Failed? Reform in the Church of England*, edited by Charles Yeats, 130–41. London: Hodder and Stoughton, 1995.

Williams, Rowan. *Anglican Identities*. Cambridge, MA: Cowley, 2004.

———. "Archbishop Rowan Williams' Presidential Address at COE General Synod." http://www.globalsouthanglican.org/blog/comments/archbishop_rowan_williams_presidential_address_at_coe_general_synod.

"The Windsor Report." London: The Anglican Communion Office, 2004. https://www.anglicancommunion.org/media/68225/windsor2004full.pdf.

Woodhouse, John. "Lay Administration of the Lord's Supper: A Change to Stay the Same." In *The Anglican Evangelical Crisis*, edited by Melvin Tinker, 144–55. Fearn: Christian Focus, 1995.

———. "The Unity of the Church." https://gotherefor.com/offer.php?intid=14973&changestore=true.

Wright, J. Robert. "The Sources and Structures of Authority in the Church." http://anglicanhistory.org/essays/wright/bishoy1990.pdf.

Wright, Tom. "A Confused 'Covenant': Initial Comments on 'A Covenant for the Church of England', Issued by Paul Perkin and Chris Sugden and Others." https://virtueonline.org/england-confused-covenant-tom-wright.

———. "Doctrine Declared." In "Where Shall Doctrine Be Found?" In *Believing in the Church: The Corporate Nature of Faith*, 109–41. London: SPCK, 1981.

Yelton, Michael. *Anglican Papalism: An Illustrated History, 1900–1960*. Norwich: Canterbury, 2005.

Zahl, Paul F. M. *The Protestant Face of Anglicanism*. Grand Rapids: Eerdmans, 1998.

———. *A Short Systematic Theology*. Grand Rapids: Eerdmans, 2000.

Index of Names

Index of Subjects

revivalistic spirituality, associated with the *balokole* ("the saved ones"), 148

Righter, Walter, 7

Righter trial, 7

Ritualist Movement, 125

Roman canon, using, 127

Roman Catholic Church, 19, 73

Roman Catholic Mass, Anglo-Catholics in England using, 117

rosary, 128

Rule of Life, 112, 116

Russian Orthodox churches, 73

sacramental confession, practice of, 31

sacramental validity, of women priests, 71

sacraments

of Baptism and the Lord's Supper, 16, 81

devaluation in Alpha of the role of, 140

less emphasis on in the COU, 151

as necessary for salvation, 71

same-sex clergy and bishops, invited to Lambeth 2020, 61

same-sex relations, views on the issue of, 56

same-sex rites, mandated by TEC in 2018, 5, 8, 61

Schreiter, Robert, 37, 143

Scotland, as liberal, 4

Scottish Episcopal Church, 27n23, 29

Scripture

appeal to as a norm, 130

as authority, 21

as a bond of unity, 44

"containing all things necessary to salvation," 16

defining orthodox Anglicanism, 85–94

as the highest authority in Anglicanism, 8, 85, 86

orthodox Anglican re-affirmation of, 86

rejection of the authority of, 7

renewed emphasis on, 27

Resolution I.10 and, 66

silence of against tradition, 94

as the ultimate standard of faith and practice, 81

"Scripture in communion," authority of, 57–58

second stage, of Anglican identity, 27–32

See of Canterbury

ACNA (Anglican Church in North America) member churches relationship with, 62

Church of Nigeria on communion with, 34n29

churches in communion with, 14, 32–33, 34, 34n29

as the primary instrument of unity, 32

service books and liturgies, as alternatives to the 1662 Prayer Book, 114

"Sheng Kung Hui," 158

A Short Systematic Theology (Zahl), 89

slavery, passion to abolish, 27

sola exegesis, in contrast to *sola Scriptura*, 131

sola scriptura with private judgment, Evangelicals placing reliance on, 89

SOMA (Sharing of Ministries Abroad), committed to Charismatic renewal, 150

songs, in Charismatic worship, 137–38

speaking in tongues, 140

spiritualities, in the Church of Uganda (COU), 147–50

spirituality. *See* Anglican spirituality

Standing Liturgical Commission, 111

"Statement on the Global Anglican Future," 63, 64–65

Stott, John, 91, 143–44

"strategy of time," dealing with the issue of autonomous provinces, 57

strength of identity, existence of, 23

Strivers, attacked church members during services in Uganda, 151

subjective definition, of Anglicanism, 161

subscription, to the Articles in the Church of England, 95, 98, 99

subsidiarity, principle of, 54–55, 68

Lightning Source UK Ltd.
Milton Keynes UK
UKHW022254200921
390918UK00005B/129